W9-AQN-109

· THE BEST OF ·
ROBERT BENCHLEY

· THE BEST OF ·
ROBERT BENCHLEY

by Robert Benchley

with illustrations by

PETER ARNO
HERBERT F. ROESE
ADAM JOHN BARTH

and others

Avenel Books • New York

This 1983 edition is published by Avenel Books, distributed by Crown
Publishers, Inc., by arrangement with Liberty Library Corporation.

Manufactured in the United States of America

Library of Congress Cataloging in Publication Data

Benchley, Robert, 1889–1945.
The best of Robert Benchley.
I. Title.
PS3503.E49A6   1983   814′.52   83-2712
ISBN: 0-517-411393

Book design by June Marie Bennett

h g f e d c b a

CONTENTS

· THE BEST OF ·
ROBERT BENCHLEY

Back in Line

FOR a nation which has an almost evil reputation for bustle, bustle, bustle, and rush, rush, rush. we spend an enormous amount of time standing around in line in front of windows, just waiting. It would be all right if we were Spanish peasants and could strum guitars and hum, or even stab each other, while we were standing in line, or East Indians who could just sit cross-legged and simply stare into space for hours. Nobody expects anything more of Spanish peasants or East Indians, because they have been smart enough to build themselves a reputation for picturesque lethargy.

But we in America have built ourselves reputations for speed and dash, and are known far and wide as the rushingest nation in the world. So when fifty of us get in a line and stand for an hour shifting from one foot to the other, re-reading the shipping news and cooking recipes in an old newspaper until our turn comes, we just make ourselves look silly.

Most of this linestanding is the fault of the Government, just as everything else which is bad in our national life is the fault of the Government, including stone bruises and tight shoes. We would have plenty of time to rush around as we are supposed to do, if the Government did not require 500 of us to stand in one line at once waiting for two civil service

1

employees to weigh our letters, thumb out income-tax blanks, tear off our customs slips or roll back our eyelids. Of course, there are times when we stand in line to see a ball game or buy a railroad ticket, but that is *our* affair, and in time we get enough sense to stop going to ball games or traveling on railroads.

The U.S. Post Office is one of the most popular line-standing fields in the country. It has been estimated that six-tenths of the population of the United States spend their entire lives standing in line in a post office. When you realize that no provision is made for their eating or sleeping or intellectual advancement while they are thus standing in line, you will understand why six-tenths of the population look so cross and peaked. The wonder is that they have the courage to go on living at all.

This congestion in the post offices is due to what are technically known as "regulations" but what are really a series of acrostics and anagrams devised by some officials who got around a table one night and tried to be funny. "Here's a good gag!" one of them probably cried. "Let's make it compulsory for the package to be wrapped in paper which is watermarked with Napoleon's coat of arms. We won't say anything about it until they get right up to the window, so there will be no danger of their bringing that kind of paper with them. Then they will have to go away again with their bundles, find some paper watermarked with Napoleon's coat of arms (of which there is none that I ever heard of), rewrap their bundles, and come back and stand in line again. What do you say to that!" This scheme probably threw the little group of officials into such a gale of merriment that they had to call the meeting off and send down for some more White Rock.

You can't tell me that the post-office regulations (to say nothing of those of the Custom House and Income Tax Bureau) were made with anything else in mind except general confusion. It must be a source of great chagrin to those in charge to think of so many people being able to stick a stamp on a letter and drop it into a mail box without any trouble or suffering at all. They are probably working on that problem at this very minute, trying to devise some way in which the public can be made to fill out a blank, stand in line, consult some underling who will refer them to a superior, and then be made to black up with burned cork before they can mail a letter. And they'll figure it out, too. They always have.

But at present their chief source of amusement is in torturing those unfortunates who find themselves with a package to send by mail. And with Christmas in the offing, they must be licking their chops with glee in very anticipation. Although bundles of old unpaid bills is about all anyone will be sending this Christmas, it doesn't make any difference to the P.O. Department. A package is a package, and you must suffer for it.

It wouldn't be a bad idea for those of us who have been through the fire to get together and cheat the officials out of their fund this year by sending out lists of instructions

The wonder is that they have the courage to go on living at all.

(based on our own experience) to all our friends, telling them just what they have got to look out for before they start to stand in line. Can you imagine the expression on the face of a post-office clerk if a whole line of people came up to his window, one by one, each with his package so correctly done up that there was no fault to find with it? He would probably shoot himself in the end, rather than face his superiors with the confession that he had sent no one home to do the whole thing over. And if his superiors shot themselves too it would not detract one whit from the joyousness of the Christmas tide.

So here are the things I have learned in my various visits to the Post Office. If you will send me yours and get ten friends to make a round robin of their experiences, we may thwart the old Government yet.

Packages to be mailed abroad must be:

1. Wrapped in small separate packages, each weighing no more than one pound and seven-eighths (Eastern Standard Time), and each package to be tied with blue ribbon in a sheepshank knot. (Any sailor of fifteen years' experience will teach you to tie a sheepshank.)

2. The address must be picked out in blue, and reenforced with an insertion of blue ribbon, no narrower than three-eighths of an inch and no wider than five-eighths of an inch (and certainly not exactly four-eighths or one-half), or else you may have to stay and write it out a hundred times after the Post Office has closed.

3. The package, no matter what size, will have to be made smaller.

4. The package, no matter what size, will have to be made larger.

(In order to thwart the clerk on these last two points, it will be necessary to have packages of *all* sizes concealed in a bag slung over your back.)

5. The person who is mailing the package must approach the window with the package held in his right hand extended toward the clerk one foot from the body, while with the left hand he must carry a small bunch of lilies of the valley, with a tag on them reading: "Love from—[name of sender]—to the U.S. Post Office."

6. The following ritual will then be adhered to, a deviation by a single word subjecting the sender to a year in Leavenworth or both:

Clerk's Question: Do you want to mail a package?

Sender's Answer: No, sir.

Q. What *do* you want to do?

A. I don't much care, so long as I can be with you.

Q. Do you like tick-tack-toe?

A. I'm crazy mad for it.

Q. Very well. We won't play that.

A. Aren't you being just a little bit petty?

Q. Are you criticizing *me*?

A. Sorry.

Q. And high time. Now what do you want?

A. *You,* dear.

Q. You get along with yourself. What's in your hand?

A. Flowers for you—*dear.*

Q. I know that. What's in the other hand?

A. I won't tell.

Q. Give it here this minute.

A. You won't like it.

Q. Give-it-here-this-minute, I say.

The sender reluctantly gives over the parcel.

Q. What do you want to do with this?

A. I want to take it home with me and wrap it up again.

Q. You leave it here, and *like it.*

A. Please give it back. Please, pretty please?

Q. I will do no such thing. You leave it here and I will mail it for you. And shut up!

The sender leaves the window, sobbing. The clerk, just to be mean, mails the package.

The Real Public Enemies

I HAVE now reached an age when I feel that I am pretty well able to take care of myself against animate enemies. By "animate enemies" I mean living people, like burglars, drunks, or police—people who set out with a definite idea in their minds of getting me. Mind you, I don't mean that I can lick these people in a hand-to-hand encounter, but I do know, in a general way, what to do when they attack me, even if it is only to run.

It is the inanimate enemies who have me baffled. The hundred and one little bits of wood and metal that go to make up the impedimenta of our daily life—the shoes and pins, the picture books and door keys, the bits of fluff and sheets of newspaper—each and every one with just as much vicious ill will toward me personally as the meanest footpad who roams the streets, each and every one bent on my humiliation and working together, as on one great team, to bedevil and confuse me and to get me into a neurasthenics' home before I am sixty. I can't fight these boys. They've got me licked.

When I was very young and first realizing the conspiracy against me on the part of these inanimate things, I had a boyish idea that force was the thing to use. When a shoestring had clearly shown that it was definitely *not* going to be put through the eyelet, I would give it a yank that broke it in two, and feel that the bother of getting a new lace was not too much to pay for the physical pain which the old lace must have suffered. In fact, as I put in the new one I had an idea that it was pretty well frightened at the example of its predecessor and would jolly well behave itself or suffer the same fate.

But after years of getting out new laces and buying new fountain pens (my method, when a pen refused to work, was to press down on it so hard that the points spread open like a fork and then to rip the paper in a frenzied imitation of writing), I gradually realized that I was being the sucker in the battle and that the use of force didn't pay in the long run.

I then started trying subtlety. If there is one field in fighting in which a human ought to be able to win out over a piece of word, it is in tricky maneuvering. Take, for example, when you are trying to read a newspaper on top of a bus. We will start with the premise that the newspaper knows what you are trying to do and has already made up its mind that you are not going to do it. Very well, Mr. Newspaper, we'll see! (Later on you don't call it "Mr. Newspaper." You call it "you ——!" But that is after you know it better.)

Suppose you want to open it to page four. The thing to do is not to hold it up and try to turn it as you would an ordinary newspaper. If you do, it will turn into a full-rigged brigantine, each sheet forming a sail, and will crash head-on into your face, blinding you and sometimes carrying you right off the bus.

The best way is to say, as if talking to yourself, "Well, I guess I'll turn to page seven." Or better yet, let the paper overhear you say, "Oh, well, I guess I won't read any more," and make a move as if to put it away in your pocket. Then, quick as a wink, give it a quick turn inside out before it realizes what is happening.

It won't take long to catch on, but, thinking that you want to turn to page seven, as you said, it will quite possibly open to page four, which was the one you wanted.

A conspiracy to hurt me exists among household objects.

But even this system of *sotto voce* talking and deceit does not always work. In the first place, you have to have a pretty young newspaper, who hasn't had much experience, for all the older ones will be on to your game and will play it back at you for all it is worth.

The only way to be safe about the thing is to take it all very calmly and try to do your best with deliberate fierceness, folding each page over under your feet very slowly until you come to the right one. But by that time you have got the paper in such a condition that it cannot be read—so you lose anyway.

Of course, after years of antagonizing members of the inanimate underworld, you are going to get an active conspiracy against you, with physical violence on *their* part as its aim. It then becomes, not an aggressive campaign on your part, but one of defense to save yourself from being attacked.

For example, I have a pair of military brushes which have definitely signed up to put me on the spot and will, I am afraid, ultimately kill me. I have taken those brushes from the bureau and held them in a position to brush my hair, without an unkind thought in my mind, and have had them actually fly out of my hands, execute a pretty takeoff of perhaps a foot and a half, and then crash into my forehead with as deft a "one-two" as any heavyweight ever pulled on a groggy opponent.

I have placed slippers very carefully under my bed, only to have them crawl out during the night to a position where I will step into them the wrong way round when leaping out of bed to answer the telephone.

These things don't just happen, you know. They are proofs of a very clear conspiracy to hurt me physically which exists among household objects, and against which I have no defense. All that I can do is to walk about all day crouched over with one elbow raised to ward off the heavier attacks which are being aimed at me. This gives a man a cringing look which soon becomes a personal characteristic.

It is this element of physical danger which has entered my struggle with these things which has got me worried. I will match myself in an unequal fight to open a can of sardines or a bottle of water, if the issue is to be merely whether I get it open or not. But I can't face the inevitable gashing and bleeding which always follow my failure. I will tackle the closing of a trunk or suitcase, but I am already licked by the knowledge that, no matter how the fight turns out, the metal snaps are going to reach out and nip my fingers.

The only thing that I can do, as old age and experience bear down on me, is to sit with my hands in my pockets and try nothing.

I have said that, in my youth, I gave up the use of force when little things thwarted me. I *should* have given it up, but there is one enemy which I still lash out at in futile bludgeonings. It is the typewriter on which I am writing this article. In putting on a ribbon I lose myself entirely, and invariably end up completely festooned like Laocoön, ripping and tearing madly with inkstained fingers at a ribbon which long before I had rendered useless. I am also thrown into raging fits of physical violence when, owing to some technical fault which I do not understand, the letters begin getting dimmer and dimmer, finally becoming just shells of their natural selves. On such occasions I start very quietly hitting the keys harder and harder, muttering, "Oh, you won't, won't you?" until I am crashing down with both fists on the keyboard and screaming, "Take that—and *that!*"

In fact, as I write this, I detect a weakening in the pigment of the ribbon, and, as I strike each key, less and less seems to be happening. I will try to be calm.

I must try to remember that it does no good to inflict pain on inanimate things and that the best that I can do is break the typewriter. ... But really ... after all ... you xxxxx you xxxxxxxxxxxxxx take that xxxxxxxxxxxxxx and *that* xxxxxxxxxxxx.

HERBERT F. ROESE

Ripping and tearing madly at a ribbon which long before I had rendered useless.

What Time Is It?

And What of It?

By secretly consulting an old bootleg watch which I hid away (set at Standard Time) under my bed when my native state went daylight-saving, I find that it is a little over a month now since the Cossacks stormed up at the door and forced us to set our clocks an hour ahead. And, at the end of this month, I can give out a definite verdict against daylight-saving. I don't like it. I don't care what the reasons for it are. I don't like it. And beginning tomorrow I, personally, am going back to God's time. My body may belong to the State, but my soul belongs to Standard Time. If necessary, I will carry the case to the Supreme Court.

Time-keeping is a difficult enough maneuver at best, without monkeying around with an extra hour plus or minus. Just the fact that, when it is noon in New York, it is 5 P.M. in Paris has always worried me, and even now I am more or less inclined not to believe it. And when, last New Year's, greetings were radioed from New Zealand which reached here on December 31, I went into a sulk which almost spoiled the holidays for my friends. The whole idea is unpleasant to me.

The thing gets worse the farther west you go. When you cross the 180th meridian in the Pacific (so they try to tell me) you lose a whole day, which I very much doubt. If, at the

11

same time, daylight-saving is in effect just at that time, you lose one day and one hour. I suppose that, if someone were to come along and say so, you lose one day, one hour, and one minute. The thing can easily be made absurd.

If everyone knew the trouble that the Western Union goes to in order to fix Standard Time, there wouldn't be so much tampering with it on the part of the irresponsible legislators. From the United States Naval Observatory they select a list of about 150 so-called "clock stars." It is a great honor to be on this list. In order to be on it, a star has to sit very still and not wiggle or whisper, so that its permanent position can be noted in the American Ephemeris or Social Register. The person who told me all this (and who has, for obvious reasons, asked to remain anonymous) says that only stars which cross the meridian within twenty degrees of the zenith are included, "in order that the azimuth error may be small." Just how large an azimuth error has to be before it becomes large I forgot to ask, but I should imagine that six or seven feet would be pretty big for any azimuth error that you or I would likely to have anything to do with.

Well, sir, after the Western Union has selected its clock stars, it takes a look at them each night through pearl-handled opera glasses, and, according to my informant, in this way finds out what time it is. I am not quite clear on the thing yet, and don't know whether the stars, if looked at from the right angle, spell out "E-i-g-h-t-f-o-r-t-y-t-h-r-e-e." However, the experts at the Western Union can tell, and I suppose that is all that matters. If I knew what it was they did, and how they were able to tell time by the stars, I should be an expert at the Western Union. That is, of course, provided that I was socially acceptable to the present experts

But, on the whole, I think that I shall keep out of any jobs which involve an understanding of clocks and time-keeping. I can't even understand my own clocks. I have an alarm clock, a plain, unattractive piece of mechanism which I bought in a drug store about eight years ago. This clock will keep perfect time so long as it is tipped over on its face. If I humor it in this whim, however, it is obvious that I am not going to be able to tell what time it is, because I can't see the face. I tried once placing it over on its back, but it raised such a fuss that I had to turn it over instantly into its old position.

I have now solved the problem by having it on a table with a coarse wire net for a top instead of a solid piece of wood. So when I want to see what time it is, I simply get down on my hands and knees and look up through the wire, and there, clear as day, is the face of the clock looking down at me with the correct time. This maneuver also serves a double purpose, as it gets me out of bed much more surely than the mere ringing of an alarm will do.

I have had several letters from friends asking me why I

How to tell time by the Zodiac and one thing and another, as explained by Mr. Benchley.

didn't get rid of this clock and get one which would tell time without being coddled; but I have become fond of "Blushing Bennie," as I call it (because it is always hiding its face), and I wouldn't know what to do with a new clock staring directly at me every time I looked at it.

Down in the living room I have a clock which is called a "four-hundred-day" clock, which is supposed to run 400 days without winding. This feat seems to be accomplished by arranging four large cherries on a rotating stem which hangs down out of the works of the clock (clearly visible through the glass cover) and they go slowly round one way and then slowly round the other until the person who is watching them has gone mad. I have got myself trained now so that I can lean against the mantel and watch them rotate for six hours without feeling queer, but people who are not used to it should not try watching for more than fifteen minutes at first. If I have any work to do, it is a great comfort to know that I can always keep from doing it by watching these revolving cherries, for after a while I get hypnotized by the sight and am unable to take my eyes away. I have a man who does nothing else but come and lead me away from the clock whenever I have been there too long or when anyone in the room wants to talk to me.

Sometimes a dash of cold water in my face is necessary, and this is apt to irritate me and make me petulant at first, but when I am myself again I realize that it was for the best and reward the man with a warm smile and a "Well done!"

I don't know what we are supposed to do with the clock when the 400 days are up, because the directions distinctly said that under no circumstances was it to be touched once it had been started. I suppose that we shall have to throw it away. I shall want to save the cherries, however, and can perhaps learn how to twirl them myself.

All this will perhaps show you how mystified I am by any time-recording device, even the simplest. And when it comes to chronometers of a more complicated nature, I am frankly baffled. This is probably why daylight-saving not only confuses but irritates me, because I wasn't really settled in my mind about the old Standard Time and resent any further attempt to make it more difficult. I understand perfectly the attitude of Holland in the matter of so-called "Zone Time." Or perhaps you don't know what Holland's attitude was.

In 1879 a busybody named Sanford Fleming brought forward a plan for the whole earth which set out twenty-four standard meridians to be fifteen degrees apart in longitude, starting from Greenwich, England. There was to be an hour's difference in time between each two of these.

This was the guy who made all the trouble and made it possible for people in California who happened to be in the middle of a big party at midnight call up someone in New York on the telephone and wake him up out of a four A.M. slumber to say: "Hello, you big bum, you! Guess who this is!"

Well, all the nations accepted this crazy scheme of time-telling except Holland. Holland couldn't see any reason for messing around with meridians when there was so much trouble in the world as it was (and is). So Holland, although one of the smallest nations, stood out against the whole world and kept its own time, and, as a result, didn't get into the War when it came. And also makes delicious cheeses. And tulip bulbs. So you see?

My plan is to be known as "the Holland of Scarsdale," and to set all my clocks (except the one which cannot be tampered with) back to the old time we loved so well. They may throw me in jail, or they may cut off my electricity, but I am going through with this thing if it takes all summer. I don't like Time, and I never have, and I want to have as little to do with it as possible. If I am bothered much more by it, I shall take all the hands off all the watches and clocks in my house and just drift along, playing the mandolin and humming. I'm too busy a man to be worried by figuring out what time it is.

Greetings From—

DURING the Christmas and New Year's season there was an ugly rumor going the rounds of the countinghouses and salons *(Note to Printer: Only one 'o," please!)* of the town that I was in jail. I would like to have it understood at this time that I started that rumor myself. I started it, and spent quite a lot of money to keep it alive through the use of paid whisperers, in order that my friends would understand why they got no gifts or greeting cards from me. They couldn't expect a man who was in jail to send them anything. Or could they?

I have now reached an age and arterial condition where this business of selection of gifts for particular people throws me into a high fever (102) and causes my eyes to roll back into my head. It isn't the money that I begrudge. I spend that much in a single night on jaguar cubs and rare old Egyptian wines for one of my favous revels. It is simply that I am no longer able to decide what to get for whom. In other words, that splendid cellular structure once known as "my mind" has completely collapsed in this particular respect. (I am finding other respects every day, but we won't got into that now.)

It is not only at Christmas and New Year's that I am confronted with this terrifying crisis. When I am away on my summer vacation, when I go away on a business trip, or even when I wake up and find myself in another city by mistake, there is always that incubus sitting on my chest: "Which post card shall I send to Joe?" or "What shall I take back to Mae?" The result is that I have acquired a full-blown phobia for post-card stands and the sight of a gift shop standing in my path will send me scurrying around a three-mile detour or rolling on the ground in an unpleasant frenzy. If I knew of a good doctor, I would go to him for it.

On my last vacation I suddenly realized that I had been away for two weeks without sending any word home other than to cable the bank to mind its own business and let me alone about the overdraft. So I walked up and down in front of a post-card shop until I got my courage up, gritted my teeth, and made a dash for it. I found myself confronted by just short of 450,000 post cards.

Taking up a position slightly to the left and half facing one of those revolving racks, I gave it a little spin once around, just to see if it was working nicely. This brought the lady clerk to my side.

. . . in order that my friends would understand.

"Some post cards?" she asked, perhaps to make sure that I wasn't gambling with the contraption.

"I'm just looking," I reassured her. Then, of course, I *had* to look. I spun the thing around eighty or ninety times, until it began to look as if there were only one set of post cards in the rack, all showing some unattractive people in a rowboat on a moonlit lake. Then I started spinning in the opposite direction. This made me dizzy and I had to stop altogether. "Let me see," I said aloud to myself in order to reassure the lady that I really was buying cards and not just out on a lark, "who—whom—do I have to send to?"

Well, there were four in my own family, and Joe and Hamilton and Tweek and Charlie (something comical for Charlie)—oh, and Miss McLassney in the office and Miss Whirtle in the outer office and Eddie on the elevator, and then a bunch of kidding ones for the boys at the Iron Gate and— here I felt well enough to start spinning again. Obviously the thing to do was to take three or four dozen at random and then decide later who to send each one to. So I grabbed out great chunks of post cards from the rack, three out of this pack showed a water-colored boy carrying a bunch of pansies (these ought to get a laugh), and seven or eight showing peasants in native costume flying kites or something.

"I'll take these," I said, in a fever of excitement, and dashed out without paying.

For four days, I avoided sitting down at a desk to write those cards, but at last a terrific mountain storm drove me indoors and the lack of anything to read drove me to the desk. I took the three dozen cards and piled them in a neat pile before me. Then I took out my fountain pen. By great good luck, there was no ink in it. You can't write post cards without ink, now, can you? So I leapt up from the desk and took a nap until the storm was over.

It was not until a week later that I finally sat down again and began to decide which cards to send and to whom. Here was one showing an old goat standing on a cliff. That would be good for Joe, with some comical crack written on it. No, I guess this one of two peasant girls pushing a cart would be better for Joe. I wrote, "Some fun, eh, kid?" on the goat

picture and decided to send it to Hamilton, but right under
it was a colored one showing a boy and girl eating a bunch
of lilies of the valley. That would be better for Hamilton—
or maybe it would be better for Charlie. No, the goat one
would be better for Charlie, because he says "Some fun, eh,
kid?" all the time. . . . Now let's do this thing systematically.
The goat one to Charlie. Cross off Charlie's name from the
list. That's one. Now the boy and girl eating lilies of the
valley—or perhaps this one of a herd of swans—no the boy
and girl to Hamilton because—hello, what's this? How about
that for Hamilton? And how about the boy and girl eating a
herd of swans in a cartful of lilies of the valley on a cliff for

*The sight of a gift shop will send me rolling on the ground in an
unpleasant frenzy.*

Eddie or Joe or Miss McLassney or Mother or Tweek or—

At this point everything went black before me and when I came to I was seated at a little iron table on a terrace with my face buried in an oddly flavored glass of ice. Not having had a stamp, I didn't send even the card I had written to Charlie, but brought them all home with me in my trunk and they are in my top desk drawer to this very day.

The question of bringing home little gifts is an even more serious one. On the last day before I start back I go to some shop which specializes in odds and ends for returning travelers. I have my list of beneficiaries all neatly made out. Here are some traveling clocks. Everyone *has* a traveling clock. Here are some embroidered hand bags. (As a matter of fact, I have come to believe that the entire choice of gifts for ladies, no matter where you are, is limited to embroidered hand bags. You ask a clerk for suggestions as to what to take to your mother, and she says: "How about a nice embroidered hand bag?" You look in the advertisements in the newspapers and all you can find are sales of embroidered hand bags. The stores at home are full of embroidered hand bags and your own house is full of embroidered hand bags. My God, don't they ever think of anything else to make?)

I roam about in shop after shop, thinking that in the next one I shall run across something that will be just right. Traveling clocks and embroidered hand bags. Perfumes and embroidered hand bags. Perfumes and traveling clocks. And all of them can be bought at home right down on Main Street and probably a great deal better. At this point, the shops all close suddenly, and I am left with my list and lame ankles to show for a final day's shopping. It usually results in my sneaking out, the first day that I am home, and buying a traveling clock, some perfume, and an embroidered hand bag at the local department store and presenting them without the telltale wrappings to only moderately excited friends.

This is why I pretend to be in jail around Christmas and New Year's. It may end up in my pretending to be (or actually being) in jail the year round.

Defying the Conventions

WITH the advent of the political conventions there are three courses left open to the General Public (recently reduced to Major General Public on a private's pay). The private citizen who is not impressed by these two great gatherings of nominators may (1) tell the boy to stop leaving the morning and evening papers until further notice; (2) go up to the attic and hide in trunk until it is all over; (3) go to the conventions in person, take a seat up front, and when, if ever, there comes a moment of comparative quiet, deliver a long and resounding "bird," using one of those rubber contraptions especially designed for the purpose. Perhaps if enough private citizens went to the conventions in person there would be no room for the delegates and then we wouldn't have to have any election!

But since there is small chance of getting enough volunteers to crowd out the regulars, we might as well brush up on the details of how, according to the Constitution (the document, not the frigate), our Presidential candidates are nominated. We learned all about this in school, of course, but we also learned how to erect a square on the hypotenuse of a right-angled triangle and prove something by it—and where did *that* get us? I could entertain you for hours telling you where my geometry got me, but this is a political treatise.

According to the Constitution (the frigate, not the document), "each state will appoint, or shall cause to be appointed, or shall appoint to be caused, or shall go jump in the lake, as the legislature thereof may direct—" I guess that isn't the clause.

Anyway, every four years (it seems oftener, but that is because time passes so quickly when you are enjoying yourself), every four years a mysterious list of names appears in the papers, names of people who claim to be "delegates," seemingly empowered to go to the conventions, eat nuts, and vote for candidates for the Presidency. Just how they became "delegates" nobody seems to remember, but there must have been some ritual gone through with at *some* time, otherwise they would be just ordinary citizens like the rest of us. And when I say "ordinary," do I mean *ordinary!*

There is one explanation of the problem of where their delegates come from in the theory that they are chosen by taking the names that were left over in the hat after the drawings for the Irish Sweepstakes. Another school of political economists claim that they were the first ten to send in post cards making the greatest number of words out of "K-L-E-E-N-C-H-I-N Toothpaste—No More—No Less." My personal theory is that they were elected by being changed from mice into delegates by a good fairy who got to changing pumpkins into coaches and couldn't stop.

At any rate, along about February every four years they spring up and begin giving off hints as to which one of the candidates they favor, or, as the kidding phrase goes, "are pledged to." The pledge of a delegate to a national convention is embossed on tissue papeer and, when rolled up, can be exploded by pulling little strings at either end. Inside will be found a motto reading: "If in January you were born, then blow a toot upon this horn. I love you." This makes it clear which candidate they are supporting. The rule is that each candidate must either keep his pledge or else give it back to someone who will keep it for him until he gets back.

At the conventions, the main feature is the marching around the hall. No one can be a delegate who cannnot march around a hall and sing, "Hail, hail, the gang's all here!" This is what is known as the dignity of Democracy. There has been some talk of dispensing with the delegates entirely and just getting the Boys' Fife and Drum Corps of each community to go to the conventions bearing signs reading, "We want a touchdown!" and "Kiss me again!" thereby giving the same effect as the delegates and yet maintaining a certain feeling of genuine youth. If the idea is just to be boys again, why not get *real* boys and not fifty-year-old men in Ferris waists? A good convention of sixteen-year-old boys, with their girls, would be a relief. Then we should know where we stood.

The party system in the United States is rather complicated right now, owing to there being no parties and very little United States. The Republican and Democratic parties, ancient rivals, do not exist any more as such, there being more fun watching Harvard and Yale. This has brought about a condition where Republican conventions are sometimes attended by Democrats by mistake, and Democratic conventions attended by Republicans on purpose. The only way to tell them apart is by the conditions of the hotel rooms after the convention is over. The Republicans have more gin bottles and the Democrats seem to have gone in more for rye.

The hotel room as a factor in the political conventions can hardly be overemphasized. The main assembly hall or auditorium (so called because no one can hear anyone talking in it) is used chiefly for the marching and fistfighting, with an occasional round dance or hockey game. It is here also that all the photographs are taken. In the 1936 conventions it is planned to use the photographs of the 1928 and 1932 conventions and not use the auditorium at all, just sticking to the hotel rooms where the real work of the session is done. In fact, in 1936 it may not be necessary for the delegates to go to the convention city at all. They can just stay at home and march up and down in their own rooms until instructions come from the leaders as to how they are to vote.

But, you may say, what about the applause? How can there be a convention without the regulation applause which lasts ten, fifteen, or twenty minutes as each candidate's name is mentioned? This is a tough one, but there ought to be some way around it. Each delegate, if he stayed in his own home town, could send a telegram reading, "I am applauding for fifteen minutes," or "Consider that I am giving the name of George W. Glib an ovation."

This, however, will probably never receive the support of the newspapers, as attending political conventions is the only form of fun that many reporters get. In fact, if it weren't for the newspapers there would be no convention at all. With a man from each paper or news syndicate to cover the political angle, the personality angle, the woman's angle, the ginger-pop angle, the angle angle (that word is beginning to look as if it weren't spelled right), the resultant unemployment among newspaper men if the convention were abolished would be frightful and might end up in a revolution. It has been estimated that at this year's conventions there will be more newspaper men than delegates, many of them depending on the hand-outs from the various headquarters for their sandwiches and coffee for the coming year.

A revolution of half-starved and wholly parched convention reporters would be the biggest thing since the Union Square riots.

Thus we find that, for the present at any rate, it will be necessary for the so-called "delegates" to take their instructions right in the convention city itself.

And when the whole thing is over and the radio programs have settled back into the regular run of pancake recipes and Oh, Sweet Mystery of Life, At Last I've Found You without being broken up by Alabama's twenty-four votes being announced every five minutes, and when all the bottles and sevens of spades have been picked up off the floor along with some of the older delegates who haven't been able to stand the heat, and when two candidates have been chosen to carry the banners of their respective parties in the great 1932 Presidential campaign—then we can start reading the papers again.

adam
john
barth

ADAM JOHN BARTH

*My personal theory is that they were changed from mice into delegates by
a good fairy who got to changing pumpkins into coaches and couldn't stop.*

Ill Will
Toward Men

·   ·

NOBODY would like to see the Brotherhood of Man come to pass any more than I would, for I am not a very good fighter and even have difficulty holding my own in a battle of repartee. I am more the passive type, and I would be glad to have everybody else passive too.

But I am afraid that it can't be done. I am afraid that there are certain situations in which a man finds himself placed by chance where there is nothing left for him to do but hate his fellow man. It isn't that he wants to hate him, but certain chemical reactions take place in his system.

Take, for example, the case of the dining car. You come in alone and the steward waves the menu at you in a friendly fashion indicating that you are to sit right down here opposite this gentleman. At the very start, this gentleman resents your sitting opposite him and you resent his having got there first.

He doesn't take a good look at your face, or you at his, but you both concentrate an ugly glare on the buttons of each other's waistcoats. If he happens to have a fraternal watch charm on his chain you appraise it critically and say to yourself, "Oh, one of *those,* eh?" In the meantime, he has worked his inspection up to your tie, and you are conscious of the fact that he doesn't like it at all.

You take a quick look at what he is eating. It is usually

He unfolds his paper and opens it so wide that it knocks your hat askew.

steak and French-fried potatoes, with sliced tomatoes on the side. Has the guy no imagination in eating? You feel sure that he is going to top off with a piece of apple pie and a large cup of coffee. In the meantime, it has come your time to order. Now it is *his* turn to be critical.

As a matter of fact, that steak of his looks pretty good, but you wouldn't order that for a million dollars. He would know that you got the idea from him and you won't give him that satisfaction. So you order the deviled beef bones—and realize that he is laughing nastily to himself at your naïveté. The hell with him!

While your order is being prepared, you try looking out the window, but it is too dark to see anything. Here is the chance to break down the ill feeling slightly and make some remark, such as, "Dark out, isn't it?" But, unless you do it right away, the chance is lost and it is war to the death.

When your dinner comes, the advantage is all his. He can watch you serve yourself, make mental notes on *your* handling of your knife and fork, laugh inwardly at your attempts to get meat from a bone which has no meat on it. The result is that you spill large pieces of beef on the cloth, suddenly become self-conscious about holding your implements until you aren't sure just how you *have* been holding them all your life and, with the nervousness of a beginner, let your knife fly out of your hand on to the window sill. You are tempted to throw it at him, but you notice that he has divined your purpose and is grasping his. Well, let us have no bloodshed here. You can get him out in the vestibule.

Here are two citizens of the United States who should be brothers in the bond, whipped up to a state of mutual dislike and animosity without a word being spoken. He delays over his dessert much longer than he has to, and although you yourself would like some preserved figs with cream, you decide that one hog at a table is enough. You both pay your checks at the same time and sneer at each other's tip. Fortunately his car is in one direction from the diner and yours is in the other, so actual physical combat is avoided.

In elevators also we find a spirit which, without any justification whatsoever, threatens to destroy all the good work which evangelists and philanthropists have been struggling at all these years. Two people alone in an elevator, and strangers to each other, are instinctive enemies. If one says: "Ten out" and the other can beat him by two and say "Eight out," it is a victory which can hardly be measured by ordinary standards. Sidelong glances of hatred are shot across the car. If one catches the other looking in the mirror, a scornful leer passes over his face and the word "Siss" is spoken just as clearly as if the sound were actually made. If a woman gets into the car, and No. 1 takes off his hat while No. 2 keeps his on, the first man boils with a desire to snatch the other's hat from his head and dash it to the floor, while the second does everything but sneer out loud at the affectation which prompts the other to assume a gentility which is both spurious and unnecessary.

The only thing which can possibly bring these two together

is the entrance into the car of two other people who carry on their conversation over the heads of the other passengers. Our two original antagonists could almost become friends under the irritation of having to listen to the new occupants' badinage.

But probably the most common of all antagonisms arises from one man's taking a seat beside you on a train, a seat to which he is completely entitled. You get in at Bog Shore and find a seat by yourself. At any rate, you get the window, and although you know that by the time the train reaches Flithurst the car will be taxed to its capacity, you put your hat down in the seat beside you.

At Flithurst a long line of commuters files past. One of them, an especially unpleasant-looking man, spies your hat and hesitates. You are thinking: "The great hulk! Why doesn't he go into the next car?" He is thinking: "I guess I'll teach this seat hog a lesson. . . . Is this seat taken?" Without deigning a reply, you grab your hat sulkily and cram it on your head. He sits down and the contest begins.

He unfolds his paper and opens it so wide that it knocks your hat askew. He is regarding the *Post-Examiner*. He *would*. Obviously an illiterate, to add to everything else. You crouch against the window sill, in exaggerated courtesy and fold your paper up into the smallest possible compass. Go ahead, take all the room if you want it! Don't mind *me*—oh, no! He doesn't. Nevertheless, he is boiling with antagonism, while you are on the point of pulling the bell rope and getting off the train to walk the rest of the way to town. And for what?

You are enraged because a man took a seat to which he was quite entitled, and he is enraged because he knows that you are enraged and, besides, you have the seat by the window. Thus we see that Old Stepmother Nature has her own ways and means of perpetuating warfare and hatreds. Every one of us may have a daily calendar with a motto on it about loving our fellow men, but when Nature puts two people within a radius of three feet of each other and turns on the current, there is no sense in trying to be nice about the thing. It is dog eat dog.

A Word About
Hay Fever

On the eighteenth of August, at 6 A.M., I celebrate the twenty-fifth anniversary of the advent of my hay fever. I plan to make quite an occasion of it, with field sports and a buffet lunch in a tent during the day and a *soirée de gala* after dinner with fireworks (including set pieces representing the different varieties of noxious weeds) and dancing for those who can. Twenty-five years of hay fever is nothing to be—would you believe it, I almost wrote "sneezed at" without thinking! Gosh!

On the eighteenth of August, 1905, I awoke at 6 A.M. (the reason for this unnatural procedure was that I was at a boys' camp at the time and a bugle had been blowing in my ear since 5:45) and realized that something was wrong. I realized that something was wrong because I sneezed nineteen times in rapid succession. One or two sneezes on arising is not abnormal, but nineteen indicate some derangement of the apparatus. "I must have caught cold," I said, and promptly went back to bed.

But as I got again within range of the straw-filled tick which served us hardy boys as a mattress, I realized that it was no ordinary head cold which had descended on me. I had heard and seen enough of hay fever among my tribesmen at home to know that the old Gypsy's Curse which was laid on the

PETER ARNO

I shall take the aggressive, or retire to a darkened room and tear bits of paper.

Benchleys generations ago in a dank Welsh cave had caught up with me, the youngest of the clan, and that, from that date on, I was to be marked with the red eye and the tender nose of the anaphylaxis sufferer.

If anaphylaxis (or hypersensitiveness to protein) were all that the victim of hay fever suffers from, things wouldn't be so bad. He could buy a bale of soft cotton handkerchiefs and fight the thing out by himself. The real suffering comes through his relations with the rest of society and from man's recognized inhumanity to man. In other words, he is a figure of fun.

People can have sunburn, hangnails, or even ordinary head colds, and their more fortunate mates will say: "Aw, that's too bad! Why don't you just take the day off and go home?" But the minute anyone with hay fever comes along, even though he be blind and gasping for breath, the entire community stops work and screams with laughter.

"Hay fever!" they say, holding their sides. "Boy, you ought
to pose for a bunch of pomegranates!" or "What's the matter?
Did you leave your eyes at home on the bureau?" People who
are not ordinarily given to wise-cracking blossom out as the
wits of their day when confronted with someone in the throes
of a hay-fever attack. You wouldn't think there could be so
many lighthearted, facile jokesters in the world. I can imagine
no national calamity which would not be alleviated, no community depression which would not be shot through with
sunshine, by the mere presence of a poor guy poisoned with
ragweed pollen.

Hay fever has been going now for quite a number of centuries. Every year, along about August, there are editorials
in the papers (humorous, unless the editorial writer himself
happens to be a sufferer) and reports of conventions and
newly discovered cures. And yet the ignorance of the immune
citizenry on the subject is nothing short of colossal. Tell a
man that the reason why you look so funny is that you have
hay fever and, as soon as he has stopped laughing and has
delivered himself of the customary *bon mots*, he will say: "Hay
fever, eh? That's something you get from eating goldenrod,
isn't it?" Goldenrod somehow always sticks in their minds
as the sole cause of the affliction, although goldenrod is really
one of the minor excitants and practically a soothing agent
compared to ragweed and the more common grasses. But
the non-sneezing layman will have it goldenrod, and goldenrod it is in song and story.

Then there is a great deal of good-natured incredulity over
the fact that the first attack comes along about the same day
every year. "You don't mean to tell me that it comes annually
on exactly the eighteenth of August!" they say, poking the
sufferer in the ribs. "That's because you are *looking* for it
then. Suppose the eighteenth of August falls on a Sunday!"

They express no surprise that golden bantam corn comes
along at the same time each year, or that the rambler roses
on their porch are in full bloom every Fourth of July; but
say that ragweed starts shedding its pollen every August along
about the eighteenth, and they look at you suspiciously. I

have struck, and will strike again, anyone who pushes me too far in this manner.

I do not know which is worse, to meet someone who knows nothing about hay fever and asks questions, or someone who knows just enough about it to suggest a remedy. The thing being as prevalent as it is, a lot of people have relatives who are victims. "I have a cousin who used to have hay fever," they say, "and he did something, I don't exactly remember what it was, but it was something you rub on your forehead. Cleenax or something like that—anyway, he hasn't had hay

PETER ARNO

"Hay fever!" they say, holding their sides. "Boy, you ought to pose for a bunch of pomegranates!"

fever since he started using it." You never by any chance meet the cousin who has been cured, and you never find out just what this "Cleenax or something" was, but the implication is that if you don't follow the suggestion up you just like to have hay fever.

There is also quite a general, though extremely hazy, knowledge about inoculations. "Isn't there something that they shoot into your arm that fixes it up? A guy in our office had that done and is O.K. now." Well, there are plenty of things that you could shoot into your arm which would fix hay fever, among them a good, strong solution of bichloride of mercury; but most of the pollen serums which are used for this purpose have to be shot in every fifteen minutes from February 15 until November 1, and even then there is a very good chance that the result will be simply a sore arm in addition to the hay fever. I tried it one year and have gone back to the good, old-fashioned eye-and-nose infirmity.

So, beginning with my twenty-fifth anniversary, I am going to take the aggressive. Instead of letting people say to me, "What's the matter with you? You look so funny," I am going to lead off with "What's the matter with *you*? You look awful." Just as Thoreau replied to Emerson, "Why aren't you in jail?" when the great philosopher asked him why he *was* in jail, I intend to make the immune ones explain why, with so many charming and intelligent people wiping their eyes and sneezing, *they* are standing there like ninnies and breathing easily.

I shall either adopt this course or do as I have been doing for the past five years—retire to a darkened room, shut the windows, and tear bits of paper from August 18 until September 15.

Little
Noise Abatement

So now we are to have no more noise. Scientific research has disclosed the fact that the effect of harsh noises on the brain is more deleterious than that of drugs, and nowhere near so pleasant while it is happening. The bursting of a paper bag, according to the Noise Abatement Commission, increases the brain pressure more than does morphine, but you don't read of anyone smuggling paper bags into the country just to bang them in some addict's ear at so much per bang. Noise is bad for you and isn't even any fun. It's a wonder that they care about prohibiting it.

Doing away with banging paper bags is a good beginning, along with sidewalk loud-speakers and other public disturbers, but why not first do away with the people who think it is funny to bang paper bags? You would find that you were killing 500 birds with one stone, for they are the ones who make almost all other kinds of obnoxious noises. Anyone who thinks it is funny to sneak up behind you and whack an inflated paper bag (and is there anything more satisfactory than to see the chagrin on his face when the bag turns out to be a dud and refuses to bang?) will also sneak up behind you and push you off rafts into the water, will dive down and grab your legs while you are swimming, will snap rubber bands at you, and will cover his lower teeth with his lip and

35

emit piercing whistles. Get rid of one and you will have got rid of them all.

This shrill whistling through the teeth is a sure indication in a boy that he will grow up to be an obnoxious citizen. They usually practice it in public gatherings where it will attract attention to themselves. It is offered in place of any mental attainment or physical prowess and is almost always the mark of retarded development along lines other than whistling through the teeth. In a crowd, if you will watch carefully, you will see the boy who has just whistled himself into prominence sooner or later will begin to push. This is also considered funny, especially if a good flying wedge can be started which will knock over a couple of old ladies. It is all a part of the banging-paper-bags and whistling-through-the-teeth psychology and is, mental experts will tell you, the sign of an inferiority complex. Inferiority is a mild word for it.

What the scientists do not seem to have taken into consideration in their researches is that it is not so much the noise itself that irritates as the knowledge that someone is making the noise deliberately.

That is entirely a question of whether the noise is necessary or not is shown by the fact that I am not upset by the sound of celery or nuts being eaten. There is no way that I know of, unless they are ground up into a paste and dissolved in the mouth, by which celery and nuts can be eaten noiselessly. So my nerves get a rest during this course, and I have nothing but the kindliest feelings toward the eater. In fact, I don't hear it at all. But ice-crunching and loud gum-chewing, together with drumming on tables and whistling the same tune seventy times in succession, because they indicate an indifference on the party of the perpetrator to the rest of the world in general, are not only registered on the delicate surface of the brain but eat little holes in it until it finally collapses or blows up. I didn't see this mentioned anywhere in the Commission's report.

The Commission, in fact, just concentrates on the big noises, like those which go to make up what poets call "the symphony of a big city." Some of these are also the result of the activities of grownups who used to whistle through their teeth when

My nerves get a rest during this course.

they were boys and who now don't care how much they disturb other people so long as they call attention to themselves. In this class are those owners of radio supply shops who stick big horns out over their doors to give the "Maine Stein Song" an airing from nine to six every day; chauffeurs who sound their horns in a traffic jam when they know that it will do no good; and, I am sorry to say, mendicants who walk up and down the street playing shrill little instruments featuring "The Blue Danube Waltz" and "Happy Days" in rotation.

I hate to be nasty about blind men (if they really are blind) but there is one who takes up a stand right under my window on Tuesdays, Thursdays, and Saturdays and plays a clarinet most of the afternoon. He is accompanied by a helper with a banjo.

Now, a clarinet is an instrument with considerable volume and powerful reach. It sounds out above the noise of the elevator (which I don't mind) and the riveting (which I can make allowances for) and the worst of it is he plays it pretty well. When it first begins I rather enjoy it. I stop my lathe and hum softly to myself. I sometimes even get up and execute a short *pas seul* if nobody is looking. But his repertory is limited, and, after a while, "I'm Dancing with Tears in My Eyes Because the Girl in My Arms Isn't You" loses its sentimental value and begins its work on my nerve fibers. I try to say to myself: "Come, come, the man is blind and very poor," but then I remember reading about street beggars who not only are really not blind but who make more in a day than I do in some weeks (this week, for instance) and I become convinced that this man is one of those. And why can't he move on? Doesn't he ever stop to think that there are probably 5,000 people who are being driven mad by his music within a radius of one block? Aren't there *any* instruments that he can play which aren't so loud? By this time I am in a rage which is cumulative every time he stops and I hear him begin again. (The stopping and beginning again is really the peak of irritation.) The whole thing ends in my shutting all the windows and getting under the bed to sulk.

I hope that the Noise Abatement Commission will take cognizance of these things. If they don't, I have my own resources. I have a small rifle with which I am practicing every day at a shooting gallery, and I am going to try it out on that newsboy (aged thirty-five, with a voice to match) who picks out the noon hour about once a week to walk through my street announcing that "Nya-a-ya-nyaded! Onoy-naded!" in tones which would indicate that he has three other men inside him. I may not wait for the Noise Abatement Commission to get him.

As a matter of fact, I have every confidence that some of the louder and more general noises will be abated. It is the little noises that I am after, or rather the people who make the little noises. My brain cells are pretty far gone as it is, but it may not be too late. Of course, the question might arise as to what I shall use my brain for, once I have saved it. There will be time enough to figure that out when the noises have stopped.

The Truth about Thunderstorms

ONE of the advantages of growing older and putting on weight is that a man can admit to being afraid of certain things which, as a stripling, he had to face without blanching. I will come right out and say that I mean thunderstorms.

For years I have been concealing my nervousness during thunderstorms, or, at least, I have flattered myself that I was concealing it. I have scoffed at women who gave signs of being petrified, saying, "Come, come!" What is there to be afraid of?" And all the time I *knew* what there was to be afraid of, and that it was a good, crashing sock on the head with a bolt of lightning. People *do* get it, and I have no particular reason for believing that I am immune. On the contrary.

Just where any of us in the human race get off to adopt the Big-Man attitude of "What is there to be afraid of?" toward lightning is more than I can figure out. You would think that we knew what lightning is. You would think that we knew how to stop it. You would think that no one but women and yellow dogs were ever hit by it and that no man in a turtle-neck sweater and a three days' beard on his chin would give it a second thought. I am sick of all this bravado about lightning and am definitely abandoning it herewith.

Ever since I was a child old enough to have any pride in the matter I have been wincing inwardly whenever 100,000 volts of Simon-pure electricity cut loose in the air. My nervous system has about six hundred ingrowing winces stored up inside it, and that is bad for any nervous system. From now on I am going to humor mine and give a shrill scream whenever I feel like it, and that will be whenever there is a good sharp flash of lightning. I will say this for myself: I will scream when the lightning flashes and not when the thunder sounds. I may be timid but I am no fool.

My nervousness begins when I see the black clouds in the distance. At the sound of the first rumble my digestive system lays off work, leaving whatever odds and ends of assimilation there may be until later in the day.

Of course, up until now I have never allowed myself to show trepidation. If I happened to be out on the water or playing tennis when it was evident that a storm was coming, I have looked casually at my watch and said, "Ho-hum! What about going in and making a nice, cool drink?" Sometimes I even come right out an say, "It looks like a storm—we'd better get in"; but there is always some phlegmatic guy who says, "Oh, we aren't going to get that—it's going around the mountain," and, by the time it is evident that we *are* going to get that and it *isn't* going around the mountain, it is too late.

It is remarkable how slow some people can be in taking down a tennis net or bringing a boat inshore when there is a thunderstorm on the way. They must not only take the net down but they must fold it up, very carefully and neatly, or they must put things away all shipshape in the cabin and coil ropes. Anything to waste time.

My attempts to saunter toward the house on such occasions must have, at times, given away the dread I have of being the recipient of a bolt of lightning. I guess that I have done some of the fastest sauntering ever pulled off on a dry track. Especially if my arms are loaded down with cushions and beach umbrellas I make a rather ungainly job of trying to walk as if I didn't care and yet make good time.

If possible, I usually suggest that someone run ahead and shut the windows in the house, and then immediately delegate myself to this job. I am not so crazy about shutting windows during a thunderstorm, but it is better than hanging around outside.

I once got caught up in an airplane during an electrical storm. In fact, there were *two* storms, one on the right and one on the left, and we were heading right for the spot where they were coming together. We could see them quite a long time before they hit us, and I was full of good suggestions which the pilot didn't take. I wanted to put down right where we were. It was a rocky country, covered with scrub pines, but it seemed to be preferable to hanging around up in the air.

I was considerably reassured, however, by being told (or shouted to) that you are safer up in the air during a thun-

PETER ARNO

If my arms are loaded down I make a rather ungainly job of trying to walk as if I didn't care and yet make good time.

derstorm than you are on the earth, as lightning cannot strike unless the object is "grounded." It sounded logical to me, or as logical as anything connected with lightning ever could sound, and I sat back to enjoy my first electrical display in comfort. It really was great, although I hate to admit it. You couldn't hear the thunder because of the motors and there were some very pretty flashes.

It was only several months after, on reading of a plane being struck by lightning three thousand feet up, that I began to get nervous. Perhaps you can't get hit unless you are "grounded," according to all the laws of nature, but it is always the exception that proves the rule, and it would be just my luck to be one of the exceptions.

Perhaps the worst part that a nervous man has to play during a crisis like this is reassuring the ladies. If I am alone, I can give in and go down cellar, but when there are women around I have to be brave and joke and yell "Bang!" every time there is a crash. To make matters worse, I find that there are a great many women who are not frightened, and who want to sit out on the porch and play bridge through the whole thing.

This is a pretty tough spot for a man of my temperament. At best, I am an indifferent bridge player, even with the sun shining or a balmy summer night's breeze wafting around outside. I have to go very carefully with my bidding and listen to everything that is being said or I am in danger of getting a knife in my back from my partner when the game is over. But with a thunderstorm raging around my ears and trees crashing down in the yard by my elbow, I might just as well be playing "slapjack" for all the sense I make.

A good flash of lightning has been known to jolt a "Five spades" out of me, with an eight and queen of spades in my hand. Sometimes it would almost have been better if the bolt had hit me. (Only fooling, Lord! Just kidding!)
I would feel more ashamed of confessing all this if I weren't sure that I am in the right about it. I am afraid of snakes or burglars or ghosts of even Mussolini, but when it comes to lightning—boy, there's something to be afraid *of!* And anyone who says that he isn't is either lying or an awful sap.

Of course, being nervous isn't going to keep you from getting hit, but when you are nervous you don't lie around with water dripping on you and holding a copper plate in your mouth, and avoiding all this sort of thing certainly helps.

If I were running a thunderstorm I would pick out some big man who goes around saying there is nothing to be afraid of and clip a cigar or two out from between his teeth just to show him. And any nice guy like me, who knows his place and tries to keep it, I would let go scot-free and might even uproot a fine big pot of buried gold pieces for him.

The funny part about all this is that now that I am old enough to come out frankly and admit how I feel about thunderstorms, I seem to be getting too old to mind them so much. It has been a couple of years now since I had a really good scare (I am now knocking wood so hard that the man in the next room just yelled "Come in!"). Perhaps it is just that, when you get to be my age, it doesn't make so much difference. If it isn't lightning, it will be hardening of the arteries. I still would prefer hardening of the arteries, however.

Art Revolution
No. 4861

•   •

ACCORDING to advices from Paris (if you want to take advices
from such a notorious town), a new painter has emerged
from the ateliers of Montparnasse who bids fair to revolutionize Art. Art has been revolutionized so many times in the
past twenty years that nothing short of complete annihilation
can be considered even a fist fight, to say nothing about a
revolution; but it looks now, however, as if the trick finally
had been turned. A French boy of forty-five has done it.

The artist in question is Jean Baptiste Morceau Lavalle
Raoul Depluy Rourke (during the Peninsular campaigns a
great many Irish troops settled in Paris and the authorities
were unable to get them out—hence the Rourke). He is a
little man, who has difficulty in breathing (not enough, however), and not at all the type that you would think of as a
great painter—in fact, he *isn't*. But hidden away in the recesses of that small head is an idea which, some say, is destined
to make a monkey out of Art.

Here is the Idea: All Art is Relative although all Relatives
are not Art. (The gag is not mine. I am merely reporting.)
If we look at a chair or a table or an old shoe box of picnic
lunch, what we see is not really a chair, or table, or shoe box
full of picnic lunch, but a glove, a sponge, and a child's sand
set. This much is obvious.

44

Now—if Art is to be anything at all in the expression of visual images, if, as someone has said, it is to hold Nature up to the mirror, then we must (I am still quoting Rourke, although I am thinking of stopping shortly) put down on our canvas *not* the things that we see but the things that see *us*. Or do I make myself clear?

Perhaps the best way for us to study this new theory of painting is to put on our thinking caps and turn our tired little eyes to the reproduction on this page in which Mr. Arno has caught something of the spirit of Rourke's famous painting, Mist on the Marshes. The committee of the French Academy refused to hang this picture because, they said, it

Now, as you will see, what we have here is not so much a picture as a feeling for Beauty.

wasn't accompanied by a stamped, self-addressed envelope, and, besides, it didn't have enough paint on it. This, however, was an obvious subterfuge on the part of the committee. The fact was that they didn't understand it, and, in this world, what we don't understand we don't believe in. And a very good rule it is, too.

If you examine the picture closely you will see that it is really made up of three parts—Maine, New Hampshire, and Vermont. The leg, which doesn't seem to belong to anybody, is mine—and I want it back, too, when you have finished looking at the picture. The pensive-looking old party in the picture on this page who appears to be hanging on the cornice of a building which isn't shown in the picture is a self-portrait of the artist. He painted it by holding a mirror in one hand and a harmonica in the other and then looking in the other direction. In this way he caught the *feeling* rather than actual physical details.

Now, as you will see, what we have here is not so much a picture as a feeling of Beauty. Although the artist is still feeling for it, it is quite possible that it may not be as far beyond his grasp as it seems. You can't go on feeling around like that without striking something, possibly oil.

For example, a great many people resent the fried egg in the upper left hand-corner. They claim that it looks too much like the sun. On the other hand, sun worshipers claim that it looks too much like a fried egg. As a matter of fact, friends of the artist, who caught him in a communicative mood one night when he was drunk, report that it is really a badge of a parade marshal, symbolizing the steady march of Art toward the picnic grounds. Whatever it is, you cannot deny that it is in the upper left-hand corner of the picture. And that is something.

In the Sur-Réaliste school of painting (of which Monsieur Rourke was a member until he was suspended for swimming in the pool when there was no water in it) there is an attempt to depict Spirit in terms of Matter and both Spirit and Matter in terms of a good absinthe bun.

Thus, the laughing snake in the lower left-hand corner of

PETER ARNO

Mist on the Marshes is merely a representation of the *spirit* of laughing snakes, and has nothing to do with Reality. This snake is laughing because he is really not in the picture at all. It also pleases him to see that snakes are coming back as figments of delirium tremens, for there was a time when they were considered very bad form.

A good imaginative drunk of five years ago would have been ashamed to see such old-fashioned apparitions as snakes, the fad at the time being little old men with long beards who stood in corners and jeered.

"Seeing snakes" was held to be outmoded and fit only for comic characters in old copies of *Puck*. If you couldn't see little old men, or at least waltzing beavers, you had better not see anything at all.

But the Sur-Réalistes have brought back the snake, and this one is pretty tickled about it. After all, old friends are best.

The crux of the whole picture, however, lies in the fireman who holds the center of the stage. Here the artist has become almost photographic, even to the fire bell which is ringing in the background.

The old-fashioned modernist painters, like Matisse and Picasso, were afraid of being photographic, but the new boys think it is heaps of fun. This could not possibly be anything but a fireman and a fire bell, unless possibly it is a fisherman and a ship's bell. At any rate, it is a man and a bell, and that is going a long way toward photographic Art.

As for the silk hat, the ladder, the rather unpleasant un-attached face, and the arrow and target, they belong to an-other picture which got placed by mistake on top of this one when the paint was still wet. Monsieur Rourke feels rather upset about this, but hopes that you won't notice it.

Sporting Life in America:
Turkish Bathing

ONE of the more violent forms of exercise indulged in by Americans today is Turkish-bath sitting. This invigorating activity has almost entirely replaced the old-fashioned tree chopping and hay pitching which used to work our fathers up into such a rosy glow and sometimes land them in an early grave. Turkish-bath sitting has the advantage of not only making you perspire freely, but of giving you a chance to get your newspaper read while perspiring. And you can catch cold just as easily after a Turkish bath as you ever could after pitching hay. Easier.

A man seldom thinks of taking Turkish baths until it is too late. It is usually at that time of life when little diamonds of white shirt have begun peeping out between the buttons of his vest, or when those advertisements showing men with a large sector of abdomen disappearing under the influence of a rubber belt have begun to exert a strange fascination for him. Then he remembers about Turkish baths. Or when he wakes up some morning with his head at the foot of the bed and the lights all going and the windows shut. Then, somewhere in the recesses of what used to be his mind, there struggles a puny thought vaguely connected with steam rooms and a massage.

"That might do me some good," he thinks, and promptly

faints. In both of these cases he is anywhere from one day to one year too late.

However, he takes a chance. He totters to the nearest emporium which features pore-opening devices, checks his watch and what is left of his money, and allows a man to pull off his shoes. Just in time he remembers that he has on the lavender running drawers which someone once sent him as a joke, and quickly dismisses the attendant, finishing disrobing by himself and hiding the lavender running drawers under his coat as he hangs them up. Not that he cares what the attendant thinks, but you know how those guys talk.

Then, coyly wrapping a towel about himself, he patters out into the hot room. A hot room in a Turkish bath is one of the places where American civilization appears at its worst. One wonders, on glancing about at the specimens of manhood reclining on divans or breathing moistly under sheets, if perhaps it wouldn't be better for Nature to send down a cataclysmic earthquake and begin all over again with a new race. It is slightly comforting in a way, however, because no matter how far along you have allowed your figure to get, there are always at least half a dozen figures on view which make yours look like that of a discobolus.

I can imagine no lower point of self-esteem than to find yourself one day the worst-looking exhibit in a Turkish bath. They should keep a pistol handy for just such cases. And you might shoot a couple of others while you are at it. It would save them all that bother of lacing up their shoes again.

In the hot room there isn't much to do. You can read a newspaper, but in a couple of minutes it gets a little soggy and flops over on your face, besides becoming so hot that turning over a page is something of an adventure. If, by any chance, you allow an edge of it to rest on an exposed bit of your anatomy, it isn't a quarter of a second before you have it tossed to the floor and given up reading. Then comes the period of cogitation.

As you sit waiting for your heart to stop beating entirely, you wonder if, after all, this was the thing to do. It occurs to you that a good brisk walk in the open air would have done almost the same thing for you, with the added advantage of

PETER ARNO

No matter how far along you have allowed your figure to get, there are always half a dozen which make yours look like that of a discobolus.

respiration. People must die in hot rooms, and you wonder how they would identify you if you were quietly to smother.

The towel around your waist would do no good, as they are all alike. You regret that you were never tattooed with a ship flying your name and address from the masthead. The only way for them to tell who you were would be for them to wait until everybody else had gone home and find the locker with your clothes in it. Then they would find those lavender drawers. So you decide to brave it out and not to die.

Conversation with your oven mates is no fun either. If you open your mouth you get it full of hot air and you are having trouble enough as it is keeping body and soul together. In the second place, you know that you look too silly to have your ideas carry any weight.

I remember once sitting on a sheet-covered steamer chair with my head swathed in a cold towel to keep my hair from catching on fire and thinking that there was something vaguely familiar about the small patch of face which was peering at me from under a similar turban across the room. As the owner of the face got up to go into the next torture chamber I recognized him as an English captain whom I had last seen in the impressive uniform of those Guards who sport a red coat, black trousers, and an enormous fur busby with a gold strap under the chin. I at once hopped to my feet, and, clutching my towel about me with one hand, extended my other to him.

"Well, fancy seeing you here!" was about all that seemed suitable to say. So we both said it. Then we stood, perspiring freely from under our head cloths, while he told me that he was in New York on some military mission, that the King and Queen were both well, and that England was counting a great deal on the coming Naval Conference to establish an entente with America.

In my turn, I told him that I was sure that America hoped for the same thing and that, to my way of thinking, the only impediments to the success of the conference would be the attitude of France and Italy. He agreed in impeccable English, and said that he had some inside information which he wished that he might divulge, but that, all things considered—

And then, as my mind began to stray ever so slightly, the idea of this gentleman in a sheet and a head towel having any secrets from *anyone* stuck me as a little humorous. To make things worse, a picture came to my mind's eye of how he would look if he had that busby on right now, with the gold strap under his chin, and I gave up my end of the conversation.

He must have, at the same time, caught a picture of me standing behind a none-too-generous towel, giving it as my

opinion that France and Italy were the chief obstacles to
international accord in naval matters, for he stood slightly at
attention and, bowing formally, said: "Well, I'll be toddling
along. See you again, I hope." There was an embarrassed
shaking of hands and more formal bowing and he went his
way, while I went out and flung myself in the pool.

There is one feature of Turkish bathing which I have not
had much experience in, and that is the massage. Being by
nature very ticklish, I usually succeed in evading the masseur
who follows me about suggesting salt rubs, alcohol slaps, and
the other forms of violence. I tell him that I am in a hurry

PETER ARNO

He played a powerful stream from two hydraulic hoses on me,
which threw me against the wall and dazed me.

and that I really shouldn't have come at all. He chases me from one room to another, assuring me that it won't take long. Then I plead with him that I have got a bad knee and am afraid of its flying out again. This just spurs him on, because bad knees are his dish.

Once in a while I slip on the wet tiles and he gets me, but I prove to be such a bad patient, once he has me down on the slab, that he passes the whole thing up and gives that irritating slap which means, in the language of the masseur: "All right! Get up—if you can."

Once, while I had my back turned, he played a powerful stream from two high-powered hydraulic hoses on me from clear across the room, which threw me against the wall and dazed me so that I went back into the hot room again instead of getting dressed. I would rather that the masseurs let me alone when I am in a Turkish bath. *I* know what I want better than they do.

As a matter of fact, I don't know why I go to a Turkish bath at all. I emerge into the fresh air outside looking as if I had been boiled with cabbage for five hours, with puffy, bloodshot eyes, waving hair, and the beginnings of a head cold. It is all I can do to get back to my room and go to bed, where I sleep heavily for eleven hours.

And invariably, on weighing myself, I find that I have gained slightly under a pound.

However, it is a part of the American sporting code and we red-blooded one hundred percenters must carry on the tradition.

A Little Sermon
on Success

A FAMOUS politician once remarked, on glancing through a copy of *Jo's Boys* by Louisa M. Alcott, that he would rather have written *Three Men in a Boat* than to have dug the Suez Canal. As a matter of fact, he never did either, and wasn't quite as famous a politician as I have tried to make out. But he knew what he meant by Success.

Lord Nelson is quoted as having said to one of his subordinates just before he went into action that there was no such thing as a good war or a good peace; in fact, that he doubted if there was a good anything. Now, Lord Nelson was a successful man in the sense that the world means Success, but he was unhappy because he had on his conscience the fact that he had imprisoned those two little princes in the Tower of London and had been instrumental in having them dressed in black velveteen and wear long blond curls like a couple of sissies. He was a successful man, but had only one eye.

I could go on indefinitely citing examples of great men who said things. I guess I will.

One hundred and seventy-five years ago General Wolfe Montcalm (sometimes called General Wolfe and sometimes General Montcalm, but always found on the Plains of Abra-

55

ham) wrote to his adjutant: "I sometimes wonder what it is all about, this incessant hurry-scurry after Fame. And how are *you*, my dear adjutant? And that bad shoulder of yours? Look out for that. And look out for a girl named Elsie, who may drop in on you and say that she knows me. She doesn't know me at all; in fact, who of us can say that he really knows anyone else? I often wonder if I know myself."

There was a great deal more to the letter, but I have quoted enough to show that the famous general saw through the phantom which men call Success. He won Quebec, but, after all, what is Quebec? He had to pay eight to ten, and even then he had that long hill to climb. His knowledge of what Life really means came too late for him, just as it comes too late for most of us.

There is a tribe of head-hunters who live in the jungle of Africa who reverse the general practice of seeking Success. When they are little babies they are all made head of the tribe, the highest office known in the jungle, and are given great bags full of teeth (the medium of exchange corresponding to our money, only not so hard to get and certainly not so easy to get rid of, for who wants a lot of teeth around the house?).

The idea then is for each young man to spend his life trying to get out of the office of tribal head, to dispose of his legal tender, and to end up in the gutter. The ones who succeed in doing this are counted the happy ones of the tribe, and it is said that they are "successful" men. The most successful man in the history of the tribe ended up in the gutter at the age of seven. But he had luck with him. He lived in the gutter anyway and all that he had to do was to lie over.

Now, perhaps these head-hunters have the right idea. Who knows? Charles Darwin once said that it isn't so much the Little Things in Life which count as the Little Life in Things. The less life there is in a man, the happier he is, provided there aren't mosquitoes in the room and he can get his head comfortable. (If Charles Darwin didn't say that, it is the first thing he *didn't* say.)

People often come to me and ask what I would recommend for this and that, and I ask them, "This and that what?" And

Lord Nelson was unhappy because he had imprisoned those two little princes in the Tower.

they go away sadly and think me a very wise man. I am not a wise man. I am just a simple man. "Simple Simon" they used to call me, until they found out that my name is Robert. I take Life as it comes, and although I grouse a great deal and sometimes lie on the floor and kick and scream and refuse to eat my supper, I find that taking Life as it comes is the only way to meet it. It isn't a very satisfactory way, but is the *only* way. (I should be very glad to try any other way that anyone can suggest. I certainly am sick of this one.)

Once upon a time, in a very far-away land, before men grew into the little boys they are now (Emerson once said that a little boy is just the lengthened shadow of one man), there was a very, very brave Knight who had a very, very definite yen for a beautiful Princess who lived in a far-away castle (very, very far away, I mean).

Now, there was also in this same land a Magician who could do wonders with a rabbit. People came from far and near to watch him at his egg-breaking and card-dropping, and now and again someone from the country would cry out, "Pfui!" But for the most part he was held to be as good as that feller who came down from Boston once. And, by one of those strange oddments of Fate which so often bring people together from the ends of the earth, the Magician was also in love with the very, very lovely Princess who lived you-know-where.

And it happened that the Knight went riding forth one day on his milk-white charger (or, at any rate, he had been milk-white until he thought it would be comical to lie down and roll in his stall) and set out to find the Princess, whom he still though the loveliest lady he had ever seen, although he had not yet seen her. He was a little in doubt as to which direction to take, for the Princess' castle, besides being very, very far away, was very, very hazy in the Knight's mind, he having heard of it only as "the Princess' castle" with no mention of its location. That's nothing to go by.

Now, at the same hour, the Magician himself was setting out on a horse he had brought out of a silk hat, bent on the same errand as the Knight—to get that Princess. And he, too, knew no more of where he was going than did the Knight—with the result that, after riding about in circles for three years, they both ended up at the same inn, eight miles from the town from which they started.

Now, the Knight was very fond of magic and the Magician was very fond of Knights. So, after a few tankards of mead together, the Magician got out his kit and began to pull paper roses out of the landlord's neck, much to the delight of everyone present except the landlord, who said that it was done with mirrors.

And so the Knight and the Magician became bosom friends and forgot about the very, very lovely Princess, and the Knight took the Magician home with him to his castle, so that every evening he could have another sleight-of-hand show. And the Princess, who by this time had got pretty sick of waiting, went back to her husband—who, it must be admitted, was a little disappointed at the way things had turned out.

Now, this little fable shows us that Success may be one of two things: first, getting what we want; and second, *not* getting what we want.

It was Voltaire who is reported to have said: *Plus ça change— plus ça reste,*" meaning, "There isn't much sense in doing anything these days." Perhaps it wasn't Voltaire, and perhaps that isn't what the French means; but the angle is right.

Can you say the same of yourself?

HERBERT F. ROESE

The Magician began to pull paper roses out of the landlord's neck, much to the delight of everyone except the landlord.

How
the Doggie Goes

A WELL known goldfish once referred to someone as having no more privacy than Irvin Cobb, but I would like to bet that the most publicly mauled and openly examined human being in the country today is the child of three. A child of three cannot raise its chubby fist to its mouth to remove a piece of carpet which it is through eating without being made the subject of a psychological seminar of child-welfare experts, and written up, along with five hundred other children of three who have put their hands to their mouths for the same reason, in a paper entitled: The Ratio of Mouth-Thumbing in Children of Sub-School Age in Its Relation to Carpet-Eating.

Now they have begun to examine children to see why they say "I won't!" when Mummy asks them to tell nice Mrs. Kalbfleisch what the mooley-cow says. Up until now when a child has said "I won't!" to such a demand it has seemed merely that it was the only possible reply to make. Just why a person, simply because he is only two years old, should feel any obligation to tell Mrs. Kalbfleisch what the mooley-cow says, is a mystery which any open-minded observer has difficulty in fathoming.

Who wouldn't say "I won't!" and pretty sharply, too, if asked to say "Moo-oo!" to Mrs. Kalbfleisch? Is there anything strange in a child's making the same reply?   But the child-welfare people seem to think that the matter has to be gone into. They took children ranging in age from eighteen to forty-eight months (who probably, in the first place, were pretty sore at being dragged in from the sand pile and old fish just to answer a lot of questions) and subjected them, according to the report, to "2,352 items of a verbal nature and 2,057 requiring some degree of physical reaction." That must have taken the best part of an afternoon and I guess that along about four thirty there must have been quite a bit of snarling and sulking going on, even among the examiners. I know, if I had been on the grille, what *one* of my 2,057 physical reactions would have been and it would have landed squarely between somebody's eyes.

"In each case," continues the report, "the child's resistance to the test was carefully recorded as one of the four criteria. Some children simply ignored the question." (Those children will go far. They are the white hopes of the future generation.) "Others verbally resisted with a shrill but determined 'I won't tell you!' " (The more excitable type, on the right track, but using up too much nervous energy in making their point. They should be told to watch the ones who simply ignored the questions and pattern after them.) "A third group resisted physically by running from the room or scampering into a corner." (This would have been my own personal reaction as a child, or even now for that matter, and it is a trait which has got me nowhere, as you have to come back sooner or later and there they are with the question again.) "Still others indicated inability to answer by whining 'I can't' or 'I don't know.' " (This was probably a lie on the part of the children, but it is a pretty good way out. You get the reputation for being stupid, but after a while you are let alone. I would say that the best methods were the first and the last, either ignoring the thing entirely or saying "I don't know." If you say "I won't" or scamper into a corner it just eggs the examiners on.)

The tests included the fitting of geometrical figures into a special form board ("I can't" would be my answer right now);

attaching limbs to the body of a manikin; putting square and round pegs into a perforated board; responding to such commands as "Stand on your left foot" or "Cross your feet" (to be ignored unless the examiner added "please"); recognizing one's self in a mirror (a great deal of fun could be had with the examiner by saying "I never saw this person before in my life," and sticking to it); fitting a nest of cubes together (Oh, hell! You might as well do that one for them!); and answering "What does a doggie say?" and "What mews?" To the question "What mews?" you could kid along and say you haven't seen a mewspaper that day, adding that no mews is good mews. This would confuse the examiner and perhaps make him discouraged enough to go home.

Such questions as "What does the doggie say?" and "How does the mooley-cow go?" come in a group by themselves. In the first place, any self-respecting child should insist that the question be rephrased, using "dog" instead of "doggie" and "cow" instead of "mooley-cow." This is simple justice. Then, if any answer is to be given at all (and I recommend against it), it should be delivered with considerable scorn as follows: "The dog doesn't *say* anything. It barks, if that is what you mean."

Presumably the child, while it is at the business of learning to talk, is supposed to be learning the kind of talk it will have some use for in after years, otherwise it would be taught only to make gargling noises in its throat and phrases like "Glub-glub." Now the chances are very small of its wanting ever to say "Bow-wow" in ordinary conversation unless it is going to give imitations when it grows up or else is planning to drink heavily. So why make it say "Bow-wow" in answer to the dog question, especially as that isn't what a dog says anyway? No child should allow itself to be made a fool of like that.

I personally was made to see the error of this system by a very small child who took matters into his own hands and made a fool out of me even before I had begun to do it for myself. When I would ask him what the dog said, he would reply "Moo-oo," and when I persisted, he would change it to "Toot-toot" and "Tick-tick."

At first I thought I had a cretin on my hands and got to

brooding over it. Then one day, when I had got "Bow-wow" as an answer to what the "choo-choo train" said, I detected a slight twinkle, not unmixed with scorn, in the child's eye, and as he walked off, a trifle unsteadily, I was sure that I heard a hoarse guttural laugh, not unlike what the goat says. So I stopped asking him to imitate animals and machines and took him to ball games instead. It has since transpired that he knew what he was doing and was planning to start throwing things at me if I had gone on much longer.

I *will* say this for the Child Development Institute, however. The conclusions which they made from their investigations were that the children had been asked to do so many things during the day, usually prefaced with "Come on, Junior. Won't you, please?" or told to "say please" or "say thank you," that they just simply got so damned sick of the whole silly mess that they refused to do anything. Or, in the words of the report, "a total of 161 resistances were noted. . . . The specific question, 'What is your name?' was resisted nine times out of a hundred, probably because the child's previous experience in being asked his name on each and every occasion by well meaning adults has already conditioned him negatively to this question."

Although the wording of the foregoing is a bit formal, it

PETER ARNO

is very sensible. It says "conditioned him negatively" instead of "pretty damned sick of it," but the meaning is the same. Sometime I would like to get a group of children to ask a lot of silly questions of one grown-up at a time, such as "What is your name?" and "How does the bossy go?" and see just how long it would be before the grown-ups were down on the floor kicking and screaming, or, along with me, scampering into a corner. Then perhaps we would all begin at scratch again and live and let live.

"Here You Are—
Taxi!"

It looks now, or rather it did the last time I looked, as if taxicabs in New York were going to be all put under one management and one franchise, like gas mains and trolley cars. Before this plan goes into effect, I have a few words that I would like to say to the Committee in Charge. If the members of the Committee wish, they may leave the room while I am talking.

I want taxicabs to be more standardized. I want to know, when I hail a cab at night, just what sort of conveyance it is that I am going to get into. Many's the time I have stepped out into the street on a dark night all dressed up in my pretty things and raised my gold-headed cane with an imperious gesture signifying that I am ready, nay eager, to be carried somewhere in considerable splendor, only to find, on entering the first cab which stops for me, that I am in the old sleigh which used to stand up in the attic at Grandpa's barn in Millbury. How they ever got it down to New York I don't know.

I know that it is Grandpa's old sleigh by the musty smell inside. If you can tell me why some taxicabs, with motors and exhaust pipes and complete transmissions, should smell of horses and old oats and ancient whip sockets, I will—well, I will be much obliged. (A pretty weak return for all your trouble, I realize.) I have found myself in so-called taxicabs whose heavy plush seats, with nice big holes in the middle in which to hide from the other boys, have had every accessory of the old-time surrey except the horse. And the horse had been there only a few hours before, I am sure. Sometimes there is even a lap robe, one of those old gray lap robes which, on being unfolded, always were found to contain a handful of corn kernels and some bits of leghorn fluff. What I want to know is, are these really old surreys which have had motors installed, or is it all my imagination and am I going through a form of second childhood? If it is the latter, I want to do something about it right away before it goes any farther. Otherwise I may start clucking at an imaginary horse before long.

This is the sort of thing that I want to avoid when they get around to standardizing taxicabs. I want to have it so that I can hail a cab at night and not be taken for a straw ride. I want to know what it is that I am getting into.

Of course, you can always count on finding yourself in one of these musty ghosts of an elder day if you take one of the cabs forced on you by the doorman at any of our most exclusive hotels. We call ourselves a free nation, and yet we let ourselves be told what cabs we can and can't take by a man at a hotel door, simply because he has a drum major's uniform on. The ritzier the hotel, the worse, and the more expensive, are the cabs standing in its own hack stand, and if you try to hail a passing cab which looks as if it might have been built after 1900, the doorman will be very, very cross with you and make you go back into the hotel and come out again all over. I once got quite independent when a doorman told me that I couldn't take the cab I wanted and I stepped out into the street to take it, his orders to the contrary notwithstanding. The only trouble with my revolution was that the cab I wanted hadn't seen me hail it and drove right by, and I was left standing in two inches of slush with nothing at all to ride in. So I had to make believe that I was going across the street anyway, a process which almost resulted in complete annihilation and in losing one shoe.

If all the taxis were the same, there would not be this

. . . only to find it already occupied by people who do not want to see me at that particular time.

constant struggling back and forth with doormen, for it wouldn't make any difference which cab you took. Or, rather, the only difference would be in the drivers.

Taxi drivers are always going to differ, I suppose, whether the state runs the business or not, but there might be some way of showing a prospective fare just what the personality of his driver is going to be. A red light on the starboard side could mean that the chauffeur is conversationally inclined, a green light that he would rather be left to himself. I, personally, prefer the conversational kind as a general rule, but there might be times when I wanted to do some reading or take a tardy shave, and then a good, quiet, even sullen, companion would be appreciated. On the whole, though, I have

found taxi drivers to be much more consistently agreeable
and sensitive to your wishes than any other class of the citizenry. If you want to talk, they will talk (and very delightfully,
too). If you want to sit quietly and sob or read, they sense it
and look straight ahead. Find me any other type of person
who will do that.

This matter of reading in cabs could stand a little preliminary planning, too. Reading in a cab at night is bad enough,
for, after groping up and down the sides and pushing screws
and hinges and ineffectual protuberances in a search for the
tiny light switch, it is nine times out of ten discovered that
the light doesn't work, or that it goes on only when the door
is opened.

And you can't go whizzing through the streets with a door
swinging open just to find out who won the football game.

But in the daytime it is much more tantalizing to try and
catch a few paragraphs between jounces, for you think that
the windows are going to be some help in letting in light—
and they are not. You try to hold the paper up to the little
back window, with your head twisted off to the right to avoid
a shadow, but that doesn't give *quite* enough light to get beyond the headlines. You then try leaning over toward one
of the door windows, but that necessitates getting halfway
off the seat and leaves you in no position at all to cope with
the next jounce. I have a scar on one of my cheekbones to
this day resulting from a nasty reading wound incurred while
trying to hold a paper where I could see it just as we went
over an uncovered water main.

All of this could be remedied, if the new scheme goes
through, by a little care in the construction of cabs and perhaps a poll of patrons giving suggestions.

Aside from the installation of reading lamps and character
guides to drivers' personal traits, I would like to offer the
following list of possible accessories which would make it
easier for us to hail a taxi and ride in it with a certain degree
of comfort:

(1) A light on top reading "Taxi," so that I shall not constantly be hailing private cars and incurring the displeasure
of their owners.

(2) Another light reading "Taken" or "Not to Be Disturbed until 9 A.M.," so that I shall not snatch open the door of a stalled cab only to find it already occupied by people who do not want to see me at that particular time.

(3) Some elevation of the door frame which will make it possible to enter a cab wearing a tall hat without having to go back immediately for a new one.

(4) Little hooks on which tall hats or derbies may be hung to avoid having them jammed over the ears by contact with roofs when going over bumps.

(5) Special helicopter attachment on the roof, making it possible for a cab stuck in traffic to rise, fly over the blockade, and land where it will have some chance of reaching its destination.

Or perhaps it would be simpler just to not use taxicabs at all.

Tell-Tale
· Clues ·

UNLESS you are very smart and remember all that was taught you in school about how to cover up your tracks after you have committed a crime, you are going to be surprised at some of the things that I am going to write down for you. And I, in turn, shall be surprised if you read them. The average criminal has no idea how careful he has to be in order to keep on being a criminal and not just an ex-. He may think that he is being careful while he is at work, wearing silk gloves and walking on his ankles and all that, but unless he spends as much time looking around for telltale bits of evidence after he commits the crime as he spent in committing it, then he is leaving himself open for a terrible panning by *some*one, even if it is only the Chief of Police.

For example, on April 7, 1904, the vault in the Lazybones National Bank and Fiduciary Trust Co. of Illville, Illinois, was blown off, and if there had been anything in there worth taking away, it could easily have been done. As it was, the vault contained nothing but a hundred shares of Goldman Sachs, and the robbers, instead of taking these, added two hundred more shares of their own and made their get-away, leaving the bank stuck with three hundred shares instead of one hundred.

Attracted by the oaths of the safe-crackers as they walked down the street, the police rushed first to the Farmers' and

Drovers' Bank, then to the First Congregational Church, and then to the Lazybones National where the explosion had taken place. They found that not only had the front been blown off the vault but the handle to the front door of the bank building was gone. It had evidently been pulled off in

A policeman, approaching him, said, "There is a payment due on an artificial limb bought from us last year."

pique by one of the robbers when he found that the door would not open as easily as he thought it ought to.

After a thorough investigation of the premises, Captain Louis Mildew of the detective force turned to his aide and said, "If we can find the man who has this door knob in his hand, we shall have the man who cracked the safe." A week later a man was picked up in Zanesville who was carrying a door knob which corresponded in every detail with the one missing from the bank building. In spite of the fact that he claimed that it belonged to him and that he was carrying it to ward off rheumatism, he was arrested and later confessed.

Another case where carelessness on the part of the criminal led to his ultimate arrest and embarrassment is found on the records of police in Right Knee, New Jersey. A puddleworker had been killed in a fight and his assailant had escaped, evidently several days before the crime was discovered (in fact, the evidence pointed to the killer having escaped several days before the murder, which didn't make sense). On looking over the ground where the body was found, the police discovered a man's wooden leg firmly gripped in the teeth of the dead man.

The name of the makers of the wooden leg, the Peter Pan Novelty Co., was also broadcast.

On the fourth day of the search a policeman saw a one-legged man sitting at a bar and, approaching him in a businesslike manner, said "I represent the Peter Pan Novelty Co. and there is a payment due on an artificial limb bought from us last year. Could you see your way clear to giving us something at this time?"

The one-legged man immediately bridled and said hotly, "I pay you no more on that leg. It came off when I needed it most, and I haven't been able to find it since. If you wish, I will put this in the form of a letter of complaint to the company."

"You can put it in the form of testimony before a judge, buddy," said the policeman, turning back his lapel where he had forgotten to pin his badge. "Come along with me."

And so, simply through careless haste in getting away without looking about for incriminating evidence, the man was caught, and had a pretty rough time convincing the jury that he had done the killing in self-defense and to save his sister's honor. It was later found that not only did he have no sister but that she had no honor.

Perhaps the most famous instance of carelessness was the discovery of the abductor of the Sacred White Elephant of Mistick, California. This was an inside job, for the elephant had been confined in a hut which was several sizes too small for her, making it impossible for anyone to enter from the outside. This much was certain.

The elephant, when it was first discovered in Mistick, had been neither white nor sacred, but was a camp follower of a circus, who had liked the town and stayed behind when the rest moved on. So the town whitewashed her and spread the report about that she was sacred, and used to charge two bits to take a walk around her, once around one way and back around the other.

The man who had turned the trick was a very wily elephant thief who had been in the business a long time but had never worked in white elephants before. He made all provisions for a quick get-away and, before the loss was discovered, had the prize out of town and well on its way down the coast. What he had neglected to do, however, was to brush off the sleeve of his coat, not realizing that, when frightened, a white elephant gives off a fine dusty powder which settles on the nearest objects and marks them as having been near a white elephant. And so it was that, as the crook was walking along a country road leading his ill-gotten gain, he was accosted by a local constable. Stopping Potts (the thief's name was Potts), he said, "What's that white dust on your coat shoulder?"

"I just left my girl," said Potts. "Does your girl wear white elephant powder?" asked the constable, very comical. "That's white elephant powder and it's off that elephant."

"What elephant?" said Potts in surprise, looking behind him. "Oh, *that* elephant?"

The thief tried to escape by hiding behind the beast; but the constable could see his legs and feet from the other side and placed him under arrest.

So you will see that it is the little things that count in successful police evasion, and the sooner our criminals realize this the fewer humiliating arrests there will be.

Sporting Life in America:
• Dozing •

WE Americans are a hardy race, and hardy races need a lot of sleep. "Sleep, that knits up the ravell'd sleave of care," Shakespeare has called it, and, except for the fact that it doesn't mean much, it is a pretty good simile. I often think of it myself just as I am dropping off into a light doze: "Sleep, that sleeves up the raveled care of . . . knit, that sleeps up the shaveled neeve of—pfor—pff—prpf—orpffff" *(trailing off into a low whistle)*.

One of the most charming manifestations of sleep which we, as a nation, indulge in as a pastime is the Doze. By the Doze I mean those little snatches of sleep which are caught now and then during the day, usually with the collar on and choking slightly, with the head inclined coyly to one side, during which there is a semiconscious attempt to appear as if we were really awake. It is in this department of sleep that we are really at our best.

Of course, there is one form of doze which, to the casual observer or tourist, gives the appearance of legitimate sleep. This is the short doze, or "quickie," which is taken just after the main awakening in the morning. The alarm rings, or the Lord High Chamberlain taps us on the shoulder (in the absence of a chamberlain a relative will do. And right here I would like to offer for examination that type of sadistic relative who takes actual delight in awakening people. They hover about with ghoulish anticipation until the minute arrives when they may legitmately begin their dirty work, and then, leering unpleasantly, they shake the sleeper roughly with a "Come, come! Time to get up!" and wait right there until he is actually out on the cold floor in his bare feet. There is something radically wrong with such people, and the sooner they are exposed as pathological cases the better it will be for the world). I'm sorry. I didn't mean to be nasty about it.

At any rate, we are awakened and look at the clock. There are five minutes before it is absolutely necessary to get out of bed. If we leave shaving until night, there might even be fifteen minutes. If we leave dressing until we get to the office, snatching our clothes from the chair and carrying them downtown on our arm, there might even be half an hour more for a good, health-giving nap. Who knows? Perhaps those few minutes of extra sleep might make us just ten times as efficient during the day! That is what we must think of— efficiency. We must sacrifice our petty opinions on the matter and think of the rest of the day and our efficiency. There is no doubt that fifteen minutes' more sleep would do wonders for us, no matter how little we really want to take it.

PETER ARNO

They hover about with ghoulish anticipation until the minute when they may begin their dirty work.

By the time we have finished this line of argument we are out pretty fairly cold again, but not so cold that we are not conscious of anyone entering the room. We feel that they are going to say: "Come, come, don't go back to sleep again!" and we forestall this warning with a brisk "I know! I know! I'm just thinking!" This is said with one eye partially open and one tiny corner of the brain functioning. The rest of our powers add up to a total loss.

It is one of Nature's wonders how a man can carry on an argument with someone standing beside his bed and still be asleep to all intents and purposes. Not a very good argument, perhaps, and one in which many important words are missing or indistinct, but still an argument. It is an argument, however, which seldom wins, the state of justice in the world being what it is today.

Dozing before arising does not really come within the range of this treatise. What we are concerned with are those little lapses when we are fully dressed, when we fondly believe that no one notices. Riding on a train, for example.

There is the short-distance doze in a day coach, probably the most humiliating form of train sleeping. In this the elbow is rested on the window sill and the head placed in the hand in an attitude of thought. The glass feels very cool on the forehead and we rest it there, more to cool off than anything else. The next thing we know the forehead (carrying the entire head with it) has slid down the length of the slippery pane and we have received a rather nasty bang against the woodwork. They shouldn't keep their glass so slippery. A person is likely to get badly hurt that way.

However, back again goes the forehead against the pane in its original position, with the hand serving more or less as a buffer, until another skid occurs, this time resulting in an angry determination to give the whole thing up entirely and sit up straight in the seat. Some dozers will take four or five slides without whimpering, going back each time for more with apparently undiminished confidence in their ability to see the thing through.

It is a game that you can't beat, however, and the sooner

you sit up straight in your seat, the sooner you will stop banging your head.

Dozing in a Pullman chair is not so dangerous, as one does not have the risk of the sliding glass to cope with, but it is even less lovely in its appearance. Here the head is allowed to sink back against the antimacassar—just for a minute to see if the headrest is really as comfortable as it seems. It is then but the work of a minute for the mouth to open slightly and the head to tip roguishly to the right, and there you are—as pretty as a picture as one would care to see. You are very lucky if, when you come to and look about, you do not find your neighbors smiling indulgently at some little vagaries of breathing or eccentricities of facial expression which you have been permitting yourself.

The game in all this public dozing is to act, on awakening, as if you had known all along what you were doing. If your neighbors are smiling, you should smile back, as if to say: "Fooled you that time! You thought I was asleep, didn't you?"

If they are not quite so rude as to smile, but look quickly back at their reading on seeing your eyes open, you should assume a brisk, businesslike expression indicating that you have been thinking out some weighty business problem with your eyes closed, and, now that you have at last come on its solution, that it is snap-snap! back to work for you! If, after a furtive look around, you discover that no one has caught you at it, then it will do no harm to give it another try, this time until your collar chokes you into awakening with a strangling gasp.

The collar, however, is not always an impediment to public dozing. In the theater, for example, a good, stiff dress collar and shirt bosom have been known to hold the sleeper in an upright position when otherwise he might have plunged forward and banged his head on the back of the seat in front.

In my professional capacity as play reviewer I have had occasion to experiment in the various ways of sitting up straight and still snatching a few winks of health-giving sleep. I have found that by far the safest is to keep one's heavy overcoat on, especially if it is made of some good, substantial

material which will hold a sagging torso erect within its folds.
With a good overcoat, reinforced by a stiff dress shirt and a
high collar, one may even go beyond the dozing stage and
sink into a deep, refreshing slumber, and still not be made
conspicuous by continual lurching and plungings. Of course,
if you are an uneasy sleeper and given to thrashing about,
you will find that even a heavy overcoat will let you down
once in a while. But for the average man, who holds ap-
proximately the same position after he has gone to sleep, I
don't think that this method can go wrong. Its only drawback
is that you are likely to get a little warm along about the
middle of the second act.

If you don't want to wear your overcoat in the theater, the
next best method is to fold the arms across the chest and
brace the chin against the dress collar, exerting a slight upward pressure with the arms against the shirt front. This,
however, can be used only for the lightest of dozes, as once
unconsciousness has set in, the pressure relaxes and over you
go.

Dozing at a play, however refreshing, makes it a bit difficult
to follow the argument on the stage, as occasionally the nap
drags itself out into a couple of minutes and you awake to
find a wholly fresh set of characters on the scene, or even a
wholly fresh scene. This is confusing. It is therefore wise to
have someone along with you who will alternate watches with
you, dozing when you are awake and keeping more or less
alert while you are dozing. In this way you can keep abreast
of what has been happening.

This, unfortunately, is impossible in personal conversa-
tions. If you slip off into a quick coma late some evening
when your *vis-à-vis* is telling you about South America or a
new solvent process, it is usually pretty difficult to pick up
the thread where you dropped it. You may remember that
the last words he was saying were "—which is situated at the
mouth of the Amazon," but that isn't going to help you much
if you come to just as he is asking you: "What would *you* say
are?" As in the personal-conversation doze the eyes seldom
completely close (it is more of a turning back of the eyeballs

A good, stiff dress collar and shirt bosom have been known to hold the sleeper in an upright position.

than a closing of the lids) you may escape detection if you have a ready answer for the emergency. I find that "Well, I don't know," said very slowly and deliberately, will fit almost any question that has been asked you. "Yes" and "No" should never be offered, as they might make you sound even sillier than you look. If you say: "Well, I—don't—know," it will give you a chance to collect your wits (what few there are left) and may lead your questioner into answering the thing himself.

At any rate, it will serve as a stall. If there are other people present, some one of them is quite likely to come to your rescue and say something which will tip you off as to the general subject under discussion. From then on, you will have to fight your own battle. I can't help you.

The whole problem is one which calls for a great deal of thought. If we can develop some way in which a man can doze and still keep from making a monkey of himself, we have removed one of the big obstacles to human happiness in modern civilization. It goes without saying that we don't get enough sleep while we are in bed; so we have got to get a little now and then while we are at work or at play. If we can find some way to keep the head up straight, the mouth closed, and just enough of the brain working to answer questions, we have got the thing solved right there.

I am working on it right now, as a matter of fact, but I find it a little difficult to keep awake.

The Helping Hand

I HAVE tried to be as public-spirited as I could and yet save out a little time to myself for running and jumping. That is, when the Fuel Administration wanted us all to save coal, I saved coal with a will; when it was Anti-Litter Week, I anti-littered; when the nation was supposed to be devoting itself to eating apples, I drank applejack until the cows came home—and very funny-looking cows they were, too.

So when the head of the Unemployment Commission came out over the radio and asked every good citizen to set about "sprucing up" his home and give employment to as many men as possible, I saw my duty and set about doing it.

My house could stand a little "sprucing up," for we have been hoping to sell it for eight to ten years (centrally located in Westchester County, three minutes from the station, co-lonial type, four master's bedrooms and three masters, ser-vants' quarters at the foot of the plantation, two chimneys, of which one is imitation; just try naming a price and see what happens), and when you expect to sell a house any minute you more or less put off "sprucing up." So I figured that I could help out the situation considerably merely by fixing up the house so that the owls didn't fly in through the roof at night.

Aside from having the roof patted down, I decided that a

couple of eaves troughs could stand a little humoring; that
one of the master's bathtubs might very well be given a new
porcelain filling; that the furnace could easily be looked into
by an expert, possibly using a ferret to get out that clinker
which got stuck in the grate four years ago; and that we
needed a new lock on the front door (or perhaps it was a
new key; at any rate, the front door couldn't be locked).

This shaped up like quite a boon to the unemployed of
the town. All that remained was for me myself to find enough
work to do to pay for it.

We had quite a little trouble in finding a carpenter and a
plumber who could promise to come before the following
week (no matter how serious the unemployment situation,
no individual carpenter or plumber can ever come before
the following week, doubtless out of habit), and the locksmith
and the furnaceman just didn't seem interested. But we finally got a little group of experts who agreed to drop in the
next day and see what could be done.

In the meantime, we had discovered that the electric range
needed tampering with and that a fresh coat of paint wouldn't
hurt the back porch. So we engaged an electrician and a
painter to come in the next day also.

The next day was one of those crisp late fall days when
everyone feels so good that he wants to stay right in bed
under the blankets all the morning. I was surprised, therefore, in my bathrobe by Mr. Margotson, the carpenter, and
Mr. Rallif, the electrician, who arrived together at eight thirty.
This started the thing off on an informal basis right at the
beginning, and as Mr. Shrank, the locksmith, came a few
minutes later, it seemed only hospitable to ask them if they
wouldn't like a second cup of coffee before starting to work.
At this point the furnaceman, Mr. Thurple, arrived in the
painter's automobile (I didn't quite catch the painter's name,
but I think it was Schnee; at any rate, I called him Schnee
and he seemed quite pleased), and so our little coffee party
was now six, including the host, which just filled the breakfast
table nicely.

"Do you take cream in your coffee, Mr. Margotson?" I
asked. Mr. Margotson and Mr. Rallif having been the first to

arrive, it seemed to me that they should be served first.

"It's strange that you should have asked me that," replied Mr. Margotson, "for I was saying to Mrs. Margotson at breakfast only this morning, 'I see in the paper where a man says that cream *and* sugar together in coffee set up a poison which sooner or later results in toxemia!' "

"Don't you think," put in Mr. Thurple, helping himself to cream and sugar, "that we are, as a nation, becoming a little too self-conscious about what we eat and drink? As a nation, I mean."

Mr. Schnee, or whatever his name was, laughed a low, tinkling laugh. This, although Mr. Schnee said nothing, somehow broke the ice and we all laughed. I had never seen five more congenial and delightful men together at one table (six, if you want to count me; I couldn't very well have said it myself). As soon as we all had our coffee cups well poised, the conversation became general and drifted from dietetics to religion and then quickly back to dietetics again. When Mr. Ramm, the plumber (true to the jokes in the funny papers, the last to arrive), came bursting in he found us deep in a discussion of whether or not ransom should be paid in kidnaping cases.

"The late Mr. Ramm!" taunted Mr. Thurple, the furnaceman, who had already established himself as the clown of the crowd by having seven cups of coffee. At which sally Mr. Schnee again laughed his low, tinkling laugh and set us all off again. As soon as Mr. Ramm had recovered from his embarrassment at being the butt of Mr. Thurple's joke, I set the round of day's activities in motion.

"How many here play badminton?" I asked, springing to my feet.

"I," "I," and "I," came with a will from three hearty throats, and Messrs. Margotson, Rallif, and Thurple had their coats off and their sleeves rolled up as an earnest of their intentions.

"Take me, I like backgammon," said Mr. Ramm.

"You're my man then," said Mr. Shrank. "I am the backgammon king of Locksmiths' Row." It looked for a minute as if we were in for a rather nasty argument, but Mr. Schnee's low, musical laugh came again to the rescue, and the party was on. The room which had been full of men only a minute before was now emptied in a trice, some rushing pell-mell to the badminton court and some to the backgammon room.

Luncheon was a gay affair, with favors for those who had won at their various games and speeches of acceptance which convulsed even the low-laughing Mr. Schnee.

"I am sorry, gentlemen," I said, in part, when it came my turn, "that I have got you all here to do certain jobs to which you are severally suited by training and study, for I find that I have not the money to pay you with, even if you were to carry out your commissions. But what there is of good cheer and good fellowship in this house is yours, and we are all going to make the most of it while it lasts."

That was a month and a half ago and they are still living with me. We are the best of friends and still the small boys at heart that we always were. The house is in much worse condition than it was before; but, as it turned out that they all had more money than I, I am not worrying. They have each promised to buy a story from me as soon as I can get around to writing it.

Announcing
a New Vitamin

DR. ARTHUR W. MEEXUS and the author of this paper take great pleasure in announcing the discovery of vitamin F on August 15, 1931. We ran across it quite by accident while poking through some old mackerel bones, trying to find a little piece of fish that we could eat.

"By George," exclaimed Dr. Meexus, "I think this is a vitamin!"

"By George," I said, examining it, "it is not only a vitamin, but it is vitamin F! See how F it looks!" And, sure enough, it was vitamin F all over, the very vitamin F which had been eluding Science since that day in 1913 when Science decided that there were such things as vitamins. (Before 1913 people had just been eating food and dying like flies.)

In honor of being the first vitamin to be discovered, this new element was called vitamin A, and a very pretty name it was, too. From then on, doctors began discovering other vitamins—B, C, D, and E, and then vitamin G. But vitamin F was missing. It is true vitamin G looked so much like vitamin B that you could hardly tell them apart, except in strong light, and vitamin E was, for all practical purposes, the same as vitamin A (except a little more blond), but nobody seemed able to work up any discovery by which a vitamin F could be announced.

The sad suicide of Dr. Eno M. Kerk in 1930 was laid to the fact that he had just got a vitamin isolated from the E class and almost into the F, when the room suddenly got warm and it turned into a full-fledged vitamin G. The doctor was heartbroken and deliberately died of malnutrition by refusing to eat any of the other vitamins from that day on. If he couldn't have vitamin F, he wouldn't have any. The result was a fatal combination of rickets, beriberi, scurvy, East Indian flagroot, and all other diseases which come from an undersupply of vitamins (most of them diseases which nice people up North wouldn't have).

First in our search for a vitamin which would answer to the name of F, we had to figure out something that it would be good for. You can't just have a vitamin lying around doing nothing. We therefore decided that vitamin F would stimulate the salivary glands and the tear ducts. If, for instance, you happen to be a stamp licker or envelope sealer, or like to cry a lot, it will be necessary for you to eat a great deal of food which is rich in vitamin F. Otherwise your envelopes won't stay stuck, or, when you want to cry, all you can do is make a funny-looking face without getting anywhere.

For research work we decided that the natives of one of the Guianas (British-French, or French-British, or Harvard-Yale) would present a good field, so we took a little trip down there to see just what food values they were short of. Most of the food in the Guianas consists of Guiana hen in its multiple variants, with a little wild Irish rice on the side to take away the taste. The natives reverse the usual order of tribal eating, placing the hen and rice outside a large bowl and getting into the bowl themselves, from which vantage point they are able to pick up not only the food but any little bits of grass and pebbles which may be lying on the ground beside it. This method of eating is known as *hariboru,* or "damned inconvenient."

Naturally, a diet consisting entirely of Guiana hen and wild Irish rice is terribly, terribly short on vitamin F, with the result that natives are scarcely able to lick their lips, much less a long envelope. And when they want to cry (as they do whenever anyone speaks crossly to them) they make a low, grinding noise with their teeth and hide their eyes with one hand to cover up their lack of tears. We played them "Silver Threads Among the Gold" one night on our ukuleles, with Dr. Meexus singing the tenor, and although every eye in the house was dry, the grinding sound was as loud as the creaking timbers on an excursion boat. (As loud, but nothing like.)

The next thing to do was to discover what foods contain vitamin F. Here was a stickler! We had discovered it in a mess of mackerel bones, so evidently mackerel bones contain it. But you can't tell people to eat lots of mackerel bones.

Now, from a study of vitamins A, B, C, D, E, and G, we knew that all one really needs to have, in order to stock up

HERBERT F. ROESE

We played them "Silver Threads Among the Gold" one night, with Dr. Meexus singing the tenor.

on any of these strength-giving elements, is milk. Milk and cod-liver oil. Milk has vitamin A, vitamins B, E, and G—so it is pretty certain to have vitamin F. For all we knew, it might also contain vitamin F sharp. So we picked milk as the base of our prescribed diet and set about to think up something else to go with it.

Then it occurred to Dr. Meexus that he had a lot of extra radishes growing in his garden, radishes which he was sure he had not planted. He had planted lots of other vegetables, beans, peas, Swiss chard, and corn, but radishes were the only things that had come up in any quantity. He was radish poor. And he figured out that practically six million amateur gardeners were in the same fix. Where you find one amateur gardener in a fix, you are pretty likely to find six million others in the same one. And, according to the Department of Agriculture's figures for 1931 (April–September), practically every amateur gardener in the country was in some sort of fix or other, mostly due to a bumper crop of radishes.

We therefore decided that radishes must contain a lot of vitamin F, since they contain nothing else, unless possibly a corky substance which would be used only in the manufacture of life preservers. "Milk and radishes" was selected as the slogan for vitamin F.

We figured it out that our chief advantage over the other vitamin teams was in the choice of conditions which our vitamin would cure. The vitamin B group had taken over beriberi, but who wants to have beriberi for a disease to be avoided? Vitamin D is a cure for rickets, but most of our patients ought to know by now whether they are going to have rickets or not. (We planned to cater to the more mature, sophisticated Long Island crowd, and, if they haven't had rickets up until now, they don't much care. If they *have* had them, it is too late anyway, and you can always say that your legs got that way from riding horseback.)

Vitamin C is corking for scurvy, but, here again, scurvy is not in our line.

In fact, I don't know much about scurvy, except that it was always found breaking out on shipboard when sailing vessels went around the Horn. But Dr. Hess, one of the discoverers of vitamin C, has pointed out that scurvy need not always be present in cases demanding vitamin C.

According to Hess (you must always call doctors who discover something by their last names without the "Dr."), the frequency among children in which irritability can be cured by vitamin C is proof that it has more uses than one.

This was pretty smart of Hess to pick on such a common ailment as irritability among children, for, up until the discovery of vitamin C, the only cure for this had been a good swift smack on the face.

.However, it looks now as if we were stuck with a perfectly good vitamin and nothing for it to cure. Licking stamps and crying aren't quite important enough functions to put a vitamin on its feet. We have announced its discovery, and have given to the world sufficient data to show that it is an item of diet which undoubtedly serves a purpose. But what purpose? We are working on that now, and ought to have something very interesting to report in a short time. If we aren't able to, we shall have to call vitamin F in, and begin all over again.

Inherent Vice:
• Express Paid •

SOME evening, when you haven't anything to read, why not light a cozy fire, draw up your chair, and browse around among your old express receipts and bills of lading? You will learn a lot. Here you have been going on for years, sending parcels and crates like mad, and I'll bet that not one of you really knows the contractual obligations you have been entering into with the companies who serve you. For all you know, you have been agreeing to marry the company manager at the end of sixty days.

As I write this, I am sitting in the gloaming of a late autumn afternoon with an express company's receipt on the table before me. As I read over the fine print on the back of it, my eyes cross gradually with the strain and I put on the light. (What a wonderful invention—electricity! I am sure that we should all be very proud and happy to be living in this age.)

As my eyes adjust themselves, I find that when I sent that old bureau to Ruth's folks, I agreed to let the express company get away with the following exceptions to their liability. (If you are going to read this article, I would advise studying the following. It will probably amuse you more than what I have to say afterward.)

The company shall in no event be liable for any loss, damage, or delay to said property or to any part thereof occasioned by act of God, by perils or accidents of the sea or other waters, [That "other waters" makes a pretty broad exemption, when you come to think of it. It means that they can upset tumblers on your stuff, or let roguish employees play squirt guns all over it, and yet not be responsible.] or of navigation or transportation of whatsoever nature or kind; by fire or explosion . . . by theft or pilferage [What about garroting?] by any person whatsoever; by arrest or restraint of governments,

PETER ARNO

It would almost be better to get a sled and drag your package to wherever you want it.

princes, rulers, or peoples or those purporting to exercise governmental or other authority; by legal process or stoppage in transit; by fumigation or other acts or requirements of quarantine or sanitary authorities; [Tell me when you are getting tired.] by epidemics, pestilence, riots; or rebellions, by war or any of the dangers incident to a state of war, or by acts of any person or group of persons purporting to wage war or to act as a belligerent; [Come, come, Mr. Express Company—aren't you being just a little bit picayune?] by strikes or stoppage of labor or labor troubles, whether of carrier's employees or others; by unseaworthiness of any vessel, lighter, or other craft whatsoever, [Not even just a teeny-weeny bit of a rowboat?] although existing at the time of shipment on board thereof; . . . . by water, [You said that once before.] heating, or the effects of climate, frost, decay, smell, taint, rust, sweat, dampness, mildew, spotting, rain or spray, [Ninety-five-a-hundred-all around my goal are it.] INHERENT VICE, [Remember that one; we're coming back to that later.] drainage, leakage, vermin, improper or insufficient packing, inaccuracies or obliterations, errors, [Why don't they just say "errors" and let it go at that?] nor for the breakage of any fragile articles or damage to any materials consisting of or contained in glass; nor shall this company [Beginning all over again, in case you should have forgotten who it is that isn't responsible.] be held liable or responsible for any damage to or resulting from dangerous corrosives, explosives, or inflammable goods, even if the true nature has been declared to the company; nor for neglect, damage, accident to or escape or mortality of any animals or birds [Ah-ha! They forgot fish!] received by the company hereunder, from any cause whatsoever.

That's all! Aside from that, the express company is responsible for your package.

Aside from that, your little crate or barrel is as safe as it would be in your own home. It would almost be better to get a sled and drag your package yourself to wherever you want it taken.

At least you could personally fight off vermin and princes (or those purporting to be vermin and princes).

But the thing that worries me most about this contract between me and the express company is that clause about "inherent vice."

The company is not responsible for any damage to that bureau of mine if it is caused by inherent vice. This makes you stop and think.

Wholly aside from the Calvinistic dourness of the phrase "inherent vice" (I thought that the theory of Original Sin and Inherent Vice went out with the hanging of witches), the question now arises—*whose* inherent vice? The company's officials? The bureau's? Aunt Alice's? We are up against quite a nice problem in ethics here.

I can't imagine what you could send by express that would be full enough in inherent vice to damage it en route. Certainly nothing that you could pack in a bureau.

You might send some very naughty rabbits or squirrels by express, but it seems a little narrow-minded to put all the responsibility for their actions on the little creatures themselves. No one has ever told them that they are vicious, or that they were conceived in sin. They don't *know* that they are being bad.

I have known one or two very smart dogs who were pretty self-concious about being wicked and couldn't look you in the eye afterward, but aside from cases like that it seems a bit arbitrary for a big public-service corporation like an express company to frown on the peccadillos of five or six squirrels.

Would the private lives of the company officials themselves bear looking into so well that they must prate of inherent vice? Live and let live, say I.

Which brings us to the other theory—that inherent vice in the company's officials or employees cannot be held responsible for any damage to my bureau.

Do you mean to tell me that if one of the company's employees is a man who, ever since he was a boy, has been willfully and maliciously destructive, and that if he takes my bureau out of its crate and chops the whole thing up into kindling—do you mean to tell me that I am without recourse to the law?

If the president of the express company or any one of his employees goes monkeying around with my bureau and then pleads "not guilty" because of his inherent vice, I will start a *putsch* that will bring our government crashing down around our ears.

I refuse to discuss the remaining possibility—that the inherent vice referred to means inherent vice in Aunt Alice, or consignee.

This brings us to the conclusion that what is meant by that package or bale or crate (or articles purporting to be packages, or bales, or crates) might have inherent vice enough to spoil it, and that, in this event, the company washes its hands of the whole affair.

The only alternative to this almost incredibly silly reservation is that there has been a misprint and that what the company is so afraid of is "inherent *mice*." In this case, I have taken up all your time for nothing. But I do think that you ought to know what you are agreeing to when you send an express package. Or perhaps you don't care.

Can We Believe
Our Eyes?

• ————————————————————————— •

It is pretty generally agreed by now that Seeing is not Believing. Along with those exploded saws (watch out for ex-
ploding saws!) that Old Friends Are Best and the Longest
Way Round is the Shortest Way Home (I could kill the guy
who made that one up—it cost me eight dollars and a half
in taxi fare once), the old dictum about seeing and believing
has been shown to be just another flash in the pan.

In fact, according to scientists, if your eyes tell you that a
thing is so, it is a very good reason for believing the opposite.

This will eventually make for a lot of trouble in the world.

However, all you have to do is read the Sunday papers to
see what little monkeys your eyes really are. Even the ad-
vertisments are getting into the game of confusing us with
pictures showing large arrows and small arrows with captions
like:

"Which is the larger of these two arrows?" Of course, it is
perfectly obvious which is the larger, but when you come to
measure them you find that, through some trickery, they are
both the same size.

I will put up with just so much of this sort of thing, and
then I will stop measuring.

This unreliability on the part of visual images is only one
part of Nature's way of making saps out of us, her children.

You may see two girls at a party, or two wire-haired fox terriers in a dog-shop window, and you say, pointing deliberately to one:

"The one on the right is the one for me. I can tell just by looking that this is what I have been searching for all my life." If you want to know what this leads to all you have to do is read the divorce notices or the list of wire-haired fox terriers for sale "cheap."

For example, take Figure 1 of the accompanying illustrations. Which of these acorns would you say was the taller? (One is a hydrant, but you are not supposed to know that.) You would naturally say that the acorn on the left was at least twice as tall as the one on the right. Taller and handsomer.

FIG. 1

Well, you would be right. But, when you see two objects like these in an eye test, you *think*: "There is a trick here! I am supposed to say that the one on the left is taller, so it can't be. I will say the one on the right, much against my better judgment." And so you lose five dollars.

This is only one of the fascinating things that you can do with your eyes. Another is to wink one of them very slowly at a young lady sitting at the next table in a restaurant, and, the first thing you know, the other eye will be all blue and bulging and *very* sore, owing to her escort having shown you that optical illusion isn't everything. (See Figure 2.)

FIG. 2

In Figure 3 we have another common form of self-deception. If you will take these concentric circles and rotate them slowly in front of your eyes, you will soon be dizzy enough to be quite ill. (In order to rotate the circles it will be necessary for you to buy another copy of this magazine and cut out the diagram with a pair of scissors. If you try rotating the whole magazine, you will find, not only that you will get tired quickly, but that you will be unable to read the type matter. And as in the type matter are contained the directions for *stopping* the rotary movement, you may go on twirling the paper for hours without knowing what to do next.) But after you have rotated the concentric circles for some time, you will find yourself believing that the thing is *actually turning itself!* After a while you will think that you are

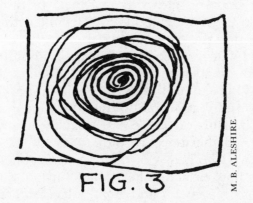

FIG. 3

M. B. ALESHIRE

on a bicycle and will start working your feet on the pedals. If you keep the thing up much longer, you will faint.

Thus we see that our eyes play their pranks—as well as our other senses—and that the best thing to do with them is to keep them shut entirely.

There is a well known case of optical illusion recorded in the files of the British War Office at the Old Vic. It seems that during the Crimean War a detachment of British troops was isolated in a lonely village in a clump of trees. (The natives were tree dwellers, silly as it may seem.)

They had nothing to do but drink a sort of mixture of heartsease (absinthe) and wormword (absinthe) which the local doctor put up for people who rather be dead.

Thus the days wore on.

One night when three subalterns were sitting around a fire and sipping at this strange mixture (no longer strange to them however, more like a mother), one, a seargeant (British spelling), Villiers, turned to his companions and said:

"Don't look now, boys, but there go the Devonshire Reds, all but O'Day."

(The Devonshire Reds was a regiment which was stationed in Ottawa at the time, and O'Day was the only man in the regiment whom Villiers knew.)

"I rather doubt if the Devonshire Reds are right here in the Crimea right at this minute," said Athoy, one of the three, "but I see what you mean. It is a body of moving figures going quickly, in a swaying motion, from left to right, but it is my guess that they are penguins.

"See! See! There is a penguin now—leading the band!"

The third member of the party, a Leftenant Merley, who had said nothing up until this time, still said nothing. It was later discovered that his mouth had, in some unaccountable way, sunk into his cartridge belt, making it impossible for him to talk. Furthermore, he didn't care.

But the two who had seen the passing regiment (of either Devonshire Reds or penguins) argued far into the night over the phantom marchers, and finally decided that they had been really nothing but a crowd of rather ungainly sheep, walking on their hind legs.

In the morning, however, it was found that, as far as the sentries knew, *nobody had passed through the camp at all!*

This, one of the most famous examples of optical illusion, is only one item in the testimony to back up the contention that we cannot believe our eyes. And if we cannot believe our eyes, what *can* we believe?

The whole thing becomes frightening once you start to think of it.

So don't think of it.

M. B. ALESHIRE

The two finally decided that they had been a crowd of sheep, walking on their hind legs.

Sand Trouble

It doesn't seem much more than a month since I shook the remaining grains of last season's sand out of my shoes. Here's another summer nearly gone, and I find I am doing it again.

By "it" I mean the process of getting sand on and into things and then getting it off and out of things, at which most of us spend our summers. If, during the winter months when we are in the city, we had to cope with an element as cussed as sand, we would be writing letters to the papers and getting up committees to go to the City Hall about it. If, every night when we got home from work, we had to shake out our shoes and empty out our pockets to get rid of a fine scratchy substance which was infesting the city, there would be such a muttering all over town that you would think there was a thunderstorm coming up. And yet, when it is a part of our vacation, we take it, along with all other inconveniences, and pay money for it. It sometimes seems as if we weren't very bright.

Of course, there is sand and sand. I am a great admirer of nice, hard, smooth sand which knows its place, especially if I can draw pictures in it with a stick. I guess there is no more exquisite pleasure. It is a little more enjoyable if you happen to be able to draw well, but even just little five-pointed starts and egg-and-dart designs are a great comfort. Sand is also a good place on which to write, "I love you," as it would be difficult to get it into court after several years have passed.

But a great majority of the grains of sand on the earth's surface do not know their place. They are always wanting to go somewhere—with you. Just how several hundred grains of sand work it to get up from the beach and into the short hair on the back of your neck is one of Old Mother Nature's mysteries, but they do it, and with a great deal of dispatch, too. I can go on to a beach and stand perfectly upright, touching nothing but the soles of my feet to the ground, for four minutes, with my hands held high above my head, and at the end of that time there will be sand in my pockets, on the back of my neck, around my belt line (inside), and in my pipe. It is marvelous.

Smoking is one of life's pleasures which is easiest marred by this little trick of sand. After a swim in the ocean or lake there is nothing more refreshing than the tang of tobacco smoke, yet the risks incident to lighting a pipe or a cigarette are so great that it is hardly worth while. A pipe is particulary susceptible. You can wait until you have had your swim and then have a man come down from the bathhouse with a fresh pipe in a chamois bag, which he himself can insert in your mouth (naturally, not still in the chamois bag) and which he can light for you with matches also brought freshly to the beach, handled only with silk gloves. And yet, at the first drag, there will come that sickening crackling sound like an egg frying in deep fat, indicating that the stem is already as full of sand particles as a shad is of roe, and presently your teeth are a-grit (and on your teeth three grains of sand will do the work of thousands) and in no time sand is in your eye.

Just to avoid this blight on beach smoking I had a leathersmith make me a little box, with compartments just fitting my pipe, a box of cigarettes, a box of matches, and my watch. (Sand in watches would make a whole treatise in itself.) Although I came under suspicion of carrying a vanity case when I appeared on the beach with this outfit, it nevertheless seemed worth it to keep my smoking utensils free from the usual pulverized rock. But the very first day, when I came out of the water and, unwrapping my box from two towels, unlocked it with a combination known only to myself and my banker, I found that my pipe, cigarettes, and matches were merely parts of a sand design such as men build along by the boardwalk at Atlantic City. In fact, there was more sand on them than usual, because the box had served as a catchall in which sand could concentrate and pile up without being blown away by the breeze. Since then I have given up smoking on the beach.

Lying supine (or even prone, for that matter) on the sand is one of those activities which always seem more fun just before you do them. You think how wonderful it would be to stretch out under the sun and bake, letting the world, as the Duncan Sisters used to do in soprano and alto, go drifting by. So you take up your favorite position (which very shortly turns out to be *not* your favorite position, much to your surprise) and, shutting your eyes, abandon yourself to a pagan submission to the sun and its health-giving beams.

Gradually small protuberances arise from the beach underneath you, protuberances which were not there when you lay down but which seem to have forced their way up through the sand for the express purpose of irritating you. If you are lying on your face, the sand just at the corner of your mouth raises itself up in a little mound just high enough to enter between the upper and lower lip. If you are lying on your back, the same sand raises itself into an even higher mound and one with a curve at the top so that it still gets into the corner of your mouth. All this happens without outside aid.

But there is plenty of outside aid available. One small boy playing tag fifty feet away, and running past anywhere within radius, can throw off enough sand to blind an ordinary man. And, as there must be at least two small boys to make a game of tag anything but a mockery, enough sand is thrown off to blind two ordinary men. A dog, merely by trotting by, can get almost the same effect. And it is very seldom that a dog is content with merely trotting by. I have never yet stretched myself on a beach for an afternoon's nap that a dog, fresh from a swim, did not take up a position just to the left of my tightly closed eyes, and shake himself. I need hardly go into this.

Aside from the initial fright at the sudden shower, there is the subsequent irritation at the humiliation (it is quite apparent that the dog picked you out deliberately to do it to) which ends in your leaping up and going home to lie down on a couch. It usually ends up that way even without the dog.

I am perhaps working myself up into a phobia for sand which I did not originally feel. Simply by putting all this down on paper I have got myself wiping my lips to get off imaginary particles of sand. And there is no sense in my getting myself into this state of nervous susceptibility, for in fifteen minutes I have got to go down to the beach and romp with the children. Perhaps I can persuade them to go to the movies. Perhaps I shall even *make* them go to the movies.

One small boy can throw enough sand to blind an ordinary man.

The Wreck of the
Sunday Paper

WHAT is to be done with people who can't read a Sunday paper without messing it all up? I just throw this out as one of the problems with which we are faced if we are to keep our civilization from complete collapse.

There is a certain type of citizen (a great many times, I am sorry to have to say, one of the "fair" sex) whose lack of civic pride shows itself in divers forms, but it is in the devastation of a Sunday newspaper that it reaches its full bloom. Show me a Sunday paper which has been left in a condition fit only for kite flying, and I will show you an antisocial and dangerous character who has left it that way.

Such a person may not mean deliberately to do the things to a newspaper that he or (pardon my pointing) *she* does. They really couldn't achieve such colossal disarrangement by any planning or scheming. It has to come from some cataclysmic stroke of a giant force, probably beyond their control. Let them but touch a nice, neat Sunday edition as it lies folded so flat and cold on the doorstep, and immediately the rotogravure section becomes entwined with the sporting section and the editorial page leaps out and joins with the shipping news to form a tent under which a pretty good-sized child could crawl. The society page bundles itself up into a ball in the center of which, by some strange convulsion, the real-estate news conceals itself in a smaller and more compact ball. It is the Touch of Cain that these people have, and perhaps we should not blame them for it.

But they needn't *leave* this mound of rumpled newsprint this way. They could recognize their failing and at least try to correct its ravages before handing the paper on to someone else.

I once knew a man whose wife was a newspaper builder. She built things out of newspapers when she read them. There wasn't much to show for it when she had finished in the way of definite objects; that is, you couldn't quite make out just what she had thought she was building. But there had very evidently been some very clear idea of making each section of the newspaper into an object of some sort—anything so long as it made the newspaper absolutely unsuited for reading purposes.

Now the man usually tried to get down on Sunday morning ahead of his wife so that he could have first crack at the paper before the Great Disintegration set in. But, owing to a habit he had formed in his youth of staying out late on Saturday nights, he found it difficult to beat her to it. By the time he got downstairs the room looked like a militia encampment.

"What do you do with a newspaper?" he once asked her, as quietly as he could. "Try to dress yourself in it? You'll never get anywhere without buttons, you know."

But she didn't seem to mind his taunts, and, in fact, more or less put him on the defensive by calling him "an old maid"; so he decided that the time had come for action. He ordered *two* editions of each Sunday paper, one for his wife to mux about with and one for himself.

It was then that he discovered that his helpmeet's rolling herself up in the paper was not just an unconscious weakness on her part but a vicious perversion from which she got a fiendish pleasure. She would sneak upstairs and get his personal edition before he was awake and give it the works, pretending that she couldn't find her own.

She was simply doing it to be mean, that was all. Often her

own copy would be untouched and he would find it on Monday morning hidden away behind the sofa in its pristine smoothness.

I suppose, in a way, that the inability to read a newspaper which someone else has wrapped around himself or which is in any way disarranged is a sign of abnormality in itself and that we are the ones who are in the wrong.

I have tried to open a newspaper while riding on the top of a bus on a windy day and, after personifying the sheet and endowing it with malign purposes of its own, talking to it under my breath and waitly slying until I thought that it wasn't expecting an attack before rushing into a maneuver which I fondly hoped would take it at a disadvantage, have then been unable to read what was printed on it because the page was in the general condition of a relief map of North America. This may show a hypersensitivity to tactile sensations and mark *me* as the one needing medical attention and not the one who can read anything so long as the print is visible.

All right, then—*I'm* the one to blame. *I'm* the enemy to society and the one to be locked up. But the fact remains that I am going to stand just so much more of this thing and then away *some*body goes to the police station.

*She would sneak upstairs and get his personal edition
and give it the works.*

The Tourist Rush
to America

ACCORDING to statistics or whatever you call those long tables
of figures with "1929" and "1930" at the tops of the columns,
there weren't so many Americans vacationing in Europe last
summer as there were the summer before. Of course, it was
impossible to get accommodations back to New York on any
boat leaving after the middle of August, but that may have
been because a lot of Americans adopted Frenchmen and
Germans and brought them home. The boats were filled up
*some*how. But figures will show that, full boats or not, Americans stayed away from Europe this year in great droves. (I
know why, but I am not going to tell. You must guess. It
begins with a W and is the name of a street in New York.)

Now, if it is true that American tourist trade to Europe is
falling off, then European tourist trade to America will have
to begin. There has simply got to be a tourist trade somewhere, otherwise the world will be flooded with picture post
cards which nobody will buy and there will be a plague of
them.

So far, the only Europeans who have come over here have
come to sell something or to lecture. They land in New York,
rush right to an import house or lecture platform, do their
stuff, and take the next boat back. They very seldom stop to
look around, probably because there isn't much to stop to

look around at. We have never gone in much for the tourist trade, but, if the future is going to bring great hordes of Europeans to this country to behave as we have been behaving in Europe all these years, we had better begin to look picturesque. We can also begin to jack up prices a bit, having one set of prices for us natives and one for the foreign visitors. Maybe it won't be a pleasure to get one of those French hotel-keepers with a long black mustache into a corner of a real old New England inn with spinning wheels in the lobby and just nick him good and plenty for a sheaf of those little lavender francs he has in his sock!

But we shall have to give them something for their money. Not much, perhaps, but a little more than we have to offer now in the way of local color. They will want to see the quaint old streets of Lawrence, Massachusetts, or Portage, Wisconsin. We shall have to make them quaint. They will want to see the natives in native costume. We shall have to rig up something for the residents of Massillon, Ohio, and Denver, Colorado, to wear which will bring forth gasps of delight from our foreign friends—at twenty dollars a gasp.

Of course, some of our citizenry may object to being stared at while they are at their supper, but Americans have been staring at French and German natives for years and it is only fair that they have their chance now. There may be a little trouble if, some warm summer evening, when the Perkinses are sitting out on their front porch getting what breeze there is, a group of French tourists from the local hotel stop and make remarks about Mr. Perkins' suspenders and offer to buy the straw mat out from under Mrs. Perkins as she sits on the steps.

The boys who hang around the corner drug store and make wise cracks at passers-by are going to resent just a bit being pointed out from an automobile-full of Italian visitors as the "the lower element of the village, wearing the native headgear," and having their pictures taken by elderly Tyrolese couples who happen to be spending the night in town on their way to Chicago. Mrs. Durkins, on Sycamore Street, isn't going to fancy being interrupted in her housework by having a German artist poke his head in her kitchen window and ask if she will pose for a sketch.

But these things will have to be done if we are going in
for getting foreign business. We have made no bones about
peering into Dutch windows. We can't object to the Dutch
peering into ours. Of course, we *shall* object, but we shouldn't.

In fact, sooner or later we shall probably get used to it and
make a little effort to be picturesque. You will find different
sections of the country brushing up on the distinctive local
dishes and serving them in costume. Our own tea rooms have
given us a start on the thing, and in many places the serving
of a simple lettuce-and-tomato sandwich involves the dressing
up of the waitress like Betsy Ross and the execution of a short
minuet by the customer and the cashier.

The step from this sort of thing to catering to foreign
visitors is not so drastic. Up around Boston they can put the
regular Sunday morning baked beans and fish balls up in
little earthenware pots and serve tham at a dollar and a half
a throw. Everybody in Boston will, I am afraid, have to dress
up like Puritans during the summer months, because that is
the way that the Europeans will have read about them in
their guidebooks. In Philadelphia, scrapple can be elevated
to the status of a rare old *vin du pays* and served by Quaker-
esses or little Ben Franklins. Of course, the South will just
drive the foreigners crazy with its famous dishes and local
color. It would not be surprising to see corn pone, if dished
out by a dear old mammy with a bandanna on, reach an
importance where it could draw down three dollars a portion
in the open market.

The present batch of guidebooks to points of interest in
the United States will have to be revised to make them more
like books we get abroad explaining the intricacies of France
and Germany, with phrases for use by the foreign traveler.
They can be divided up into sections like this:

PHRASES FOR THE STEAMSHIP PIER

What country is this? . . . That is too bad, I wanted Brazil.
. . . In which direction is the night-club life? . . . Get the hell
out of that trunk! . . . No, that bottle of cognac is not mine. . . .
I do not know how it got in there. . . . I am surprised to see

that you have discovered yet another bottle of cognac. . . .
They must have been in the trunk when I bought it. . . . Here,
porter, take these bags and my arm. . . . I want to go first to
the corner of Michigan Avenue and Goethe Street, Chicago.

AT THE HOTEL

Please assign me to a room overlooking the Mayor and the
City Council. . . . It need not have a bath so long as the bureau
drawers are wide enough to accommodate my dress shirts. . . .
What shall I write here? . . . How do I know that you will not
use my signature to further some nefarious financial coup

*The boys who hang around the corner drug store are having
their pictures taken.*

of your own? Boy, take those three bags of mine and the nice-looking one next to them to Room 1473.

IN THE RESTAURANT

What are your most typical native dishes? . . . Then give me a couple of eggs. . . . I do not care how they are cooked so long as they do not contain sentimental mottoes or confetti. . . . Won't you sit down yourself and have a bit to eat? . . . You seem tired. . . . Perhaps you would like to have *me* serve *you*? . . . What would you like? . . . The chicken pie is very nice today. . . . No, I am *not* nice. I am simply being polite. . . . I would much rather not dance, if you don't mind.

IN THE AVIARY

What type of bird is that? . . . Ugh! . . . Are all three of those one bird, or do they come separately? . . . I am not very crazy about birds. . . . Let us go.

IN THE REPAIR SHOP FOR CIGARETTE LIGHTERS

I would like a new flint for my briquet. . . . I'm sorry, I thought that this was a repair shop for cigarette lighters. . . . Good day.

ON THE WAY BACK TO EUROPE

That is the last time I shall make a voyage to America. . . . Such robbers! . . . I did not see a pretty woman all the time I was there. . . . It will certainly seem good to get back home and have some bad coffee. . . . Well, I suppose everyone ought to see America once, but, for me, give me little old Bucharest every time!

The Eel-Snooper

COME, come! What's all this we hear about eels? Some Danish ichthyologist (look it up yourself—I had to) named Schmidt comes back from a scientific cruise and says that every single one of the eels on the eastern cost of the United States and the western coast of Europe came originally from the Sargasso Sea (the Sargasso Sea behind that small area of the Atlantic Ocean down around the Antilles which is always full of tea leaves and old bits of grass). He says that whenever our eels get to feeling sappy and foolish and want to become parents, they pack up and leave the fresh waters of New England or Virginia or wherever they happen to be living at the time, and glide all the way south to the Sargasso Sea. Here the eggs are deposited and (pardon me) fertilized, and here the happy event takes place. Or perhaps it should be happy events, since they hatch out in litters of ten million per mother.

At this point, according to the Danish Dr. Schmidt, the parents die, evidently disgusted at the prospect of cutting up food and picking up toys for ten million babies. The offspring, finding themselves orphans, immediately turn tail and wriggle north, where they, too, stay until Joe feels that he is earning enough to have kiddies. Then the whole rather silly procedure takes place all over again.

At least, this is what the Danish Dr. Schmidt says. Just what anyone named Schmidt is doing in Denmark (unless his parents, like the eels, went somewhere else for the time being) is beside the point. What I want to know is how does he know that our eels come from, and go back to, the Sargasso Sea? How do you keep track of an eel?

According to the story told by the ichthyologist (don't tell me you haven't look that up *yet!*), he "banded" thousands of eels and then followed them all over the various seas. I take this to mean that he tied little markers on each eel, labeled "Georgie" and "Fred" or perhaps just "No. 113,539." While he was at it, it would have been just as easy to have the plate engraved "This is Rover, and belongs to Dr. Johannes Schmidt, 114 Nvjeltidg Boulevard, Copenhagen," or "Please put me off at Jacksonville, Fla." He might even have gone so far as to put little false mustaches on those eels which he particularly wanted to keep track of and to give them each seventy-five cents to spend for candy on the trip south. The whole thing sounds just a little bit fishy to me.

An eel must be an awful sap to let himself be caught just for the sake of being tagged and thrown back into the water again. My experience with eels is rather limited, having got hold of one for only a few seconds once and then decided that it wasn't worth the struggle. But I should think that any self-respecting eel would resent being caught and "banded" and then tossed back, making him a figure of fun among the other eels, and perhaps laying himself open to the charge of being a sissy. For a breed of fish (or are they fish?) which has gone proudly through the centuries without ornamentation of any kind, it must be very humiliating for one particular member to find himself wearing a shiny new band around his tail reading "Prince."

No wonder those eels who have been subjected to this indignity rush off to the Sargasso Sea. They probably can't bear to stay around the home town with all the kidding they must get. I shouldn't be surprised to find that it was *only* those eels who wore bands that fled to the south. The rest are probably still in the northern fresh waters, laughing their heads off and saying: "Whatever became of that pansy who used to wear a tin ring on his tail?"

And from then on, just what is Dr. Schmidt's course of action? Does he follow the eels down the coast, fishing them out every few days to see if their bands are on tight? Or does he rush right off by airplane to the Sargasso Sea in order to be there when his pets arrive? It must be rather confusing for a bunch, or covey, or flowk of eels to leave New England after their distressing experience with Dr. Schmidt, and swim all the way down to Central America only to be fished out by the same Dr. Schmidt at the other end and made mock of all over again. If eels figure out anything at all, they must

PETER ARNO

He might even have put false mustaches on those eels he particularly wanted to keep track of.

have evolved the theory that there are two Schmidt brothers who look exactly alike.

"For the love of Mike," they must say, "didn't we just *leave* this guy? What is this—a racket? Can't we *ever* shake him?" The twin-brother theory would be the only one that would satisfy a clear-headed eel, especially when he finds out that the name is Schmidt again. The wonder is that they have enough patience left to go ahead with the breeding.

The behavior of the young eels on the return trip is even more extraordinary, according to the Doc. They start out for the north just as soon as they are born (which is not surprising when you consider that the Sargasso Sea is full of pretty unpleasant stuff, even for an eel) and, if they don't swim fast enough, or, as Dr. Schmidt phrases it, "are dilatory," they outgrow their salt-water days and perish before they reach fresh water. I am not so sure that the ones who are "dilatory" are not the smart ones, for at least they have had the pleasure of being dilatory, than which there is no greater pleasure in the world.

The rest, who rush along to fresh water, have only just time to swim around once at their destination, be fished out and banded, and then rush right back to die in the Sargasso Sea.

The little ones who are aggressive enough to make the grade northward sound very unattractive. They are "transparent, gelatinous creatures of which the only substantial parts are two disembodied eel eyes like mother-of-pearl." This presents a rather horrid picture, I am sure. I am just as glad that my bailiwick does not include the swarming grounds of these young eels, for coming home late at night and seeing a group of disembodied eyes with nothing to back them up must be a pretty trying experience. I still don't understand how a fish can have nothing but eyes, but there are a lot of things in this world that I don't understand.

When this unprepossessing-looking crowd of larvæ reach a point about the latitude of Bermuda, they split up into east-bound and west-bound parties, those who are more sober-minded going up to the New England territory and the gayer ones heading for the coast of France. I doubt if many of those who go to France ever bother about coming back to the Sargasso Sea to have children. They probably go up a river to some nice, rich, farming territory and settle down to salt away their money, or swim down the Seine to Paris and drink themselves to death.

Dr. Schmidt will only be wasting his time to band any of these.

In fact, I wonder if Dr. Schmidt isn't wasting his time anyway. Suppose it *is* proven that all eels come from, and go back to, the Sargasso Sea. What then?

The rest are probably saying: "Whatever became of that pansy who used to wear a tin ring on his tail?"

What Are
Little Boys Made Of?

Dɪᴅ you know that you have enough resin in your system to rub up a hundred violin A strings? Or enough linoleum to carpet two medium-sized rooms (without bath)? You were probably not aware of these valuable properties lying dormant in your physical make-up, and yet scientists tell us that they are there.

As you all were taught in school, our body is made up of millions and millions of tiny particles called the Solar System. These tiny particles are called "æons," and it would take one of them fifteen billion years to reach the sun if it ever broke loose and *wanted* to get to the sun.

Well, anyway, these millions and millions of tiny particles are composed of hydrogen, oxygen, iodine, phosphorus, Rhode Island, Connecticut. There is also a blueplate dinner for those who don't like iodine. The action of all these elements sets up a ferment (C_2HN_4, or common table pepper) which sometimes ends in digestion but more often does not. If any of these agents is lacking in our make-up, due to our having dressed in a hurry, we say we are "deficient," or perhaps we "feel awful." Even with everything working I don't feel so hot.

It is only recently that doctors have discovered that we have many more elements in our systems than was originally thought. Whether we have always had them and just didn't know it, or whether they were brought there and left by some people who wanted to get rid of them has not been decided.

They tell us that the average 150-pound body (and a very pretty way to phrase it, too) contains enough carbon alone to make 9,000 lead pencils (not one of them ever sharpened, probably).

Another item which the doctors tell us we have in abundance is hydrogen—"enough in excess," they put it, "to fill about a hundred child's balloons." There's a pretty picture for you! As if we didn't have troubles enough as it is, we must go about with the consciousness that we have the makings of one hundred child's balloons inside us, and that under the right conditions we might float right off our chairs and bounce against the ceiling until pulled down by friends!

Thinking of ourselves in terms of balloons, lead pencils, whitewash (we have enough lime in us to whitewash a chicken coop, says one expert), and matches (we are fools to bother with those paper books of matches, for we are carrying around enough phosphorus to make 2,200 match heads), all this rather makes a mockery of dressing up in evening clothes or brushing our hair. We might just as well get a good big truck and pile ourselves into it in the raw whenever we want to go anywhere, with perhaps some good burlap bags to keep the rain off. There is no sense trying to look nice when all that is needed is a sandwich-board sign reading: "Anything on this counter—15 cents."

And that is the ultimate insult that these inventory hounds have offered us: they tell us just how much all this truck of which we are made is worth in dollars and cents. They didn't have to do that. Put all our bones, brains, muscles, nerves, and everything that goes into the composition of our bodies on to scales and, at the current market prices, the whole lot would bring just a little over a dollar. This is on the hoof, mind you. If we wanted to tie each element up in little packages with Japanese paper and ribbon, or if we went to the trouble to weather them up a bit and call them antiques, we might be able to ask a little more.

For example, the average body, such as might meet another

Under the right conditions we might float off our chairs and bounce against the ceiling.

body comin' through the rye, contains only about one tenth of a drop of tincture of iodine at any one time, and one tenth of a drop would hardly be worth the dropper to pick it up for the retail trade. And yet, if *we* don't have that tenth of a drop something happens to our thyroid gland and we sit around the village grocery store all day saying "Nya-ya!" Or to our pituitary gland and we end up wearing a red coat in a circus, billed as Walter, the Cardiff Behemoth: Twice the Size of an Ordinary Man and Only Half as Bright.

I don't see why scientists couldn't have let us alone and not told us about this. There was a day when I could bounce out of bed with the lark (I sometimes let the lark get out first, just to shut the window and turn on the heat, but I wasn't far behind), plunge into a cold tub (with just a dash of warm to take off the chill), eat a hearty breakfast, and be off to work with a light heart.

But now I get out of bed very carefully, if at all, thinking of those 9,000 lead pencils which are inside me. Too much water seems to be a risk, with all that iron lying around loose. Exercise is out of the question when you consider 2,200 match heads which might jolt up against each other and start a very pretty blaze before you were halfway to work.

Suppose that we *are* as full of knickknacks as the doctors say. Why not let the whole matter drop and just forget about it? Now that they have put the thing into our heads, the only way to get it out is for some expert to issue a statement saying that everyone has been mistaken and that what we are really made of is a solid mechanism of unrustable cast iron and if anything goes wrong, just have a man come up from the garage and look it over.

The Five- (or Maybe Six-) Year Plan

IF I hear any more about this five-year-plan business I am going to start one myself. Russia has been working on hers for a couple of years now, and England is thinking of starting one, and what Russia and England can do, I can do. All that is necessary is for me to find out just what a five-year plan is.

As I understand it, you take five years to start all over again. You throw out all your old systems, clean out the rubbers in the hall closet, give to the Salvation Army all those old bundles of the *National Geographic* you have been saving, and tell your creditors to wait for five years and that they will be surprised to see how well you pay. It sounds like a good plan to me. I haven't asked my butcher about it yet.

When a nation goes in for a five-year plan it reorganizes everything, eliminates competition, buys everything on a large scale, sells everying in amalgamations, and, in general, acts up big. I can't do that, because I shall be working alone and on my own, but I *can* reorganize, and I figure that it will take me about five years to do the thing right. Let's say six and be on the safe side.

In the first place, my whole financial system has got to be gone over. It is in such bad shape now that it can hardly be called a system. In fact, I don't think that it can even be called

122

financial. It is more of a carnival. I shall have to go through
all those old checkbook stubs and throw them out, for, under
my present method of keeping books, there was no need of
saving them, anyway. You see, it has been quite some time
since I subtracted the amounts of checks drawn from what
I smilingly call the "balance." In fact, there are often great
stretches of time when I don't even enter the amounts at all.
This latter irregularity is due to a habit of making out checks
on blank forms supplied by hotels and restaurants, on which
even the name of the bank has to be filled in, to say nothing
of the number of the check and its amount. I like to make
these out, because I print rather well and it is a great satisfaction to letter in the name of my bank in neat capitals
exactly in the middle of the space provided for that purpose.
I have sometimes made out a blank check just for the satisfaction of seeing "BANKERS' TRUST CO., 57th St. Branch"
come out in such typographical perfection from the point of
my pen. I am sure that it is a satisfaction to the bank, too.
They often speak of it. What they object to is the amount
which I fill in below. It seems too bad, they say, to have such
a neat-looking check so unnegotiable. All of this will be
changed under my five-year plan, for I intend not only to
give up making out blank checks, but to enter and subtract
those which I do make out. I cannot guarantee to subtract
them correctly, for I am not a superman and can do only
one thing at a time, but I will at least get the figures down
on paper. The bank can handle the rest, and I am sure that
they will. That is what they pay men to do, and they have
never failed me yet.

Which brings us to the second part of my new economic
reorganization—production. Some way has got to be found
to turn out more work. One solution would be, I suppose,
to do more work, but that seems a little drastic. If Russia and
England can combine all their forces to speed up production,
I ought to be able to combine with somebody to speed up
mine without making a slave of myself as well. If I could get
a dozen or so fellows who are in the same line of business, we
could work up some division of labor whereby one of them
could think up the ideas, another could arrange them in

notes, another could lose the notes, and yet another could hunt for them. This would take a lot of work off my hands and yet save time for the combination.

By then we would be ready for a fifth member of the pool to walk up and down the room dictating the story from such of the notes as can be found, while a sixth took it down in shorthand. We could all then get together and try to figure out the shorthand, with a special typing member ready to put the story down on paper in its final form. All that would now remain would be to put the stories in envelopes and address them, and it is here that I would fit in. That neat printing that I have been doing on blank checks all my life could be turned to good account here. It makes a great difference with an editor whether or not the contribution is neat, and it might turn out that I was the most important member of the pool. I don't think there is any doubt that the stories would be better.

So much for production. With my financial system reorganized and my production speeded up, the problem would be my world market. Here is where the fun would come in. You can't get a world market without personal contact. You couldn't very well write letters to people in Germany and Spain and say: "I am a little boy forty years old and how would you like to buy a piece that I have written?"

You would have to *go* to Germany and Spain and see the people personally. This is why I feel that my five-year plan may take possibly six years to carry out. I shall have to do so much traveling to establish a world market. And I *won't* want any of my associates in the pool along with me, either. They will have plenty to do with thinking up ideas at home—and writing them.

Now, I may have this five-year plan all wrong. I haven't read much about Russia's, except to look at pictures showing Lenin's tomb. But I do know that the principle of the thing is that five years are supposed to elapse before anyone can really judge of its success. In five years Russia expects to have increased production of wheat to 3,000,000,000,000 bushels (or is it 3,000,000,000?) and before that time everyone has

PETER ARNO

You can't get a world market without personal contact. This is why I feel that my five-year plan may take six. I shall have to do so much traveling.

got to take Russia's word for it. This is what appeals to me about the idea. I want to be given a little rest from all this nagging and eyebrow-lifting and "What about that article you promised?" and "Your account shows a slight overdraft." I want to have something definite to hold out to these people, like: "In five years' time I will have my whole system reorganized, with a yearly production of 3,000,000 articles and monthly deposits of $500,000. Can't you have a little faith? Can't you see that a great economic experiment is being carried on here?" (This, I think, ought to do the trick, unless they have no interest in progressive movements at all. And, from what I hear about them, they haven't.)

The Mystery of the
Poisoned Kipper

Who sent the poisoned kipper to Major General Hannafield of the Royal Welch Lavaliers? That is the problem which is distorting Scotland Yard at the present moment, for the solution lies evidently in the breast of Major Hannafield himself. And Major General Hannafield is dead. (At any rate, he doesn't answer his telephone.)

Following are the details, such as they are. You may take them or leave them. If you leave them, please leave them in the coat room downstairs and say that Martin will call for them.

One Saturday night about three weeks ago, after a dinner given by the Royal Welch Lavaliers for the Royal Platinum Watch, Major General Hannafield returned home just in time for a late breakfast which he really didn't want. In fact, when his wife said, rather icily, "I suppose you've had your breakfast," the Maj. Gen. replied: "I'll thank you not to mention breakfast, *or* lunch, *or* dinner, until such time as I give you the signal." Mrs. Hannafield thereupon packed her bags and left for her mother's in New Zealand.

Along about eleven thirty in the morning, however, the Maj. Gen. extricated himself from the hatrack where he had gone to sleep, and decided that something rather drastic had to be done about his mouth. He thought of getting a new mouth; but as it was Sunday all the mouth shops were closed, and he had no chance of sending into London for anything. He thought of water, great tidal waves of water, but even that didn't seem to be exactly adequate. So naturally his mind turned next to kippered herring. "Send a thief to catch a thief" is an old saying but a good one, and applies especially to Sunday-morning mouths.

So he rang for his man, and nobody answered.

The Maj. Gen. then went to the window and called out to the gardener, who was wrestling with a dahlia, and suggested

HERBERT F. ROESE

General Hannafield returned home just in time for a late breakfast which he really didn't want.

that he let those dahlias alone and see about getting a kipper, and what's more a very salty kipper, immediately. This the gardener did.

On receiving the kipper, the Maj. Gen., according to witnesses, devoured it with avidity, paper and all, and then hung himself back up on the hatrack. This was the last that was seen of Major General Hannafield alive, although perhaps "alive" is too strong a word. Perhaps "breathing" would be better.

Mrs. Hannafield, being on her way to New Zealand, has been absolved of any connection with the crime (if causing the Maj. Gen.'s death can be called a crime, as he was quite an offensive old gentleman). The gardener, from his cell in the Old Bailey, claims that he bought the kipper from a fish stall in the High Street, and the fish vendor in the High Street claims that he bought the kipper from the gardener.

According to the officials of Scotland Yard, there are two possible solutions to the crime, neither of them probable: revenge, or inadvertent poisoning of the kipper in preparation. Both have been discarded, along with the remainder of the kipper.

Revenge as a motive is not plausible, as the only people who could possibly seek revenge on the Maj. Gen. were killed by him a long time ago. The Maj. Gen. was notoriously hot-tempered, and, when opposed, was accustomed to settling his neck very low in his collar and rushing all the blood available to his temples. In such states as this he usually said: "Gad, sir!" and lashed out with an old Indian weapon which he always carried, killing his offender. He was always acquitted, on account of his war record.

It is quite possible that some relatives of one of the Maj. Gen.'s victims might have tracked him from the Punjab or the Kit-Kat Club to his "diggings" in Diggings Street, but he usually was pretty careful to kill only people who were orphans or unmarried.

There was some thought at first that the Maj. Gen. might have at one time stolen the eye of an idol in India and brought it back to England, and that some zealot had followed him

Mrs. Hannafield and the ship's doctor have struck up an acquaintance.

across the world and wreaked vengeance on him. A study of the records, however, shows that the Maj. Gen. once tried to steal an emerald eye out of an Indian idol, but that the idol succeeded in getting the Maj. Gen.'s eye instead, and that the Maj. Gen. came back to England wearing a glass eye—which accounted for his rather baffling mannerism of looking over a person's shoulder while that person was talking to him.

Now as for the inadvertent poisoning of a kipper in the process of being cured. Herring are caught off the coast of Normandy (they are also caught practically everywhere, but Normandy makes a better story), brought to shore by Norman fishermen dressed up as Norman fishermen, and carried almost immediately to the kippering room.

The herring kipperers are all under state control and are examined by government agents both before and after kippering. They are subjected to the most rigid mental tests, and have to give satisfactory answers to such questions as "Do you believe in poisoning herring?" and "Which of the following statements is true? *(a)* William the Norman was really a Swede; *(b)* herring, placed in the handkerchief drawer, give the handkerchiefs that *je ne sais quoi; (c)* honesty is the best policy."

If the kipperers are able to answer these questions, and can, in addition, chin themselves twelve times, they are allowed to proceed with their work. Otherwise they are sent to the French Chamber of Deputies, or Devil's Island, for ten years. So you can see that there is not much chance for a herring kipperer to go wrong, and practically no chance for Major General Hannafield to have been poisoned by mistake.

This leaves really nothing for Scotland Yard to work on, except an empty stomach. The motive of revenge being out, and accidental poisoning being out, the only possible solution remaining is that Major General Hannafield was in no state to digest a kippered herring and practically committed suicide by eating it. This theory they are working on, and at the coroner's inquest (which ought to come along any day now) the whole matter will be threshed out.

An examination of the Maj. Gen.'s vital organs has disclosed nothing except a possible solution of the whereabouts of the collier Cyclops, which was lost during the Great War.

Here the matter stands, or rather *there*. (It was here a minute ago.) Mrs. Hannafield may have some suggestions to offer, if she ever will land in New Zealand, but, according to radio dispatches, she is having an awfully good time on the boat and keeps going back and forth without ever getting off when they put into port. She and the ship's doctor have struck up an acquaintance, and you know what that means.

Your Boy and
His Dog

PEOPLE are constantly writing in to this department and asking: "What kind of dog shall I give my boy?" or sometimes: "What kind of boy shall I give my dog?" And although we are always somewhat surprised to get a query like this, ours really being the Jam and Fern Question Box, we usually give the same answer to both forms of inquiry: "Are you quite sure that you want to do either?" This confuses them, and we are able to snatch a few more minutes for our regular work.

But the question of Boy and Dog is one which will not be downed. There is no doubt that every healthy, normal boy (if there is such a thing in these days of Child Study) should own a dog at some time in his life, preferably between the ages of forty-five and fifty. Give a dog to a boy who is much younger and his parents will find themselves obliged to pack up and go to the Sailors' Snug Harbor to live until the dog runs away—which he will do as soon as the first pretty face comes along.

But a dog teaches a boy fidelity, perseverance, and to turn around three times before lying down—very important traits in times like these. In fact, just as soon as a dog comes along who, in addition to these qualities, also knows when to buy and sell stocks, he can be moved right up to the boy's bedroom

"You could have knocked me over with a feather," he said.

and the boy can sleep in the dog house.

In buying a dog for a very small child, attention must be paid to one or two essential points. In the first place, the dog must be one which will come apart easily or of such a breed that the sizing will get pasty and all gummed up when wet. Dachshunds are ideal dogs for small children, as they already are stretched and pulled to such a length that the child cannot do much harm one way or the other. The dachshund being so long also makes it difficult for a very small child to go through with the favorite juvenile maneuver of lifting the dog's hind legs up in the air and wheeling it along like a barrow, cooing, "Diddy-app!" Any small child trying to lift a dachshund's hind legs up very high is going to find itself flat on its back.

For the very small child who likes to pick animals up around the middle and carry them over to the fireplace, mastiffs, St. Bernards, or Russian wolfhounds are not indicated—that is, not if the child is of any value at all. It is not that the larger dogs resent being carried around the middle and dropped in the fireplace (in fact, the smaller the dog, the more touchy it is in matters of dignity, as is so often the case with people and nations); but, even though a mastiff does everything that it can to help the child in carrying it by the diaphragm, there are matters of gravity to be reckoned with which make it impossible to carry the thing through without something being broken. If a dog could be trained to wrestle and throw the child immediately, a great deal of time could be saved.

But, as we have suggested, the ideal age for a boy to own a dog is between forty-five and fifty. By this time the boy ought to have attained his full growth and, provided he is ever going to, ought to know more or less what he wants to make of himself in life. At this age the dog will be more of a companion than a chattel, and, if necessary, can be counted upon to carry the boy by the middle, and drop him into bed in case sleep overcomes him at a dinner or camp meeting or anything. It can also be counted upon to tell him he has made a fool of himself and embarrassed all his friends. A wife could do no more.

The training of the dog is something which should be left to the boy, as this teaches him responsibility and accustoms him to the use of authority, probably the only time he will ever have a chance to use it. If, for example, the dog insists on following the boy when he is leaving the house, even after repeated commands to "Go on back home!" the boy must decide on one of two courses. He must either take the dog back to the house and lock it in the cellar, or, as an alternate course, he can give up the idea of going out himself and stay with the dog. The latter is the better way, especially if the dog is in good voice and given to screaming the house down.

There has always been considerable difference of opinion as to whether or not a dog really thinks. I, personally, have no doubt that distinct mental processes do go on inside the dog's brain, although many times these processes are hardly worth the name. I have known dogs, especially puppies, who were almost as stupid as humans in their mental reactions.

The only reason that puppies do not get into more trouble than they do (if there *is* any more trouble than that which puppies get into) is that they are so small. A child, for instance, should not expect to be able to fall as heavily, eat as heartily of shoe leather, or throw up as casually as a puppy does, for there is more bulk to a child and the results of these practices will be more serious in exact proportion to the size and capacity. Whereas, for example, a puppy might be able to get only the toe of a slipper, a child might well succeed in eating the whole shoe—which, considering the nails and everything, would not be wise.

One of the reasons why dogs are given credit for serious thinking is the formation of their eyebrows. A dog lying in front of a fire and looking up at his master may appear pathetic, disapproving, sage, or amused, according to the angle at which its eyebrows are set by nature.

It is quite possible, and even probable, that nothing at all is going on behind the eyebrows. In fact, one dog who had a great reputation for sagacity once told me in confidence that most of the time when he was supposed to be regarding a human with an age-old philosophical rumination he was really asleep behind his shaggy overhanging brows. "You could have knocked me over with a feather," he said, "when I found out that people were talking about my wisdom and suggesting running me for President."

This, of course, offers a possibility for the future of the child itself. As soon as the boy makes up his mind just what type of man he wants to be, he could buy some crêpe hair and a bottle of spirit gum and make himself a pair of eyebrows to suit the rôle: converging toward the nose if he wants to be a judge or savant; pointing upward from the edge of the eyes if he wants to be a worried-looking man, like a broker; elevated to his forehead if he plans on simulating surprise as a personal characteristic; and in red patches if he intends being a stage Irishman.

In this way he may be able to get away with a great deal, as his pal the dog does.

At any rate, the important thing is to get a dog for the boy and see what each can teach the other. The way things are going now with our Younger Generation, the chances are that before long the dog will be smoking, drinking gin, and wearing a soft hat pulled over one eye.

ADAM JOHN BARTH

If necessary, the dog can be counted upon to carry the boy by the middle and drop him into bed in case sleep overcomes him at a dinner or camp meeting or anything.

The Big
Coal Problem

A GREAT deal of thought has been devoted to the subject of how we are going to meet the problems of this winter; but I haven't seen any attention being paid to the Coal Question. Of course, there has been some expert speculation on how to *get* any coal without twenty dollars, but no one seems to have written anything helpful on what we are going to do with it once we have got it. Or is that just my personal problem?

I have been trying to get coal into a furnace fire box now for about fifteen years, and I should say that my average was about .002, or two pieces of coal to each half ton shoveled. I can get it anywhere else in the cellar—the ash cans, the preserve closet, the boxes behind the furnace, and even back into the bin again. But I can't quite seem to hit the fire box in the furnace.

It may be that there is something wrong with my aim or my eyesight, but I have always had a feeling that the coal itself had something to do with it. I think that my coal man sells me live coal; that is coal which lives and breathes and has a mind of its own. You can't tell me that just ordinary dumb, inanimate coal could act the way mine does!

I would not tell this to many people, because they wouldn't believe me, but I have actually seen pieces of coal which I had successfully tossed into the fire box *turn around and fly back out on to the floor!* Now, you can't fight a thing like that. I have watched coal on a shovel which I was carrying from the bin to the furnace actually set itself in a state of ferment and bound about like corn in a popper in its attempt to get off the shovel and on to the floor. Things of this nature come under the head of the Supernatural. You know that, don't you?

I remember one night back in 1926 when I went down into the cellar to fix the furnace for the night (and what a misleading phrase that "fix the furnace" is! I'd *like* to fix a furnace just once. It wouldn't pull any more of its tricks on me again, I'll tell you. The only way furnace can be fixed is with nitroglycerin.) Anyway, I went down to give the furnace its head for the night, and to this end I went over to the bin to get the customary three shovelfuls of coal.

The bin was about half full (it then being about the middle of October and the fire about two weeks in operation) and I picked out my favorite shovel—which I had built like a dredge, with sides which closed up around the coal—and started for the opening. Remember, I could *see* the coal in there.

I dug in the shovel, felt the coal settle on it, and pulled it out. There was no coal there! I then poked down from over the top of the bin with a long poker until I was absolutely sure that I felt great piles of coal descend, all the time saying to myself: "Come, come, Benchley! Pull yourself together! Of course there will be some on the shovel this time." But no! I could not even get those black diamonds out of the bin, much less into the furnace. This was disturbing enough—but wait!

I turned to look at the open door of the fire box into which I had planned to toss at least six or seven pieces, and there, on the floor between the bin and the furnace, was all the coal which hadn't come out on the shovel! It had come out by itself, possibly over my head through the air, and had strewn itself all over the cement in just the position it would have taken anyway, but without a sound! Some of it had even wound its ghostly way over into its favorite nest in the preserve closet and was lying there, looking up at me as if to say: "Beat you to it, old man!" Without another look I turned and fled upstairs, striking my head on the cellar stairs even harder than usual. I know enough not to monkey around with devil's coal.

This experience rather made me afraid to go down cellar again, and I hired a man to do it for me. He, however, seemed to have no trouble, and I used to hear the coal crashing into the furnace below (and what a lovely sound that is, to lie in bed in the morning and hear some other poor sucker downstairs putting on the coal, even if it is only your wife) and my pride became piqued.

If an Italian who had got only an A.B. in a university could get coal into a furnace without spilling it, why couldn't I, with my Ph.D., do it? Or better yet, why couldn't I actually build the fire with my Ph.D.? This was, however, out of the question, as I had lost it that time when the Salvation Army took those old army blankets in which it had been tucked away. But I determined to try my hand at the fire at least once a day, and then, if it didn't work, let Mike go on doing it all the time.

The result of this was that Mike would build the first in the morning (I chose the evening service for my experiments) and I would put it out at night. Then Mike would build it in the morning again. He finally said that he would have to get more money for tending it just once a day than he did when he tended it twice, as he had more work to do, what with taking out the things that I had put into it the night before (I may not be able to get *coal* into a fire box, but I can get some dandy other things, such as hunks of larva, old bottles, and bits of the cement floor) and then rebuilding the whole business. So I gave it up entirely for the time being. But this winter I had to start in again; for because of the unemployment, Mike has too much work to do on public improvements to bother with us.

I am now thinking of having a furnace built with the coal bin *on top*. Then, when it comes time for me to put on more coal, I can just open a chute and let the stuff dribble down into the fire box at any speed and to any amount that I want.

As for the ashes and clinkers, I shall have a great cavern dug underneath the furnace, with perhaps a small boy who will stand down there with a searchlight and a rifle and who can shoot the clinkers to bits as they stick in the grate.

When the winter is over I can have the house moved right off the cavern and the whole thing dug out.

This, of course, is going to be pretty expensive, and I haven't the slightest idea that it will work. But it will at least restore my self-respect by making it unnecessary for me to go at the thing with that shovel again. And a failure in a rather gigantic effort like that wouldn't be half as humiliating as not being able to get a few pieces of coal into a fire box with my own hands.

There was all the coal which hadn't come out on the shovel!

HERBERT F. ROESE

Hiccoughing
Makes Us Fat

So many simple little actions have been recently discovered to be fattening, there is hardly any move we can make, voluntary or involuntary, which does not put on weight for us. We have been told that laughing makes us fat, that sleeping after meals makes us fat, that drinking water makes us fat (or thin, according to which day of the week you read about it); and, although I haven't seen it specifically stated, I have no doubt that it has been discovered that yawning and sneezing are in the class with all the rest of the fatty tissue builders (who, by the way, seem to be just the busiest little builders since the days when the pyramids were being thrown together).

But, if you will notcie, all of these fatty functions are rather pleasant ones.

Laughing, dozing, and yawning are certainly lots of fun.

Though there may be some opposition to sneezing as a pastime, I am pretty sure that, if you will be quite honest, you will admit that a good rousing sneeze, one that tears open your collar and throws your hair into your eyes, is really one of life's sensational pleasures. You may say, "Oh, darn it!" in between sneezes and try to act as if you weren't enjoying it, but, as an old hay-fever sufferer, I know the kick that can lie in a good sneezing spell, provided you have the time to give to it and aren't trying to thread a needle.

In the midst of all these pleasures of life which are to be denied us if we want to keep thin, it seemed to me that hiccoughing ought to be proved fattening, thereby introducing something we *don't* like to do. I don't know of anyone who has a good word to say for hiccoughing. It is pretty easy to prove that almost anything makes people fat. All you have to do is drag out the old cells and gland secretions and talk about how they secrete fat in the blood and hide it away for the winter months. If you can get a dog or a cat in a cage and can make them do whatever the thing is you are studying, you ought to be able to prove your point in about fifteen minutes.

They put a dog and a cat in cages side by side the other day, and made them awfully cross at each other by telling the dog what the cat had been saying about him and the cat what the dog was telling his cronies about her, and, by testing the animals' blood before and after the hard feeling began, they discovered that they were both quite a bit thinner by supper time. It wasn't stated what their weight was *after* supper, or when the two had made up their little tiff, but it is safe to say that they both put on about three pounds each. I've tried those reducing gags myself and all that they do is make me hungry.

However, as not many people know what hiccoughing really is—except that it is a damned nuisance—it will be perfectly safe to go ahead on the cellular theory for a starter. You must know that our wonderful Human Machine (wonderful except for about three hundred flaws which can be named on the fingers of one hand) is made up of countless billions of cells called "cells," and that it is the special duty of some of these little body cells to store up fat. And I will say this for them: they do their duty.

I have got a set myself which lean over backward in their devotion to their duty. They must have little mottoes up on the walls of their workshop reading: Do It Now! and A Shirker Never Wins.

I sometimes think that they get other cells in from an agency to help them when it looks as if they weren't going to get their quota of fat secreted by five o'clock, for they haven't fallen down once on the job as yet. I wish I could say as much for the cells whose duty it is to *destroy* fat. I suspect that my fat-destroying cells drink, or else they don't get enough sleep. Something is slowing them down, I know that.

Now, let us say for the purposes of argument (not a very hot argument, just kidding) that the process of hiccoughing is a muscular reaction caused by an excess secretion of the penal glands (I made that one up, but there ought to be a penal gland if there isn't). You have been sitting, let us say, at a concert, or have been trying to play the flute, and have become exhausted. This exhaustion sets loose a nervous toxin which, in turn, sets loose five homing pigeons which try to fly out of your mouth. This is what we know as hiccoughs, or "the hicks."

If it were not for these hiccoughs, the fatigue poison set loose by the exhaustion would act on the cells and destroy great quantities of fat, making it necessary for us to take in our clothing two or three inches. But the hiccoughs, or escaping pigeons, step in and relieve the toxic condition, thereby leaving the fat where it was—and you know where *that* is. In my experiments I had no cats or dogs to place in cages, but I used an aunt who was visiting us and who hadn't been doing much around the house to pay for her keep. I placed her in a cage, and in the cage next to her placed a parrot which she insists on carrying about visiting with her wherever she goes. After testing the blood of both the aunt and the parrot and giving them some candy to keep them quiet, I tried to induce hiccoughs in the aunt. This was not so easy, as she didn't want to hiccough.

Now, hiccoughing is all very easy to fall into when you don't want to, but there doesn't seem to be any way in which to induce it out of thin air. I showed the aunt pictures of people hiccoughing, thinking to bring it on by suggestion. But she wouldn't look. I tried giving imitation hiccoughs myself, but succeeded only in bringing on an acute attack of real ones which I didn't want. (Unfortunately, I had neglected to test my own blood beforehand, so these were of no use in the experiment.)

I am sure you will admit that a good rousing sneeze is one of life's sensational pleasures.

My own hiccoughing, however, got my aunt laughing, and that, together with the candy, set up quite a decent little attack of hiccoughs. This, in turn, excited the parrot, who was accustomed to mock my aunt to the point of rudeness, and he began a series of imitation hiccoughs which were as irritating as they were unskillful.

Things went on like this for several days, when finally the parrot gave up the whole thing and took to singing instead. My aunt and I were spasmodically hiccoughing, but it was nothing to what it had been when the fit was at its height. In fact, I had plenty of time between hiccoughs to make blood tests of the aunt and to try to make one of the parrot. The parrot, however, would have none of it, and so I am unable to report on the effect of hiccoughing on the weight of birds.

As far as my aunt goes (and that is pretty far) I have data to show that she gained four pounds during the seizure, owing entirely to the elimination of the fat-destroying poisons through the agency of hiccoughing.

Thus we find that all fattening pastimes are not pleasurable. This is going to revolutionize the science of weight reduction, for the whole thing has been hitherto based on the theory that we mustn't do the things we want to do and must do the things we dislike (I mention no names in this latter group, but certain forms of lettuce and green vegetables will know whom I am referring to). Now, if we are to keep from doing even one disagreeable thing, like hiccoughing, the whole tide may turn, and by 1933 it may be so that the experts will tell us *not* to do the unpleasant things (and then where will you be, my fine lettuce?) and to go in strong for everything that gives us pleasure.

The Dear Dead
Table d'Hôte Days

I REALIZE as well as anybody that to talk about dieting at this late date is like discussing whether or not the polka causes giddiness or arguing about the merits of the coaster brake on a bicycle. Dieting, as such, is no longer a subject for conversation.

But the whole question has been brought to my mind with a fresh crash by the finding of an old menu among my souvenirs (several of the souvenirs I cannot quite make out—even if I knew what they were, I can see no reason for having saved them), an old menu of a Christmas dinner dispensed to the guests of a famous Chicago hotel in the year 1885. I was not exactly in a position to be eating a dinner like this in 1885, but some of my kind relatives had saved it for my torture in 1930. If you don't mind, I would like to quote a few more poetic passages.

That dinner was, of course, table d'hôte. When you bought a dinner in those days, you bought a *dinner*. None of this skimming over the card and saying: "I don't see anything I want. Just bring me an alligator pear salad." If you couldn't see anything you wanted on one of the old-fashioned table d'hôte menus, you just couldn't *see,* that's all.

This particular menu went out of its way. Even for 1885 it must have represented quite a snack. As I look at it today,

I am hungry most of the time. I feel like a crook every time I take a furtive forkful of potato.

I can only stand, hat in hand, and bow my head in reverence for the imagination, as well as the capacity, of that earlier day. Listen:

After the customary bluepoints and soup, with a comparatively meager assortment of fish (just a stuffed black bass and boiled salmon), we find a choice of broiled leg of mountain sheep or wild turkey. This is just a starter. The boys didn't get down to business until the roast. There are thirty-six choices among the roasts. Among the more distinguished names listed were:

Leg of moose, loin of elk, cinnamon bear, black-tail deer, loin of venison, saddle of antelope [the National Geographic Society evidently did the shopping for meat in behalf of this hotel], opossum, black bear, and then the duck.

The duck will have to have a paragraph all by itself. In fact, we may have to build a small house for it. When this chef came to the duck, he just threw his apron over his head and said: "I'm going crazy, boys—don't stop me!" He had canvasback duck, wood duck, butterball duck, brant, mallard duck, blue-winged teal, spoonbill duck, sage hen, green-winged teal, and pintail duck, to say nothing of partridge, quail, plover, and some other of the cheap birds.

I am not quite sure what a sage hen is, and I doubt very much if I should have ordered it on that Christmas Day, but *some*body thought enough of it to go out and snare two or three just in case, and it seems to me that this is the spirit that has made America what it is today. (And what is that?)

So, after toying with all the members of the duck family except decoys and clay pigeons, the diner of 1885 cast his eye down the card to what were called "Broiled," a very simple, honest name for what followed. Teal duck (evidently one of the teal ducks from the roast column slipped down into the broiled and liked it so well that it stayed), ricebirds, marsh birds, sand snipe, reedbirds, blackbirds, and red-winged starling. One wonders why there were no ruby-throated grosbeaks or Baltimore orioles, but probably the dinner was sort of an impromptu affair with guests taking potluck on whatever happened to be in the house.

By this time you would have supposed that they had used up all the birds within a radius of 3,000 miles of Chicago, leaving none to wake people up in the morning. But no. Among the entrées they must have a fillet of pheasant *financière*, which certainly must have come as a surprise to the dinner parties and tasted good after all that broiled pheasant and roast pheasant. Nothing goes so good after a broiled pheasant as a good fillet of pheasant *financière*. And, in case you didn't want that, there were also cutlets of antelope with mushroom sauce, stewed squirrel with dumplings, and opossum with a nice purée of sweet potatoes. (I suppose you think it is fun to sit here and write these names out, and before lunch at that.)

There then seemed to have come over the chef a feeling that he wasn't quite doing the right thing by his guests. Oh, it had been all right up to this point, but he hadn't really shown what he could do. So he got up a team of what he called "ornamental dishes," and when he said "ornamental" I rather imagine he meant "ornamental." They probably had to brought in by the town fire department and eaten standing on a ladder. Playing left end for the "ornamental dishes" we find a pyramid of wild turkey in aspic. Perhaps you would like to stop right there. If you did you would miss the aspic of lobster Queen Victoria. I rather imagine that it made quite an impressive ornamental dish—that is, if you looked anything like Queen Victoria, who was a very fine-looking woman.

Then, in a little group all by itself (after the pâté of prairie chicken, liver *royale*, and boned duck *à la* Bellevue), comes a strange throwback to the old days at the top of the menu, including boned partridge, snipe, duck (how simple just the word "duck" looks after all we have been through), and wild turkey. There seem to have been a lot of the birds who couldn't find places among the roasts and broils and so just took anything they could get down at the bottom of the card.

It is doubtful if many patrons, by the time they got down to this section, did much with quail or duck again. It is doubtful if they ever wanted to see the names in print again.

Now the question arises—what did people look like after they had eaten a dinner like that? Were people in 1885 so much fatter than those of us today who go around nibbling at bits of pineapple and drinking sips of sauerkraut juice? I personally don't remember, but it doesn't seem that people were so much worse off in those days. At any rate, they had a square meal once in a while.

I am not a particularly proud man and it doesn't make an awful lot of difference to anyone whether I am fat or not. But as I don't like to run out of breath when I stoop over to tie my shoes, I try to follow the various bits of advice which people give me in the matter of diet. As a result, I get very little to eat, and am cross and hungry most of the time. I feel like a crook every time I take a furtive forkful of potato, and once, after sneaking a piece of hot bread, I was on the verge of giving myself up to the police as a dangerous character.

Now, all this must be a wrong attitude to take toward life. Surely there are more noble aspects (aspect of lobster Queen Victoria, for instance) than that of a man who is afraid to take a piece of bread. I am going to get some photographs of people in 1885 and give quite a lot of study to finding out whether they were very much heavier than people today. If I find that they weren't, I am going to take that menu of the Chicago Christmas dinner and get some chef, or organization of chefs, to duplicate it.

The worst that can happen to me after eating it will be that I drop dead.

PETER ARNO

Even for 1885 it must have represented quite a snack. They didn't get down to business until the roast.

"Abandon Ship!"

THERE has been a great deal of printed matter issued, both in humorous and instructive vein, about ocean travel on those mammoth ships which someone, who had never ridden on one, once designated as "ocean greyhounds." "Ocean camels" would be an epithet I would work up for them, if anyone should care enough to ask me. Or I might even think of a funnier one. There is room for a funnier one.

But, whether one calls them "ocean greyhounds" or "ocean camels" or something to be thought up at a later date, no one can deny that the ships which ply between this country and foreign lands get all the publicity. Every day, throughout this "broad" land of ours, on lakes, rivers, gulfs, and up and down the coast line, there are plying little steamers carrying more American passengers than Europe, in its most avid moments, ever dreamed of. And yet, does anyone ever write any travel hints for them, other than to put up signs reading: "Please leave your stateroom keys in the door on departure"? Are colorful sea stories ever concocted, or gay pamphlets issued, to lend an air of adventure to this most popular form of travel by water? I hope not, for I had rather hoped to blaze a literary trail in this tantalizing bit of marine lore.

There are three different types of boat in use on our inland waterways and coastwise service: (1) Ferries, which are so silly

151

that even *we* won't take them up for discussion. (2) Day, or excursion, boats, which take you where you are going, and, if you get fascinated by the thing, back in the same day. (3) Night boats, mostly in the Great Lakes or coastwise service, which have, as yet, never fascinated anyone to the point of making a return trip on the same run. And then, of course, you can always row yourself.

There is one peculiar feature of travel on these smaller craft of our merchant marine. Passengers are always in a great hurry to embark and in an equally great hurry to disembark. The sailing of an ocean liner, on which people are really going somewhere and at considerable expense, is marked by leisurely and sometimes haphazard arrivals right up to the last minute. But let an excursion boat called the *Alfred W. Parmenter* announce that it will leave one end of a lake at 9 A.M. bound for the other end of the lake and return, and at 6 A.M. there will be a crowd of waiting passengers on the dock so great as to give passers-by the impression that a man-eating shark has just been hauled up. On the other hand, fully half an hour before one of these "pleasure" boats is due to dock on its return trip, the quarter-deck will be jammed with passengers who evidently can hardly wait to get off and who have to be restrained by the officers from jumping overboard and beating the boat in to shore. At least a quarter of the time on one of these recreation trips is spent in standing patiently in a crowd waiting for a chance to be the first ones on and the first ones off.

Just why anyone should want to be the first one aboard an excursion boat is one of the great mysteries of the sea. Of course, there is the desire to get good positions on deck, but even if you happen to be the first one on board, the good positions are always taken by people who seem to have swum around and come up from the other side. And then there is the question: "What *is* a good position?" No matter where you settle yourself, whether up in the bow or 'way aft under the awning, by the time the boat has started it turns out to be too sunny or too windy or too much under the pattering soot from the stack. The first fifteen minutes of a trip are given over to a general changing of positions among the passengers. People who have torn on board and fought for preferred spots with their lives are heard calling out: "Here, Alice, it's better over here!" and "You hold these and I'll go and see if we can't get something out of the wind." The wise tripper gets on board at the last minute and waits until the boat has swung around into her course. Then he can see how the sun, wind, and soot are falling and choose accordingly.

Of course, getting on a day boat at the last minute is a difficult thing to figure out. No matter how late you embark, there is always a wait of twenty minutes before the thing starts, a wait with no breeze in the broiling sun to the accompanying rumble of outbound freight. I have not the statistics at hand, but I venture to say that no boat of less than 4,000 tons ever sailed on time. The captain always has to have an extra cup of coffee up at the Greek's, or a piece of freight gets caught against a stanchion or the engineer can't get the fire to catch. The initial rush to get on board and the scuffle to get seats is followed by a great deal of tooting and ringing of bells—and then a long wait. People who have called out frantic good-bys find themselves involved in what seems to be an endless and footless conversation over the rail which drags on through remarks such as "Don't get seasick" and "Tell mother not to worry" into a forced interchange of flat comments which would hardly have served for the basis of any conversation on shore. It finally ends by the relatives and friends on the pier being the first to leave. The *voyageurs* then return dispiritedly to their seats and bake until the thing sails. Thus, before the trip has even begun, the let-down has set in.

It has always been my theory that the collapsible chairs on a day boat are put out by one firm, the founders of which were the Borgias of medieval Italy. In the old sadistic days, the victim was probably put into one of these and tied so that he could not get out. Within two hours' time the wooden crosspiece on the back would have forced its way into his body just below the shoulder blades, while the two upright knobs at the corners of the seat would have destroyed his thigh bones, thereby making any further torture, such as the Iron Maiden or the thumbscrews, unnecessary. Today, the steamboat company does not go so far as to tie its victims in, but gives them no other place to sit on deck, and the only way in which a comfortable reading posture can be struck is for the passenger to lie sideways across the seat with his left arm abaft the crossbar and his left hip resting on the cloth. The legs are then either stretched out straight or entwined around another chair. Sometimes one can be comfortable for as long as four minutes in this position. The best way is to lie down flat on the deck and let people walk over you.

This deliberate construction of chairs to make sitting impossible would be understandable if there were any particular portion of the boat, such as a good lunch counter, to which the company wanted to drive its patrons. But the lunch counters on day boats seem to run on the theory that Americans, as a nation, eat too much. Ham, Swiss cheese, and, on the dressier boats, tongue sandwiches constitute the *carte du jour* for those who, driven from their seats by impending

PETER ARNO

"Don't run so hard, Ethel; you'll tire yourself all out!"

curvature of the spine, rush to the lunch counter. If the boat happens to be plying between points in New England, that "vacation-land of America," where the business slogan is "The customer is always in the way," the customer is lucky if the chef in attendance furnishes grudgingly a loaf of bread and a piece of ham for him to make his own sandwiches. And a warm bottle of "tonic" is considered all that any epicure could demand as liquid refreshment.

All this would not be so bad if, shortly after the boat starts, a delicious aroma of cooking onions and bacon were not wafted up through ventilators, which turns out to be coming from the galley where the crew's midnight meal is being prepared.

If the boat happens to be a "night boat" there is a whole new set of experiences in store for the traveler. Boarding at about five or six in the afternoon, he discovers that, owing to the *Eastern Star* or the *Wagumsett* having been lying along-side the dock all day in the broiling sun, the staterooms are uninhabitable until the boat has been out a good two hours. Even then he has a choice of putting his bags in or getting in himself. A good way to solve this problem is to take the bags with him into one of the lifeboats and spend the night there. Of course, if there are small children in the party (and there always are) two lifeboats will be needed.

Children on a night boat seem to be built of hardier stock than children on any other mode of conveyance. They stay awake later, get up earlier, and are heavier on their feet. If, by the use of sedatives, the traveler finally succeeds in getting to sleep himself along about 3 A.M., he is awakened sharp at four by foot races along the deck outside which seem to be participated in by the combined backfields of Notre Dame and the University of Southern California. Two children can give this effect. Two children and one admonitory parent yelling out, "Don't run so hard, Ethel; you'll tire yourself all out!" can successfully bring the half-slumbering traveler to an upright position, crashing his head against the upper bunk with sufficient force to make at least one more hour's un-consciousness possible.

It is not only the children who get up early on these night

boats. There is a certain type of citizen who, when he goes on a trip, "doesn't want to miss anything." And so he puts on his clothes at 4:30 A.M. and goes out on deck in the fog. If he would be careful only not to miss anything on the coast line it might not be so bad, but he is also determined not to miss anything in the staterooms, with the result that sleepers who get through the early-morning childish prattle are bound to be awakened by the uncomfortable feeling that they are being watched. Sometimes, if the sleeper is picturesque enough, there will be a whole family looking in at him, with the youngest child asking, "Is that daddy?" There is nothing left to do but get up and shut the window. And, with the window shut, there is nothing left to do but get out into the air. Thus begins a new day.

Sometime a writer of sea stories will arise who will immortalize this type of travel by water. For it has its heroes and its hardships, to say nothing of its mysteries, and many a good ringing tale could be built around the seamen's yarns now current among the crews of our day and night excursion boats. I would do it myself, but it would necessitate at least a year's apprenticeship and right now I do not feel up to that.

How I Create

IN an article on How Authors Create, in which the writing methods of various masters of English prose, like Conrad, Shaw, Barrie are explained (with photographs of them in knickerbockers plaguing dogs and pushing against sun-dials), I discover that I have been doing the whole thing wrong all these years. The interviewer in this case hasn't got around to asking me yet—doubtless because I have been up in my room with the door shut and not answering the bell—but I am going to take a chance anyway and tell him how I do my creative work and just how much comes from inspiration and how much from hashish and other perfumes. I may even loosen up and tell what my favorite hot-weather dishes are.

When I am writing a novel I must actually live the lives of my characters. If, for instance, my hero is a gambler on the French Riviera, I make myself pack up and go to Cannes or Nice, willy-nilly, and there throw myself into the gay life of the gambling set until I really feel that I *am* Paul De Lacroix, or Ed Whelan, or whatever my hero's name is. Of course this runs into money, and I am quite likely to have to change my ideas about my hero entirely and make him a bum on a tramp steamer working his way back to America, or a young college boy out of funds who lives by his wits until his friends at home send him a hundred and ten dollars.

Often I wait weeks for inspiration, my quill pen posed in the air.

One of my heroes (Dick Markwell in *Love's How-do-you-do*), after starting out as a man about town in New York who "never showed his liquor" and was "an apparently indestructible machine devoted to pleasure," had to be changed into a patient in the Trembly Ward of a local institution, whose old friends didn't recognize him and furthermore didn't want to.

But, as you doubtless remember, it was a corking yarn.

This actually living the lives of my characters takes up quite a lot of time and makes it a little difficult to write anything. It was not until I decided to tell stories about old men who just sit in their rooms and shell walnuts that I ever got around to doing any work. It doesn't make for very interesting novels, but at any rate the wordage is there and there is something to show the publishers for their advance royalties. (Publishers are crotchety that way. They want copy, copy, copy all the time, just because they happen to have advanced a measly three hundred dollars a couple of years before. You would think that printing words on paper was their business.)

And now you ask me how I do my work, how my inspiration comes? I will tell you, Little Father. Draw up your chair and let me put my feet on it. Ah, that's better! Now you may go out and play!

Very often I must wait weeks and weeks for what you call "inspiration." In the meantime I must sit with my quill pen poised in the air over a sheet of foolscap, in case the divine spark should come like a lightning bolt and knock me off my chair on to my head. (This has happened more than once.) While I am waiting I mull over in my mind what I am going to do with my characters.

Shall I have Mildred marry Lester, or shall Lester marry Evelyn? ("Who is Evelyn?" I often say to myself, never having heard of her before.) Should the French proletariat win the Revolution, or should Louis XVI come back suddenly and establish a Coalition Cabinet? Can I afford to let Etta clean up those dishes in the sink and get them biscuits baked, or would it be better to keep her there for another year, standing first on one foot and then on the other?

You have no idea how many problems an author has to face during those feverish days when he is building a novel, and you have no idea how he solved them. Neither has he.

Sometimes, while in the throes of creative work, I get out of bed in the morning, look at my writing desk piled high with old bills, old gloves, and empty ginger-ale bottles, and go right back to bed again. The next thing I know it is night once more, and time for the Sand Man to come around. (We have a Sand Man who comes twice a day, which makes it very convenient. We give him five dollars at Christmas.)

Even if I do get up and put on a part of my clothes—I do

all my work in a Hawaiian straw skirt and a bow tie of some neutral shade—I often can think of nothing to do but pile the books which are on one end of my desk very neatly on the other end and then kick them one by one off on to the floor with my free foot.

But all the while my brain is work, work, working, and my plot is taking shape. Sometimes it is the shape of a honeydew melon and sometimes a shape which I have never been quite able to figure out. It is a sort of amorphous thing with two heads but no face. When this shape presents itself, I get right back in bed again. I'm no fool.

I find that, while working, a pipe is a great source of inspiration. A pipe can be placed diagonally across the keys of a typewriter so that they will not function, or it can be made to give out such a cloud of smoke that I cannot see the paper. Then, there is the process of lighting it. I can make lighting a pipe a ritual which has not been equaled for elaborateness since the five-day festival to the God of the Harvest. (See my book on Rituals: the Man.)

In the first place, owing to twenty-six years of constant smoking without once calling in a plumber, the space left for tobacco in the bowl of my pipe is now the size of a medium body-pore. Once the match has been applied to the tobacco therein the smoke is over. This necessitates refilling, relighting, and reknocking. The knocking out of a pipe can be made almost as important as the smoking of it, especially if there are nervous people in the room. A good, smart knock of a pipe against a tin wastebasket and you will have a neurasthenic out of his chair and into the window sash in no time.

The matches, too, have their place in the construction of modern literature. With a pipe like mine, the supply of burnt matches in one day could be floated down the St. Lawrence River with two men jumping them. . . .

When the novel is finished, it is shipped to the Cutting and Binding Room, where native girls roll it into large sheets and stamp on it with their bare feet. This accounts for the funny look of some of my novels. It is then taken back to the Drying

If my hero is a gambler, I pack up and go to Cannes.

Room, where it is rewritten by a boy whom I engage for the purpose, and sent to the publishers. It is then sent back to me.

And so you see now how we creative artists work. It really isn't like any other kind of work, for it must come from a great emotional upheaval in the soul of the writer himself; and if that emotional upheaval is not present, it must come from the works of any other writers which happen to be handy and easily imitated.

What of Europe?

HAVING just been brought back from a brief but painful
survey of business conditions in Europe (by "Europe" I mean
three or four hundred square feet in Paris and another good
place in Rome), I am continually being besieged by bankers
and manufacturers to tell them how things are faring with
our cousins (I always insist that they are *not* our cousins except
distantly through marriage) overseas. "Watchman, tell us of
the night!" is the way the bankers and manufacturers phrase
it as they accost me. "What of Europe? Will she survive?"

Rather than go on with these individual conferences in
dingy financial establishments, I am putting all my answers
down here, where he who reads may run, and the devil may
take the hindmost.

To begin with, my economic survey of Europe notes a
startling increase in blondes in Paris. Big blondes. Being a
Nordic myself, I am accustomed to blondes; but the blondes
with which the Paris market is now being glutted through
Scandinavian and German dumping are larger than any that
I remember ever having seen before, even among my own
people. They run anywhere from five feet eleven to six feet
three, with eyes and beam to match.

This sort of thing can't go on, you know, and still have
civilization keep to its present standards. For not only are

these Parisian blondes tall and powerful but they are snooty—
very, *very* snooty—and it is as much as a medium-sized man's
life is worth just to carry on a polite conversation with one
of them. They seem to have no idea at all of bringing about
friendlier relations between Europe and America—an indifference which is, to say the least, unfortunate at this time
when Europe needs America so sorely.

Just why these amazons bother to come out of doors at all
is a puzzle, for they don't seem to be enjoying a minute of
it. They might much better be back in the army, knocking
down privates and drilling people. On meeting one of them,
with one of those little black hats hanging on the side of that
blonde coiffure, one's first instinct is to stand at attention and
salute. One's second instinct is to run. The second instinct is
better.

Now, with this sudden influx of blondes into a market
which has hitherto specialized in brunettes, what may we
expect the effect to be on the American market? (This is the
question that is being asked *me*, mind you, by American business men. I, personally, don't care. I have my books and a
good pipe, and I am looking around for a dog.) And, in
order to answer this question, a little extra research is necessary. This is not so easy to accomplish.

If, by the use of ether or a good swift crack on the jaw,
one can get close enough to these Parisian blondes to note
the texture of the goods, one discovers that they are really
American in manufacture. In other words, a large percentage
of Parisian blondes are platinum, copied after the Jean Harlow
model so popular in America last year. The *hauteur* is also
an American model, distinctly Ziegfeld (before bad business
made the Ziegfeld girls loosen up and smile a little out of
one corner of their mouths), and the only real contribution
that Europe has made to the present product is the size.

I cannot account for the size, for it certainly is not French,
unless French girls have really been tall all the time and have
just been walking along all crouched over until now. It must
be that the Scandinavian countries and Germany are working
night and day to turn out something that will sweep the world
markets, although, of course, Germany has no right to do

CAFÉ DU DÔME

Not only are these Parisian blondes tall and powerful but they are very, very snooty.

this under the Versailles Treaty. Here is something that should be looked into by an interallied commission (if one can be got together which will not immediately start ripping off each other's neckties).

Another question which my clients on Wall Street and throughout the rest of the country are asking me is, "What about Italy under Mussolini?" This I cannot answer as comprehensively as I would like, because I do not speak Italian very well. (I can say "hello" and then "hello" again, in case they didn't understand me the first time, but aside from that my conversation is carried on by an intelligent twinkling of the eyes and nodding of the head to show that I understand what is being said to me. As I do *not* understand, I often get into trouble this way.)

My chief criticism of Italy under Mussolini is that it is too Italian. It is all very well in America for tenors and other participants in a church festival who are supposed to be dressed in Neapolitan costumes to sing "O Sole Mio" and "Santa Lucia," but you don't expect real Italians to do it. It is as if real Americans were to go about singing "Yankee Doodle." "O Sole Mio" and "Santa Lucia" are the only Italian songs that members of a local American pageant know. They *have* to sing them. But surely there must be some others that Italians know, and you would think that they would want to sing them, if only to be different from the Americans. But no! They sing "O Sole Mio" and "Santa Lucia," and seem to think they are doing something rather fine.

Furthermore, there is the question of spaghetti. In New York or San Francisco, when you go to an Italian restaurant, you expect to get spaghetti, because that is supposed to be the big Italian dish. Imagine the shock, on visiting Italy, to find that it *is* the big Italian dish! I am not averse to spaghetti, mind you, and in New York have been known to do rather marvelous things with it, both with and without my vest. But I am not a spaghetti fiend, and after a week in Italy I was ready to call it quits and taper off into wheat cakes and baked beans. But they won't let you.

They are all so proud of the way they (each individual spaghettist) fix the dish, that you must not only eat three platefuls at each meal, but you must smack your lips and raise your fork and say "Wonderful!" at each mouthful, for they are standing right over you and watching with tears in their eyes to see how you are taking it. My enjoyment of the thing was hampered by the fact that I always seemed to get a plate with a self-feeding arrangement in the bottom, whereby no matter how much I ate there was a steady flow up through the table which kept my plate constantly full. I could wind it around my fork or scoop it up in my spoon or shovel it into my mouth like ticker tape by the yard, but it made no impression on the mound before me.

I would estimate that in sheer yardage alone I consumed enough spaghetti to knit sixty or seventy white sweaters. And always there was the *maestro* standing by and beaming and asking, "Was good?" I finally had to resort to a little ruse whereby I would fall screaming to the floor as if in an epileptic fit and have myself carried out of the room away from that never-ending flow of pasta.

I don't think that I shall visit an Italian restaurant in New York again for ever and ever so long.

This excess of spaghetti and Italian songs is made much worse by a Mussolini-bred efficiency which causes your various courses at a meal to be rushed in front of you before you have got the order, or the course you are eating, out of your mouth. Just as you begin coping with the noodles, you see the waiter rushing up with the macaroni, and behind him another waiter with the ravioli, and way down in the distance still a third with the cheese and fruit. It rather takes the heart out of one, especially a slow-moving American who likes to dawdle a bit over his food.

The money question in Europe is naturally the one in which American financiers are most interested. Leaving the silver standard out of it (a process which seems to be taking care of itself pretty well) and eliminating the gold supply as a factor, I would say that the question of money in European countries was just about the same as the question of money in America—a situation which can be summed up in two words: "Not enough."

A History
of Playing Cards

NOT many of you little rascals who employ playing cards for
your own diversion or for the diversion of your funds know
how playing cards were first used. And I venture to say that
not many of you care. So here we are, off on a voyage of
exploration into the History of the Playing Card, or Where
Did All That Money Go Last Week?

The oldest existing playing cards, aside from those which
I keep in the back of my desk for Canfield, are in the Staat-
liches Museum in Berlin and are Chinese. Don't ask me how
Chinese playing cards got into Berlin. Do I know *every*thing?
Suffice it to say that they are a thousand years old, which
gives them perhaps twelve or fifteen years on my Canfield
pack. My Canfield pack, however, has more thumb marks.

These thousand-year-old Chinese cards would be practically no good for anyone today who wanted to sit down for
a good game of rummy. What corresponds to our ace (I am
told there is such a card in our pack—I have never seen one
myself except once when drawing to a 5–9 straight) is a handful of scorpions, and the king and queen are not like our
kings and queens but more like dragons with beards and
headdresses. A gentleman who had been playing bridge with
a ginger-ale highball at his elbow for two hours would never
get around to bidding if he found one of those kings or

queens in his hand. It would undermine his confidence in himself.

Authorities differ on the point of the invention of playing cards. Some say that it was the Egyptians, some the Arabs, while others maintain that it was part of an old Phœnician torture system by which a victim was handed thirteen cards and made to lay them down, one by one, in the proper sequence being known only to an inquisitor known as the partner. If the cards were not laid down in the sequence prescribed by the inquisitor, the victim was strung up by the thumbs and glared at until he was dead of mortification. I rather incline to this last theory of the origin of the playing card. But that may be because I am bitter.

There is a theory that playing cards and chess were originally the same game. This might very well be, although I don't see where the card players would get the chance to sleep that chess players do. A good chess player can tear off anywhere from forty to sixty-five winks a move, if he is clever at it and hides his eyes with his hand, but a card player has at least got to sit up straight and do *something*. It may not be the thing to do, but he has got to do something.

I have often wished, as a matter of fact, that bridge plays could be handled in the same way as chess moves, for if I were given time and a good excuse for covering my face, I could do an awful lot better at bridge than I do. If, when my partner led out with a four of clubs, I could cup my hand over my brow and ponder, let us say for two minutes and a half, I might figure out what the hell it was she meant by her lead.

Whether or not chessmen and playing cards were once all a part of the same big game, the fact remains that a lot of the old playing cards look as if they belonged to some other game than bridge or poker.

For example, take the card which is shown in Fig. 1—the one involving the services of what seems to be an old anteater and three nasturtiums. I can't quite figure out what the game would be which could possibly make it desirable to draw one of these. Perhaps three of such cards as this and two of the kind showing a crane and some lily pads would be as good

Fig. 1   Fig. 2

PETER ARNO

as a full house—but I doubt it. I can't imagine thrilling to a draw which resulted in two such cards as shown in Fig. 2, in which a gentleman seems to be slapping down cockroaches. I would much rather see a simple little four spot (if I already held a five, six, seven, and eight) than any number of political cartoons like those in Fig. 3, showing the Duke of Marlborough setting Queen Anne on fire.

In the old days cards were apparently designed to fill in those intervals in a game during which the player was bored with looking at his partner (I can understand that all right) and just wanted to while away the time by looking at pictures.

Even when they got to putting pictures that one can understand on playing cards—kings, queens, jacks, etc.—it was a long time before they made them look like anything at all. If you will take a look at the queen shown in playing card number 4 you will see that she looks so much like a jack that there is not fun in it. Furthermore, she has a very unpleasant expression on her face and I'll bet that she sings soprano without being asked. If I were to draw her, together with a jack, ten, nine, and three (as I *would*, you may be sure), I would discard both her and the three in the wild hope of filling to both ends rather than hold a hand with such an unpleasant-looking girl in it. Anyway, I would probably think that she was a jack and keep the two for a possible five of a kind. (I don't play poker very well.)

My theory about the origin of the people shown on playing cards is this—

Oh, well, if you don't care, I certainly don't.

It has always seemed to me that the king and queen in an ordinary pack were based on real characters in history, a king and a queen who never got along very well together and wanted to separate. If the king saw the queen coming (in *my* hand, at any rate), he ducked up an alley and said to the jack: "Listen, son, you go that way and I'll go this, and I'll meet you when the game is over at Tony's. Don't let the old lady get in touch with you. She'll only make trouble." So the king goes one way and the jack goes another, and I am stuck with the queen and an eight-four-two, with (in case of bridge) a six spot of some other suit, and others to match.

This, according to my theory, is the real history of the characters in our playing cards. They were the most unhappy royal family in any of the old-time chronicles, and somebody thought that it would be a good idea to put them on playing cards just to torture me personally. I don't know about the early cards, with the duck shooters and anteater stalkers on them. But I venture to say that if I were playing the game, they would all be in the conspiracy, too. For this I have a very simple solution: I stick to Canfield where a man has at least a fighting chance to cheat.

Fig. 3   *Fig. 4*

PETER ARNO

Yesterday's Sweetmeats

It is a rather dangerous thing to note encouraging tendencies in our national life, for just as soon as someone comes out with a statement that we are better than we used to be, we suddenly prance into another war, or a million people rush out and buy Crude Oil, preferred, or there is an epidemic of mother murders, and we are right back in the neolithic age again with our hair in our eyes.

But in the matter of children's candy I am afraid that we shall have to come right out and say definitely that the trend is upward. When I look back on the days of my youth and remember the candy that I used to impose on my stomach, the wonder is that I ever grew up to be the fine figure of a man that I am now. The wonder is that I ever grew up at all. Perhaps that was the idea, and I fooled them.

There were two distinct brands of candy in my day: the candy you bought in the drug store on Sunday, when the candy shops were closed, and the week-day, or Colored Corrosion, brand, which, according to all present-day standards of pure food, should have set up a bright green fermentation, with electric lights, in the epiglottises of nine-tenths of the youth of that time.

We can dismiss the Sunday drug-store candy with a word, for it was bought only once a week and then only for lack of something better. Its flavor was not enhanced by the fact that it was kept in tall glass jars, like appendixes, down at the end of the store where the prescriptions were filled, and consequently always had a faint suspicion of spirits of niter and sod. bicarb. about it.

The delicacy called "calves foot," for instance, which came in long ridged sticks, to be sucked with little or no relish, not only tasted of old French coffee on the second or third brewing, but gave you the undesirable feeling that it was also good for sore throat. The Sunday licorice sticks were larger and more unwieldy, and were definitely bitter on the tongue, besides costing a nickel apiece. Although the rock candy was sweet, it lacked any vestige of imagination in its make-up and made the eating of candy a hollow mockery, and, of course, horehound was frankly medicinal and could be employed only when else had failed.

It was on week days that the real orgy of poisoned and delicious candy took place, a dissipation which was to make a nation of dyspeptics of the present generation of business men and political leaders. This candy was usually bought in a little store run by an old lady (probably an agent in the employ of the German government, in a farsighted scheme to unfit the American people for participation in the war which was to come), and your arrival was heralded by the jangle of a little bell not very cleverly concealed on the top of the door. This was followed by a long period of concentration, the prospective customer sliding his nose along the glass case from end to end, pausing only to ask the price of particularly attractive samples. The smell of those little candy shops is probably now a vanished scent of a bygone day, for it combined not only the aroma of old candies and leather baseballs, but somehow the jangle of the little bell entered into one's nostrils and titillated two senses at once.

In this collection of tasty morsels the one which haunts my memory most insistenty is a confection called the "wine cup," a cone-shaped bit of colored sugar filled with some villainous fluid which, when bitten, ran down over the chin and on to the necktie. It was capped by a dingy piece of marshmallow which was supposed to be removed with the teeth before

The excitement of mixing them was hardly worth the distinct feeling of suicide which accompanied drinking the result.

ADAM JOHN BARTH

drinking the ambrosia within, but usually at the first nibble the whole structure collapsed, with the result that inveterate "wine-cup" consumers had a telltale coating of sugared water down the front of the coat, and, on a cold day, a slight glaze of ice on the chin. What went on in the stomach no one knows, but it does not make a very pretty picture for the imagination.

Another novelty was an imitation fried egg in a small frying pan, the whole sticky mess to be dug out with a little tin spoon which always bent double at the first application and had to be thrown away. The procedure from then on was to extract the so-called "egg" with the teeth, with the chin jammed firmly into the lower part of the "frying pan" as a fulcrum. This, too, left its mark on the habitué, the smear sometimes extending as high up as the forehead if the nose was very small, as it usually was.

There was one invention which was fortunately short-lived, for even in those days of killers' candy it was a little too horrible for extended consumption. It consisted of two cubes (the forerunner of our bouillon cubes of today) which, on being placed each in a glass of water mixed with a soda-fountain technique, proceeded to effervesce with an ominous activity and form what was known either as "root beer," "ginger ale," or "strawberry soda," according to the color of the cubes.

The excitement of mixing them was hardly worth the distinct feeling of suicide which accompanied the drinking of the result, for God knows what they were or what the chemical formula for the precipitate could have been. Probably something which could have gone into the manufacture of a good, stable house paint or even guncotton.

The little mottoes, in the shape of tiny hearts, which carried such varied sentiments as "I Love You," "Skiddoo," "Kick Me," and "Kiss Me Quick," were probably harmless enough in their make-up, although I would always mistrust anything colored pink, but transporting them from shop to school and around the town loose in the pocket soon rendered them grimy and covered with gnirs (a "gnir" is a little particle of wool found in the bottom of pockets, especially constructed for adhering to candies) and unfit for anything involving an æsthetic sense.

"Chocolate babies" also made poor pocket candies, especially when in contact with "jelly beans." (The "jelly bean" seems to have survived down the ages and still is served in little bean pots from the original stock in the store. It would be interesting to discover why.) Licorice whips and "all-day suckers" (which changed color and design on being held in the mouth, a fact which seemed miraculous at the time, but which, on contemplation, sends a slight shudder down the middle-aged spine) were probably the safest of all early twentieth-century candies, but even they would probably fail miserably to pass the test of the Bureau of Standards in Washington.

Worst of all was the "prize package," a cone of old newspaper containing the odds and ends of the day's refuse—

hard marshmallows with enough thumbprints on them to convict the candy dealer ten times over, quantities of tired pop corn which had originally been pink, strange little odd- ments of green and red sugar which, even in their heyday, could not have been much, and, as the Prize, either a little piece of tin in the approximate shape of a horse or a button reading "Bust the Trusts." My gambling instinct made these "prize packages" a great favorite for my pennies, and it is to these and to old Mrs. Hill, who ran the candy shop and dispensed her largesse in this great-hearted manner, that I lay present inability to eat eggs which have been boiled for more than eight seconds. Dear, *dear* Mrs. Hill!

And so, regardless of the present generation's freedom and reputed wildness, I will take a chance on their stomachs being in better shape at forty than mine is, for bootleg alcohol, whatever its drawbacks, takes away that craving for sweets which was the ruin of my generation.

More Work Ahead

AND now, with all this work that I have on my hands, along comes the Hoover Dam. I said to them when they came to me: "You'll have to get somebody else to build it. I've got work enough ahead now to keep me busy until September." But no. They must have me. So here I am—stuck with the job. And the funny part of it is, I never built a dam in my life.

I think what I will do is this: I will draw up all the plans and get things into running order and then I will turn the whole thing over to one of my lieutenants and say: "Lieutenant, here is one of the biggest jobs a man could ask for—bigger, in fact. I have laid everything out for you—here are the blue prints, here are the maps of the Colorado (the dam *is* to be on the Colorado, isn't it?), and you will find the sugar and coffee on the top shelf in the kitchen closet. Now go to it, boy, and make a name for yourself!" Then I will go back to bed.

Now we come to laying out the plans. The building of the Hoover Dam is no dilettante job. We have all got to keep sober—except, of course, Saturdays and Sundays. We can't have any kidding around the shop or any practical jokes, like joshing up the blue prints with "X marks the spot" and "Eddie loves Mabel." Those blue prints have got to tell a story, and

they have got to tell it right. Otherwise the valley of the
Colorado River will wake up some morning and find itself
full of bluefish and old rowboats. Each and every one of us
on the job has got to work like the very devil and just make
this the best dam that has ever been built. I don't have to tell
you boys that.

The first thing to do, as I see it, is to find the river. I know
in a general way where it is, having stopped off for a day on
the way to Hollywood to look at the Grand Canyon. (Don't
tell me at this late date that *that* Colorado River isn't the one
we're working on. That *would* discourage me.) As I remember
it, it looked pretty big. Almost too big. Thinking back on
what I saw that day, I have almost a mind to give the whole
thing up. . . . Oh, well, the hell with it! Let's take a chance,
anyway.

Now, once we decide on which river it is we are going to
dam, the next thing to do is to decide how we are going to
dam it. According to the specifications which have been turned
over to me by the government the dam must be 730 feet high
(I think that we can get away with 700 feet, which is a round
number and easier to remember) and 1,100 feet long. That
is pretty long. It is the longest dam *you* ever saw and I wouldn't
be surprised if it was the longest dam that Hoover ever saw,
engineer that he is. The canal (this is the first I have heard
about a canal, by the way. I thought we were just building a
dam)—the canal has got to be 200 miles long and big enough
to float a ship drawing twenty feet of water. I am sorry to
have to intrude all these technical details, but, after all, we
are embarked on a fairly technical venture. You can't go at
this thing as you would at making a punch or a costume for
a fancy dress ball. We have got to *know* something about what
we are going to do. Otherwise people will laugh.

You see, we plan to spend about $100,000,000 on the thing.
This is the figure which the government has given me, but
I plan on slipping a little bit more over because of the fact
that we shall all have to have our lunches out there on the
job and will naturally be expected to use taxis to get to and
from work. I should think that a concern as big as the United
States government would want its employees to be well nour-

ished and travel in some sort of style, if only for appearances'
sake. So we'll call it $100,000,750. If they don't like it, they
can protest it and we'll settle for the taxi fare. I, for one, do
not intend to live right by the construction work. There must
be a good hotel somewhere up back in the hills. If there isn't,
we'll build one.

Now. Here we are, all set to begin. We have $100,000,000
to spend (with extras), a pretty fair-sized river to dam, and
a lot of mending to be done. O.K. Let's go!

I frankly haven't the slighest idea of what to do first. (Don't
let this get around!) My first idea would be to throw a lot of
stuff into the river at the point where the dam is to be until
it all fills up and we can go home. This is not as easy as it
sounds. To begin with, we have got to get stuff to throw in
which will not melt or filter through. This eliminates mud

We are embarked on a technical venture. You can't go at this thing as you
would making a punch.

and corn husks. Mud is all right for a small dam, such as the ones we have built before, but this time we have got to allow for erosion, adhesion, collusion, and depreciation. All of which have to be divided by seven and taken the square root of. So we can't use mud; or, if we do, we have got to be careful and not call it mud in the expense account. When you are spending $100,000,000 you can't have an item like "Mud ... $5,000,000." Congress would get suspicious.

All right, then. . . . The only thing left for us to do, that I can see, is to throw in a lot of concrete. And here is where our first big problem presents itself. How do we get the concrete into such a form that we can throw it into the river so that it will stay? This, I admit, is a poser. We have simply got to mix the concrete up on the bank and throw it in great blocks where we want it. But how are we to get the blocks in the *middle* of the stream? The ends are all right. We can do that in no time. But that middle? I don't like to be defeatist, but I doubt very much if it can be done at all.

If we go on this theory, *viz.,* that it can't be done at all, we are adopting the Lazy Man's attitude. What would have happened if Fulton had said: "I can't invent the steam engine?" What would have happened if Edison had said: "I can't beat Ford and Firestone at throwing horseshoes?" The work of this world has been done by men who said: "I can't"—and who *meant* it.

So now that we have got that old Colorado River just chock full of concrete blocks right where it needs it most, we must look around for some place to sit down and rest. And, unless I am very much mistaken, this is going to be our toughest job. You can't stand on the bank, as we shall have been doing, mixing concrete blocks and tossing them into a river, without making a frightful mess on the shores, what with donkey engines, concrete mixers, lemon peels, and White Rock bottles. What we shall have to do is to put in a requisition, or petty-cash voucher, for a man to pick all these things up and cart them away, so that we can sit down and rest when we have finally got the dam built.

We don't want to go back to the hotel right away, because something might happen. The dam might burst and you know what that means. Ask the people of Johnstown. They are still sore about it.

The government said nothing about it in the prospectus it sent to me, but I understand from friends that the district in which the dam is to be built gets pretty hot in summer. I have heard 120 in the shade quoted. They always add: "But, of course, it is that clear, dry heat—so you don't mind it." But I have heard that before. Natives are always telling you that the heat in their home town is clear and dry and that one doesn't notice it, but I have never been able to catch it on one of its clear, dry days.

My theory is that when it is 120 in the shade it is 120 in the shade, and I have pretty good scientific backing for my point. And 120 in the shade is too hot for work, wet or dry.

So, as far as I am concerned, things look pretty black for ever getting the Hoover Dam finished. We have, in this little summary, found that it is too big, too difficult, and too hot. That leaves practically nothing in its favor except that it might possibly be fun to tinker around with, which, you will admit, is nothing to sink $100,000,000 in.

My advice to the government (in sending in my resignation herewith) would be to drop the whole business before it is too late and stick to seeds.

Atom Boy!

WITH all that I have to do, it seems a little too bad that I should have to keep worrying about the constitution of the atom. One day Sir Arthur Reeves Reeves-Arthur comes out and says that the atom is made up of electrons and protons. The following week Dr. Hjalmar Rensnessen reads a paper before the Royal Society of Locomotive Engineers and says that the atom is composed of little pieces of old pocket lint. The hell with both of them! I can't be bothered.

There is one feature of these researches, however, which holds my attention for almost a quarter of a second. Someone (his name slips my mind right now, but I have it in my files in case you ever should want it) has figured out that, if we could utilize the energy in an atom, we would never have to do any more work ourselves. Now, *there's* a scientist! *There's* the boy for me! He doesn't say what we are going to nibble on when we go out to the ice box to get a cold snack before going to bed, or what strange medium of exchange we are going to use to buy it with, since none of us are working, but he does say that we won't be working, and that is the main thing. The eating will take care of itself. We can eat each other. And I already have a list of twenty people whom I *don't* want to eat.

As I understand it (which I don't), each atom has a so-called "nucleus" as its center, like that cute little old Daddy Worm in the center of a chestnut. This part I have decided not to think about.

But when you consider that each atom is only a hundred-millionths of an inch across (that would be even smaller than the piece of lobster in a lobster and shrimp Newburgh) and that its nucleus is only about ten-thousandths of this diameter, you will not only see how small a nucleus is but you will also go a little crazy. In fact, in just writing these figures down on paper I have whipped myself into such a state that I have got the typewriter ribbon all tangled up in my fingers and am going to have to drop everything and bathe my temples. So what?

So if we can split an atom (I am using the slang of Prof. E. N. daC. Andrade in the *London Observer*) and *then* can split the nucleus, we are going to find a lot of little things called "protons" and "electrons," and you can imagine how small they are going to be. It is absurd. The protons are positive and the electrons are negative, and, of the two, I am sure that the electrons are nicer. I hate a positive proton. They think they know everything. It is "This is so" and "That is so," until you want to smack them in the face. With the world in the state it is in today, nobody can be as positive as all that.

Now Prof. E. N. daC. Andrade (until I know what the "daC." in the professor's name stands for, I shall be tossing and turning all night) suggests that, in order to break up these atoms and nuclei (hot dickity), we shall have to use some very powerful projectile to smash into them at a tremendous rate of speed. Just who is going to pick up what is left after this projectile has hit the atom and make the pieces look like anything at all, is something I, personally, am not going to worry about.

In fact, I have lost a great deal of interest in the whole subject since starting to write this article, and I am sure that you have, too, my great big Audience of Rodeo Land. Suppose we let the whole matter drop for a while and just give ourselves over to fun and frolic?

It seems there were three Irishmen, whom we will call three

Hungarians because that was not their name. Well, these three chaps were walking along the street when one of them turned to the other two (he being on the outside) and said: "Stop your pushing!" You can imagine the hubbub which resulted from this remark. Fists flew like hot cakes and in no time at all, the only one left was the man who had made the original remark, the other two having been Scotsmen, and, being Scotsmen, had saved their strength for six per cent. This more or less makes a bum out of the original story which, if you will consult your notes, was to have been about three Irishmen. It just seems as if *nothing* held together these days. I think there was even more to the story than the tantalizing bit I have given you, but it is too late now. We are back again on the atom.

We now come to the fascinating part of our paper. According to Professor You-Know, "the gun which fires the projectiles is the nucleus of atoms of radioactive substances, such as the element called 'Radium C'; the projectiles are the so-called 'alpha' particles (*Editor's note: 'So-called' by whom?*), which are themselves small nuclei, and consist of four protons and two electrons welded together."

This makes it all a little clearer. All that we have to do in order to split an atom is to go to the nearest druggist and ask him for a small package of Radium C. Radium A and Radium B are for the big boys and can be had only by presenting an order from the Headmaster.

I am not kidding when I tell you that Dr. Ernest Rutherford has succeeded in directing a stream of alpha particles from radioactive substances on to certain light elements and has knocked several representative atoms into a cocked hat. The cocked hat has then been taken, covered with the American flag, and, when uncovered, has been found to contain an old rabbit and sixty yards of red tissue paper. The applause which greeted this trick of Dr. Rutherford's was nothing short of deafening.

"It has long been my ambition" (it is Dr. Rutherford speaking) "to have available a copious supply of atoms and electrons which have an individual energy far transcending that of the alpha and beta particles from radioactive bodies."

Now here is where the surprise comes in! A few of us are getting together, unbeknownst to Dr. Rutherford, of whom we are very fond, and are going to chip in and help him fulfull this ambition of his. We are going to get him a whole case of the atoms and electrons that he has been longing for and are going around to his laboratory some day and leave them on his doorstep, with a note reading: "Dear Doc: A little bird told us that you wanted some of these. Don't open them until your birthday. Then go to it, and *split those atoms!*"

Perhaps this is making a great deal of to-do about nothing. But if somebody thinks that he can fix it so that none of us will ever have to work again, I think that we ought to help him. It probably will come too late to be of much use to us of the present generation, but, from the looks of things now, our children are going to have to work awfully hard unless something like this comes along to save them. In the meantime, I am more or less resting on my oars and waiting. It may come sooner than we think.

The applause which greeted this trick was nothing short of deafening.

A Brief Course in
World Politics

THERE used to be a time when anyone could keep in touch with the world's history (if anyone was fool enough to want to) by consulting Rand, McNally's map or by remembering that, no matter what country it was, there were only two things that could happen: either the king could have some people beheaded, or some people could have the king beheaded. It was all very simple and cozy.

But the Great War, in addition to making the old Rand, McNally's map look like an early American sampler with "God Bless Our Home" sewn on it, and in addition to making the average man's income look like what you find in the pocket of last winter's suit, also made it a great deal more difficult to follow subsequent changes in political parties throughout the world. It has become so complicated that it is hardly worth the trouble. Beyond a certain point the thing loses interest.

For example, we read one day in the newspapers that Germany has gone over from the control of the Workers National Peoples Socialist Centrist Party (with 256 seats) to the Bavarian Naitonalist Optimist Fascist Unreinigung Party (with 396 seats), which means that trouble is brewing all over the map of Europe. Now, try as you will, it is difficult to understand this. Especially as the next day you read that the election

which hurled the Workers Nationalist Optimist Centrist, etc.,
people into office was a preliminary election or *Wahl*, and
that the finals have shown that the balance of power resides
in the hands of the Christian Hanoverian Revalorization Ge-
sellschaft Party (with fifteen seats and a bicycle), which means
that Europe is on the verge of a conflagration, beginning
with a definite rupture with the Slovenes (the Extreme Left
Slovenes, that is, not to be confused with the Conservative
Radical Slovenes).

Republicans and Democrats I can understand, but I don't
care. Liberals and Conservatives are an open book to me;
one is liberal, the other conservative, or vice versa. But when
you get twenty-four parties, all beginning with "W," on each
one of which the future peace of Europe depends, then I
am sorry but I shall have to let Europe figure it out for itself
and let me know when it is going to have another war. That
is, if it can find me. I still can run pretty fast.

I try to keep up with the political parties of Germany because I am very partial to German food and whatever that
stuff is they serve with it. But keeping track of China is
something that I can't, and won't, do. Anyone who tries to
keep track of what is happening in China is going to end up
by wearing the skin off his left ear from twirling around on
it. The only way to follow the various revolutions and army
maneuvers in China is to throw yourself on your face on the
floor and kick and scream until some Chinese expert comes
and explains them to you. Not a *Chinese* expert really, but an
American expert on China. A Chinese expert would only
serve to confuse you the more.

You simply can't get anything out of China by reading the
newspapers or the weeklies. I doubt very much if the newspapers and weeklies can get anything out of China themselves. For, in China, not only do they change parties every
twelve minutes, but the parties themselves keep changing.
The Northern Army, under Wu Wing Chang, will suddenly,
without warning, became the Southern Army under Li Hung
Chu. You may follow the Peiping forces, in their victorious
march up the left bank of the Yangtze-Kiang and then, on
Tuesday morning, read that somebody has blown a whistle,

Something goes on during the night—the change hats, or something.

that the soldiers have pulled little strings in their uniforms, changing them from red to robin's-egg blue, and that Wu Wing Chang has turned into somebody named Arthur McKeever Chamison of Oak Bluffs, Massachusetts. The last man I knew who tried to follow the Chinese armies ended up by picking little spots of light off walls and putting them in a basket.

Then there is South America. Or perhaps we should say, there *was* South America. A lot of jokes have been made about South American revolutions and their frequency, but it isn't the frequency so much that is disturbing as it is their going around all sounding alike. It really makes very little difference to me whether the cabinet of Dr. Huijos or the cabinet of General Yrobarja is in power, but I don't like to pick up the paper and find that Dr. Huijos is General Yro-barja. That, frankly, does confuse me, and I resent being confused, especially after I have been following a thing very carefully from one day to another. There must be a lot of activity going on during the night in those South American revolutions, activity that never gets into the papers. Otherwise it wouldn't be possible for one party to be in power right after the salad course at dinner and another one in power, without so much as a word to the referee, before breakfast the next day. *Some*thing goes on during the night—they change hats, or something—and I personally don't like the looks of the thing at all.

Of course, I did get a little needlessly confused over a revolution they had down there some months ago, and I am perfectly willing to admit that it was my fault. I forgot for the minute and thought that Peru was the capital of the Argentine. You can see how that would tie things up a bit in my mind. One day the revolution in the Argentine was settled and the next day it was at its peak in Peru, with no mention (naturally enough, as I later realized) of what I had read the day before about Argentina. "What is this?" was the way I phrased it to myself. One day President Leguia was thrown out and the next day President Irigoyen (who, up to this time, had taken no part in the conversation) was thrown out. And all through it ran someone named President Uriburu. "Maybe I missed the papers one day," I thought. "Maybe I slept through Friday." It was in checking up on this end of it that I came across some items which recalled to my mind that Peru is one country and the Argentine is another, and that cleared up the whole ugly mess for me. When I say "cleared up" I mean nothing of the sort.

It is this sort of thing going on all over the world which makes it so difficult for a sincere student of *Weltpolitik*. The country I like best is Sweden. They have a nice king, who shows up every once in a while in the news reels, so you can keep an eye on him. They may have Centrist and Double-

Centrist parties, and, in their own quiet way, they may fight out certain issues among themselves, but there is none of this "Overthrow of Cabinet Upsets World's Balance of Power" or "New Alignment in Ingeborg Menaces Europe's Peace." I would like to bet that they have two parties, the Harvards and the Yales, or the Blue and the Gray, and that when one party is in power the other is making snowballs to throw. That is the way the whole world should be, if you will pardon my making a suggestion.

As it stands now, I am likely to throw the whole thing up and go in for contract bridge. There, at least, you know who your partner is. You may not act as if you knew, and your partner may have grave doubts about you ever knowing, but, in your own mind, the issues are very clearly defined. And that is a lot more than you can say of the world today. (A list of what you *can* say for the world today will be found tucked away in a stamp box in the upper left-hand drawer of my desk. It may be stuck to the under side of one of the stamps, but it should be there.)

Imagination in the
Bathroom

●　　　　　　　　　　　　　　　　　　　●

ONE of the three hundred and eight (1930 census figures) troubles with American home life today is the alarming spread of Home-Making as an Art. For the past fifteen or twenty years our Little Women have been reading so many articles in the women's magazines warning them against lack of Imagination in the Home that they have let their imaginations get the upper hand and turn them into a lot of Hans Christian Andersens. All that is needed is a band of dwarfs to make any modern home a Rumpelstiltskin's castle which, at the stroke of midnight, turns back into a pumpkin again.

Before Home-Making became an Art, Mother used to feel that she had done pretty well if she and Annie could get the furniture all back into place (and by "into place" is meant "into place *again*") after the spring and fall house-cleaning, with perhaps fresh tidies on the backs of the chairs every so often. Things *had* to go back pretty much where they came from, for the casters had dug little round holes in the carpet, and you wouldn't want to have the place looking like a clam flat.

The only imagination that was necessary in the preparation of the food was to find *enough*; for in the days before dieting set in Daddy and the boys and girls stopped at nothing in the way of loading up, short of foundering with all on board.

But gradually the home-making experts have got their propaganda across, flooding the country with photographs of armchairs planted with geraniums and luncheon tables in pantalets, telling the young wives who are just beginning to worry about the far-away look in George's eyes that the trouble was lack of Imagination in fixing up the Nest. So the young wives have become Imagination-conscious.

On looking back over the past ten years, the arrival of chintz would seem to have been the first indication that things were going imaginative on us. The first designs in chintz curtains and sofa coverings were very mild, perhaps little spatterings of buttercups on a black field, or, in the more radical households, medium-sized poppies; but, compared with the old white lace curtains which used to hang in the bay window back of the rubber plant and were held back in

ADAM JOHN BARTH

I like a good warm bathroom in which I can sing (and, boy, can I take those low notes!)

place by a gold ball and chain, they were pretty hot stuff. I remember, back in 1915, a man whose mother came to visit him in his new home (she had never met his wife before) and, after one look at the chintz curtains, she took him upstairs and asked him if he was sure just who his wife's people were. She thought he had married a Chinese girl.

Today those very same chintz curtains would be considered fit only for a mortuary home (or undertaking parlor, as we used to call it; the development of undertaking parlors into mortuary homes would make a story on Home-Making in itself).

As the tide of originality swept on, the poppies began getting larger and larger until the design became one big red poppy with here and there a bit of background which hardly knew that it was a background on the same piece of goods. This obviously would never do, for the next step would have been *all* poppy, or just a good old-fashioned red curtain, which was exactly the thing they were trying to get away from.

You have to look out for that in modern decoration. Beyond a certain point you swing right around back into Grandma's house again.

I have an article before me, written in one of the Home-Making sections of the Sunday paper, which begins as follows:

> Color everywhere in the house is the keynote in present-day decorating—from the basement to the attic, from the foyer hall to the back door. Even the kitchen is as gay as a flower garden, for pots and pans have been glorified. Gone are the days of all-white bathrooms. . . .

Is that a terrifying prospect or isn't it? "Gone are the days of all-white bathrooms," are they? Well, not in *my* house. The bathroom is a sacred place, not merely a room where you rush in to wash your hands before a meal. (And, incidentally, a lady member of the party has asked me to inquire why it is that the menfolk always wait until dinner has been announced before rushing up to wash their hands.

"They have all the time in the world after they get home," says this lady member of the party, "in which to fix up for dinner. But they sit down and read the evening paper, or dawdle around with the radio, or even just smoke a cigarette standing in the middle of the living room, until somebody says, 'Dinner is ready.' Then they say, 'I'll be right down,' tear upstairs into the bathroom, and start splashing about with the soap and guest towels until you would think they were doing the week's wash. In the meantime the soup is stone cold."

And I, equally incidentally, would like to ask why, in housekeepers' parlance, everything has to be "stone cold" when it is the man's fault? They are just "cold" when it is anybody else's fault, but when the man is to blame they are "stone cold.")

To get back into the bathroom. I like a good warm bathroom, with plenty of light, in which I can sing "Old Man River" (and, boy, can I take those low notes in "Old Man River" in a good resonant bathroom! Paul Robeson is a tenor compared with me some mornings); and I like a room in which I can lie in the tub and read until well parboiled, sometimes getting nice gib blisters on the pages with wet fingers, or, if very tired, perhaps dropping the whole book into the water; and I don't want to have the feeling, every time I look up, that I am taking part in the first act of Ziegfeld Follies with Joseph Urban looking on.

I once spent a week-end in a house where the bathroom was so stage-struck that I couldn't even get the cold water to run.

The towels were lavender and the curtains were pink and green and the tub was a brilliant yellow with mottlings of a rather horrid chocolate running through it. I tried running a bath with my eyes shut, but as soon as the water hit the porcelain it began to boil, and even if I had been able to draw a decent bath that a healthy man could get into, I couldn't have kept my eyes on the book for fear that a Chinese dragon would pop out from some of the decorations and get into my slippers.

I finally went back into my room and took a sponge bath from the faucet.

I have dwelt so long on the bathroom end of Home-Making

I couldn't have kept my eyes on the book for fear that a Chinese dragon would pop out from the decorations.

ADAM JOHN BARTH

as an Art because the bathroom seems to me to be the last stronghold of the old-fashioned man. If they take our bathrooms away from us we might as well all dress in harlequin costumes and throw confetti all day instead of going to work. Imagination is all right in the living room, where we can keep our eyes shut. But please, modern home-makers, leave us our white bathrooms, where we can use the towels without feeling that we are wiping our hands on a Michelangelo and look at the walls without going into a pirouette. No wonder so many men live in Turkish baths!

"Safety Second"

IF you are one of those people who are constantly getting hurt, falling down or up, crashing into railway trains, or tumbling out of people's houses, you have probably wondered why it is. You have probably asked yourself, as soon as you could talk, "Why is it I seem to be unable to lift a piece of asparagus to my mouth without poking it in my eye, or button my clothes without catching my finger in the button-hole and tearing the ligament to shreds?"

As it is the insurance companies who really care (the hell with your wrenched ligaments—it costs them money), they have put some of their best minds to work on the subject, and a great big report, all bound in red crocodile (red with embarrassment), has been submitted by the Premium Defaulters' Service Bureau, showing that certain people get hurt oftener than certain others.

Of course it is not fair to include in this analysis those hearty guys who go around slapping people on sunburned necks or pushing them off rafts. They are going to get hurt anyway. There is nothing that insurance companies can do for them except kill them before they start out in the morning. I killed seven this year, and am looking forward to a bumper crop next summer. What we are after is the reason why certain people get hurt *in spite of themselves.* Are you one? Are you two?

Take, for example, the safety devices which were placed on certain machines when the "Safety First" campaigns were started way back in 1912. Some of them have never been used since, in spite of the pretty posters. Some of them have been used, but simply to hang jumpers on while the men were changing their clothes. But the cases with which the insurance men have the most trouble are those in which workers get hurt *on the safety devices*. This type of injury calls for special attention. There was one man in a paper mill in Massachusetts who was tending a so-called "beater," in which the pulp is taken and thrashed around until it looks something awful. (On Saturdays some of the workers used to bring their wives up for a little going-over, just to save themselves the trouble that night.) A worker whom we will call Cassidy, because his name was Cassidy, had been tending "beater" for thirty-three years and had never had an accident. The safety device was put on, under the auspices of the State Insurance and Fidelity League, and, the very first day, Cassidy got flustered and dropped one leg of his trousers in the safety device, with the result that he was caught up in the machine and swashed around until all they had to do was to dry him out and they could have printed the Sunday *Times* on him. In fact, that is just what they did do, and it was one of the best editions of the Sunday *Times* that ever was run off the presses. It had human interest.

But the case of Cassidy is still not what we are after in this survey. Cassidy's injury was a special event in Cassidy's life, and there are some workers to whom injury is just an item in the day's work, like lighting a pipe. They get cut, go and have it bandaged, get cut again, go and have it bandaged, get cut again, and by that time it is five thirty. On their days off they get cut on the edge of their newspaper. There was one man, for instance, who had been tending a saw for ten years and who got splinters in his eye regularly five times a week. There was some suspicion that he held his eye out and put it *on* the splinters as they flew off the saw, but he always denied this. Then the Safety First Committee bought goggles for the men, and the very first day he got them caught in his eye and had to have the whole thing readjusted at the drug store (for which the druggist charged nothing).

"Why is it I seem to be unable to lift a piece of asparagus to my mouth without poking it in my eye?"

He collected under the head of "Occupational Disease," but the insurance company was pretty sore and got him a job in a bank. Within a week he had what is known as "eye penny," caused by flying particles of pennies being caught under the lid, resulting in great pain.

Let us say that you start to cross a street. You are trying to look up a word in the dictionary, or are worrying about how you are going to explain to your wife that you haven't got the week's pay envelope. You are obviously in no condition to be crossing a street, but, as everyone can't live on the same side of any one street, you sometimes have to. The traffic lights are against you, but so is everything else in this world, so what difference can one little traffic light make? The next thing you know you are halfway into the cylinder head of a motor and someone is saying: "Look in his pockets and see if he has an address book there." This rather makes you stop short and give pause. Why should *you* have been hit in preference to the three dozen other people who were crossing the street against the lights?

The insurance company report says that it is because you were (1) daydreaming; (2) worried over something; (3) just a plain damn fool. The daydreaming part is something that can't very well be regulated. Stop daydreaming, and you stop Keats and Shelley (although Keats and Shelley stopped themselves pretty successfully, without outside interference). Being just a plain damn fool is another complaint over which modern medicine seems to have no control. Look at the stock market (or, rather, let's not look. There is trouble enough in the world as it is). But when investigators come right out and say that one of the big causes of accidents is the fact that people are worried, then a solution presents itself with startling clarity. Keep people from being worried.

This would be my scheme: In the center of each town or city have a big pile of money, preferably in one- and five-dollar bills (it is so hard to get larger denominations changed). Whenever anyone feels a worry coming on, let him walk up to this pile, say "Hello, Joe!" to the keeper, take whatever he needs, and go on home. In this way accidents resulting from worry could be reduced 80 percent. I don't suppose the thing could ever be put into practice, however, as in most towns and cities the central square is so full of parked automobiles there wouldn't be any place for a pile of loose money.

Future Man:
Tree or Mammal?

THE study of Mankind in its present state having proven such a bust, owing to Mankind's present state being something of a bust itself, scientists are now fascinating themselves with speculations on what Mankind will be like in future generations. And when I say "future," I don't mean 1940. Add a couple of ciphers and you'll be nearer right. It's safe enough to predict what Man will be like in that kind of future, because who'll be able to check.

We know what Man was like in the Pleistocene Age. He was awful. If he stood upright at all he was lucky, and as for his facial characteristics, I would be doing you a favor if I said nothing about them. Somehow or other he knew enough to draw pictures of elephants and mammoths on the walls of caves, but I have always had a suspicion that those elephant pictures were drawn by some wag who lived in the neighborhood along about 1830. You can't tell me that anyone who carries himself as badly as the Neanderthal Man could have held a piece of crayon long enough to draw an elephant. However, this is none of my business. I can't draw an elephant either, which is probably why I am so bitter.

But when it comes to predicting what Man will be like in 100,000 years (I put it at 100,000 years because, when it gets up into figures like that, it doesn't make any difference;

100,000 years—500,000 years—who cares?)—when it comes to predicting that far ahead, it's anybody's racket. I can do it myself.

When we look back and see how Man has developed through all those corking stages from the Paleozoic Age, from sponge to tadpole to jellyfish (maybe we're on the wrong sequence—we don't seem to be getting any nearer to Man)—anyway, through all those stages before he came on up through the ape to the beautiful thing we know today as J. Hamilton Lewis or Grover Whalen, and when we consider how many æons and æons it took for him to develop even arms and legs, to say nothing of pearl shirt studs and spats, we realize that we must go very carefully before we predict what he will be like in an equal number of æons. By then he may be a catalpa tree. Stranger things *have* happened.

The Man of 1,900,031 will be very highly colored and will have no legs.

I am basing my prediction on the part which protective coloration has played in the development of Man from the lower animals. It was only those jellyfish which had the same color as the surrounding country which survived the rigors of evolution. Birds which are the same color as the foliage in which they nest are less likely to be disturbed and therefore last longer. The chameleon is a good example of protective coloration carried to ridiculous extremes. If all the animals had been possessed of this ability to change colors at the drop of a hat, we should be living in a madhouse today.

According to my theory, however, the principle of protective coloration will be working, from now on, in exactly the opposite manner from that in which it functioned in past ages. It will be only those men and women whose color differs most sharply from the surrounding country who will survive. If you will stop that whispering and fidgeting and will come up in single file and drop your chewing gum in the wastebasket, Teacher will continue to explain what he means.

Let us say that A and B are two citizens living in a modern city. A dresses in clothes which are of a dull slate color or perhaps a low-class marble. When he goes out on the street he blends in with the color of the buildings, especially if he happens to be hung-over and not looking in the best of health. (Most people today do not look in the best of health owing to not being in the best of health.) What happens? He is run down by an automobile, the driver of which cannot distinguish him from the background of buildings and passing vehicles (unless a circus band wagon happens to be passing at the time, a contingency which it would be well not to count on too much), or he is shot by accident by a gunman who is aiming at a comrade and doesn't see the drab-colored citizen at all.

The other citizen, whom we have called B but whose name is probably W, dresses in bright reds and yellows and has a complexion which makes him stand out from his fellow men. (Drinking will do this for one.) He can cross the street with impunity, because he is conspicuous, and automobile drivers

PETER ARNO

will sometimes run right up on the sidewalk and knock down a dozen drab-colored citizens rather than crash into him. Gunmen can also see him clearly and will recognize him as *not* one of their number, for gunmen are notoriously quiet dressers. It is B then (or W, as you will) who survives.

But the man who doesn't go out into the street at all will survive even longer than B. We will call him B^1, or better yet $_2B$. This wise man stays right in his room and reads magazines all day, with an occasional look at the clock to see how late he would have been if he had kept that luncheon appointment. He has his meals brought in to him, and, when it is bedtime, he sends for a lot of friends and they play backgammon. In time, owing to never having to walk, he loses the use of his legs, and, after several centuries, his breed have no legs at all. I therefore predict that Man will, in 3,000 years, have no legs, for all of those men who once had legs and have gone out into the streets will have been killed off.

This may seem fantastic and I shall probably be refused membership to the American Academy of Sciences because of promulgating this doctrine. See if I care. I still maintain that the Man of 1,900,031 will be very highly colored and will have no legs. His arms, however, owing to the constant raising and lowering of highball glasses (to preserve the high coloring) and centuries of turning on and off television dials (by means of which he will be kept in touch with the outside world), will have attained a remarkable flexibility and may reach five times the length of the distance now attained by what we fatuously call "modern man." He will not be very pretty-looking, according to modern standards, but he will be alive, which is something.

However, since we are in a period of transition right now, the best that we can do is to hasten this pleasant state of inactivity in behalf of our descendants. We ourselves cannot hope to reap its benefits. But we can attain to something of the charm and peace of that future state by resolving to stay indoors as much as possible, to increase our coloring to what others may consider an alarming degree, and to do nothing which will impede Nature's progress toward her inevitable goal, the elevation of Mankind to the condition of the beautiful catalpa tree.

"They're Off!"

A Disrespectful View of the Sport of Kings

FOND as I am of horses when meeting them personally (and give me a handful of sugar and I will make friends with any horse—or lose my hand up to the wrist in the attempt) I am strangely unmoved when I see them racing each other up and down a track. A great calm descends on me at the cry "They're off!" and, as the race proceeds, this calm increases in intensity until it is practically a coma, from which I have to be aroused by friends telling me which horse won.

Much of this coolness toward horse racing is due to the fact that I almost never have any money up. I have no scruples in the matter (except that old New England scruple against losing money), but I never seem to be able to get the hang of just how the betting is done. By the time I have decided what horse I would like to bet on, everybody seems to have disappeared, either through indifference to my betting plans or because the race is on. I hear other people betting, but I never can quite see whom they are betting with. The whole thing is more or less chaotic to me.

I am further unexcited through my inability to see the horses after they have started. I have tried using field glasses, but that only makes things worse. I sometimes hold the glasses up to my eyes in an attempt to look sporting, but I find that my arms get tired and the gray film in front of my eyes gets a bit monotonous after several minutes of inspection. The last time I used field glasses at a horse race I thought I saw a rowboat in the distance manned by a suspiciously large number of oarsmen; so I haven't felt like using glasses since then. With my naked eye I can at least see the surrounding country, and without the complication of strange rowboats.

All these distractions to the enjoyment of horse racing I have to contend with in my native land. When, by some slip-up of Fate, I am projected into an English race meeting, my confusion is complete. At English horse races I never can see the horses at all.

This is due, in part, to the prevailing mist (corresponding to our blizzard) which usually settles down over an English course several months before the race and is nicely tucked in at the corners by the day of the big event. In most races they could use camels and no one would know the difference. I once saw a Grand National where forty-three horses left the paddock and disappeared into the fog, after which the spectators hung around and marked cards and told stories for what seemed like about an hour, at the end of which time three horses came out of the fog, one of them having won. Nobody knew what had become of the other forty, and, so far as I know, nobody ever found out. They may never have started. The whole thing might very well have been a frame-up, and all forty-three could quite possibly have just hung around at the barrier until it was time to go in, and tossed up to see which ones went in first. There is no sense in running your head off over a lot of hedges when nobody is going to know the difference. A horse is a fool to tire himself out like that.

Then, too, there are the English race courses. Even if you could see through the fog, you couldn't find them, as they seem to be built on the tunnel system. "Not a horse in sight" is their boast. Watching races in England is more a matter of divination than actual watching. You have to sense where the horses are. I was at the Cheltenham meeting this spring where the horses evidently started under the grandstand, appeared for a minute in a little gully out in right field, and then disappeared for good into the beautiful hills of Gloucestershire. I thought for a while that they were running away with their riders, as it hardly seemed possible that people could come all the way from London to watch a race which was being run in the next county, but pretty soon they seemed to have been got under control and were ridden back, through a series of underground passages, until they finished. As it happened to be a clear day (with only occasional gusts of snow and rain) you could see the finish. That is, *you* could. I couldn't because I was out in tent behind the grandstand eating meat pies.

And *there* is a feature of English racing which should not be overlooked in any enumeration of horrors—the cold meat pie. It is symbolic of the British holiday. Some one has said that the English take their pleasures sadly, and I couldn't say it any better. On a holiday they may be seen walking in great droves in the pouring rain along an esplanade by the sea, grim faces buried in raincoat collars, silently giving themselves over to their mood of merriment with all the abandon of a file of convicts. Of course, they really haven't got much to work with in the way of bacchanalia, as most of England's equipment for merrymaking was captured from the Boers in 1900 and the dampness reduces confetti to so many little dabs of cosmetic. But there is also something in the English bulldog spirit which holds out any display of hilarity beyond an occasional "pfsho" (this has to be said through mustaches) or perhaps a muffled "rippin'." I am not complaining of this as a national trait. It probably has won England her empire. But, in the mass, it is a bit depressing. And the cold meat pie is the culinary symbol of this spirit.

The cold meat pie you will find on exhibition wherever people are out for a good time. They are usually on a counter of some sort and come in shipments of a dozen, sometimes under a glass cover to keep the crows from swooping down on them. They look almost like food at first, owing to a superficial resemblance to a baking-powder biscuit. But on being pressed with a fork, or bitten into, they turn out to be a collection of pastry flakes inclosing a nubbin of meat just large enough to bait a hook for a medium-sized trout. This is to be covered with mustard and devoured greedily, leaving as much of the pastry flakes for the sparrows as you choose. (Several hundred English sparrows got up a petition to keep me in England, so lavish was I with the pastry flakes from my cold meat pies.)

Along with the cold meat pie in the racing buffet goes a sandwich which seems to be made up of those little green strands which collect on a lawn mower on a damp day, but which the sons of the bulldog breed think of as "cress." Now, cress it may be, and water cress at that, but as a man who has fought all his life to keep water cress away from public and private tables because of its unmanly qualities, I may say that the herbaceous material which goes into those English rolls makes an equal amount of water cress seem like one pound of raw meat with a dropped egg on top. One of these and a cold meat pie, and you are as well nourished as a barn swallow. And yet you will see great, red-faced colonels wolfing them down and, what is more, elbowing people out of the way to get at them. Maybe there is a trick about eating them which I didn't catch on to. I must admit that I didn't give the thing my entire attention.

My attention was mostly given over to trying to find the horses, for the race was on and I was all alone. (I always finds myself alone at a race, usually having become separated from the rest of my party shortly after entering the enclosure. One of my few excitements at horse racing is seeing how long I can stick with the rest of my party without getting lost.)

I squinted my eyes in the general direction of the course, but by this time the horses were well beyond the intervening hills and meat pies and on their way into Wales. I put my field glasses to my eyes as a desperate last-minute gesture and saw a blue ocean with several old-fashioned derbies floating around in it. This seemed to me to be obviously incorrect; so I took the glasses down again and tried the naked eye. With these I was able to detect three black objects scooting along the horizon, one quite a bit in the lead and the rest bunched.

"Who is that leading?" I asked a gentleman in a raincoat who seemed to be taking an intelligent interest in what was going on. I gathered from his appearance that he was at least one of the Vice Lords of the Admiralty.

Far from giving me an aswer to my question, the Vice Lord threw me a dirty look and moved slightly away from me, as if a Board of Health man had just come along and hung a sign on me reading "Scarlet Fever in This House." Asking questions in an American accent is hazardous business in England.

Squinting back again I recovered my three fleeting black objects, but was horrified to see one of them fly straight up into the air, followed almost immediately by the other two. Now, no horse, no matter how well trained, would do that. Certainly not in the middle of a race. A fairly tempermental horse, seeing the race going badly, might say: "Oh, well, what

If I had been watching the crows all this time, it was pretty discouraging.

of it?" and fly up into the air but he would hardly be followed by the other two.

It was through this line of reasoning that I figured out that the three black objects were not horses. That narrowed it down to crows. If I had been watching three crows all this time, it was pretty discouraging. So I gave the whole thing up and went back into the meat-pie tent.

By this time the place was deserted except for three very unattractive young ladies dressed as nurses who were sweeping up pie flakes.

"Have you any American cigarettes?" I asked, using my best enunciation.

One of the young ladies looked at me and cocked her head inquiringly.

"Do you carry any American cigarettes?" I repeated making a gesture like a cigarette.

The young lady called to some one else who was evidently accustomed to dealing with Germans and Frenchmen.

"American cigarettes?" I shortened the question this time, and did my best to sound like the English actors I have heard in New York. This threw her into a panic, and she summoned a very, very old lady dressed like a very, very old nurse, who came up quite close to me and asked belligerently:

"Qu'est ker say ker voo voolay?"

Suddenly my courage failed me.

"Never mind, I'll smoke my pipe," I said, and rushed from the tent.

I met the crowd who were leaving the course, the race being over. It was the matter of but an hour or two to find one of the members of my party.

"A great race!" I said to him.

"I guess it was," he replied. "I didn't see it."

"You are a madman," I said. "You should stick with me next time."

And I guarantee that any one who sticks with me from now on will see only American horses racing over American courses—and practically none of these.

Our News-Reel Life

WHENEVER we want to find out what life was like in the days of the Pharaohs (when I say "we," I mean people who go in for that sort of thing. Me, I can take it or leave it alone), we have to go all the way to Egypt and dig and dig and dig. And even then, what do we get? A truckload of old signet rings and scarabs, some shawls, and maybe three very unhealthy-looking mummies.

We of the twentieth century are making it lots easier for archæologists of the future to find out what we were like. Whenever they want to rummage around in the past, all they have to do will be to go to the vault, pull out a dozen tins of news-reels for 1930, and run them off in a cozy projection room. Then they will know all about what we were doing in the days of the Hoover dynasty, what we wore, and how we talked. The only trouble will be that, if they go entirely by the movie news-reels, they may get an impression like the following:

> Report on the Manners and Customs of the Inhabitants of America previous to the Great Glacier of 1942–8. Read at a Meeting of the Royal Society of Ultra-Violet Engineers by Prof. Henry Six-Hundred-and-Twelve, custodian of the Motion Picture News-Reels of the British Museum, what there is left of it. Double-April 114th 3738 A.D.

"From the motion-picture news-reels on file in the Museum, it is plain that inhabitants of America in the early decades of the twentieth century were most peculiarly constructed as far as their organs of speech went. Although they moved their lips in talking, as we of today do, the sound cavity or apparatus of articulation seemed to be located somewhere in the region of the collar bone or even as low as the hip. There was a variation of between two and five seconds from the time the words were formed by the lips until the sound issued from the torso, and then it came with great resonance, as if the megaphone were being used.

"This is all very puzzling, for, in the mummies of that period, we are unable to locate any such misplaced speaking apparatus. We have looked everywhere, under the arms, between the ribs, and even in the joints of the elbow, but so far have been able to discover traces of nothing but arms, ribs, and elbows.

"From the news-reels (and other sound pictures) we are able to gather that inanimate objects of that period had distinctive sounds of their own, now happily toned down through ages of refinement. For example, a small piece of paper, on being folded, gave off a sound comparable to the crashing of one of our giant redwoods. A door, no matter how easily closed, banged like a trench mortar. A button dropping on the floor sounded as if a large wet seal had flopped in its tracks. Nothing was too small to make a loud noise.

"The people who inhabited North America at the time we are studying seemed always to be diving from springboards, doubtless because of the intense heat of the world at that particular period of its incubation. Practically every news-reel shows us one or more unclad citizens leaping from a board into the water, a maneuver which also gave off a horrendous sound much louder than our modern water. A feature of this diving was the stationing of off-stage characters to shout what must have then been considered witty remarks at the divers, such as, 'How's the water, Bill?' One hears the voices but seldom sees the speakers—which is probably just as well.

"Public speakers of that time were not particularly proficient in the art of oratory, or, at any rate, not before the microphone, for they always seem to be confined to notes which were held just out of view of the camera, somewhere in the vicinity of the speaker's instep. Reading under these difficulties made it necessary for the orator to keep his head down and his eyes lowered, with the result that usually the bald spot on the top of his head was all that was visible. And even then he quite often forgot what he was about to say, or lost his place, making a highly unsatisfactory event of the thing. We would deplore this inaccuracy more if it were not for the fact that the speakers, when they *could* be understood, rarely seemed to be saying anything worth hearing. As historical evidence they are practically worthless.

"While we are on the subject of public speakers of that era, it might be well to point out that, almost without exception, they wore a type of linen collar which, even in 1930, was old-fashioned. The curator of our Collar Department has identified it as a turnover collar of the 1908–10 age, which comes together in a straight up-and-down line in front and gives every indication of choking the wearer. Nobody as late as 1930, except politicians, ever wore them, but, as President Weaver (or Hoever), the Chief Executive at that time, had a penchant for these affairs, it is possible that the rest wore them as a mark of allegiance to the Republican (or Democratic, as it was sometimes called) party.

"For a country as provincial as the United States was at this time, the news-reel displayed a remarkable interest in Japanese and Korean school children. Almost every film that we have in our possession shows Japanese and Korean school children in some form of intellectual activity, such as reciting in unison, 'Out of the window you must go!' or grouping themselves to form the letters of the word, 'WALCOME.'

"We are also at a loss to understand just how the world's supply of petroleum was ever garnered, for every oil tank or oil well in America was always on fire. There must have been *some* which did not send out great volumes of black smoke at all times, but we have no record of them in the movies. It is barely possible that the quality of oil drawn from the ground in that era was of such a specific gravity that a

*Usually the bald spot on the top of his head
was all that was visible.*

*The turnover collar, which gives every indication
of choking the wearer.*

PETER ARNO

*This sort of thing may very well have been
a form of folk dancing.*

certain boiling or toasting was necessary before it could be used, but it would seem that this great period of oil conflagration was the prelude to the final exhaustion of the oil supply in the southern part of the country and its discovery under the surface of what was then the island of Manhattan, now happily given over to oil wells.

"The 1930 news-reels are a splendid source of information for the present-day tacticians in their supply of pictures showing the 'floating fort' or 'battleship' of the day. There seems to have been little use for these cumbersome engines of warfare except to shoot off guns in front of movie cameras. There would be a puff of smoke, followed some seconds later by a vague booming sound, with a concurrent blare of band music playing a tune which research leads us to believe was known as 'Sail, Navy, Down the Field.' The crews of these ships trained for warfare by sitting astride the large guns and swaying back and forth in time to the music.

"The games of that age were evidently concerned more with running in all directions than our present-day games of intensive manual skill. Almost every shred of evidence which we have shows more or less shadowy men dashing back and forth in front of the camera, either after striking in the air with a stick or catching an object about the size of a man's head. At times, two men would get together under brilliant lights and hold each other's shoulders, rocking back and forth until one or the other had smothered his opponent, but this sort of thing may very well have been a form of folk dancing and not a sport. The pictures are very hazy at best, and we are unable to form any accurate judgment of just what the technique of all these games was.

"It was at this time that flying was in its initial stages and we have ample sources from which to draw our conclusions about the manner in which it was done. Hundreds of moving pictures are at our disposal showing a terrifically noisy preliminary agitation in what must have been the motor compartment (motors were used almost exclusively at that time, although there were some motorless planes called gliders which received an abnormal amount of publicity), followed by a flash of more or less formless shadow and something disappearing into the air. It is hard to imagine such public interest in an activity as natural as flying, but great crowds would sometimes assemble at the take-off or landing, and the one who was making the flight would at times deliver a short speech saying that he had every intention of reaching his destination.

"All of these films are readily accessible to those students of archæology who are interested in the period under discussion and, on application at the registrar's office, will be shown gladly. Except to postgraduate students, however, they are not very interesting."

Down with Pigeons

St. francis of Assisi (unless I am getting him mixed up with St. Simeon Stylites, which might be very easy to do as both their names beging with "St.") was very fond of birds, and often had his picture taken with them sitting on his shoulders and pecking at his wrists. That was all right, if St. Francis liked it. We all have our likes and dislikes, and I have more of a feeling for dogs. However, I am not *against* birds as a class. I am just against pigeons.

I do not consider pigeons birds, in the first place. They are more in the nature of people, people who mooch. Probably my feeling about pigeons arises from the fact that all my life I have lived in rooms where pigeons came rumbling in and out of my window. I myself must have a certain morbid fascination for pigeons, because they follow me about so much—and with evident ill will. I am firmly convinced that they are trying to haunt me.

Although I live in the middle of a very large city (well, to show you how large it is—it is the largest in the world) I am awakened every morning by a low gargling sound which turns out to be the result of one, or two, or three pigeons walking in at my window and sneering at me. Granted that I am a fit subject for sneering as I lie there, possibly with one shoe on or an unattractive expression on my face, but there is some-

216

For the first time in centuries no pigeon fell for the corn gag.

thing more than just a passing criticism in these birds making remarks about me. They have some ugly scheme on foot against me, and I know it. Sooner or later it will come out, and then I can sue.

This thing has been going on ever since I was in college. In our college everybody was very proud of the pigeons. Anyone walking across the Yard (Campus to you, please) was beset by large birds who insisted on climbing up his waistcoat and looking about in his wallet for nuts or raisins or whatever it is you feed pigeons (bichloride would be my suggestion, but let it pass).

God knows that I was decent enough to them in my undergraduate days. I let them walk up and down my back and

I tried to be as nice as I could without actually letting them see that I was not crazy about it. I even gave them chestnuts, chestnuts which I wanted myself. I now regret my generosity, for good chestnuts are hard to get these days, what with the blight and the Depression and everything.

But somehow the word got around in pigeon circles that Benchley was antipigeon. They began pestering me. I would go to bed at night, tired from overstudy, and at six thirty in the morning the Big Parade would begin. The line of march was as follows: Light on Benchley's window sill, march once in through the open window, going "Grumble-grumble-grumble" in a sinister tone. Then out and stand on the sill, urging other pigeons to come in and take a crack at it.

There is very little fun in waking up with a headache and hearing an ominous murmuring noise, with just the suggestion of a passing shadow moving across your window sill. No man should be asked to submit to this *all* his life.

I once went to Venice (Italy), and there, with the rest of the tourists, stood in awe in the center of St. Mark's Piazza, gazing at the stately portals of the church and at the lovely green drinks served at Florian's for those who don't want to look at the church all of the time.

It is an age-old custom for tourists to feed corn to the pigeons and then for the pigeons to crawl all over the tourists. This has been going on without interruption ever since Americans discovered Venice. So far as the records show, no pigeon has ever failed a tourist—and no tourist has ever failed a pigeon. It is a very pretty relationship.

In my case, however, it was different. In the first place, the St. Mark's pigeons, having received word from the American chapter of their lodge, began flying at me in such numbers and with such force as actually to endanger my life. They came in great droves, all flying low and hard, just barely skimming my hat and whirring in an ugly fashion with some idea of intimidating me. But by that time I was not be be intimidated, and, although I ducked very low and lost my hat several times, I did not give in. I even bought some corn from one of the vendors and held it out in my hand, albeit with bad grace. But, for the first time in centuries, no pigeon fell for the corn gag. I stood alone in the middle of St. Mark's Square, holding out my hand dripping with kernels of golden corn, and was openly and deliberately snubbed. One or two of the creatures walked up to within about ten feet of me and gave me a nasty look, but not one gave my corn a tumble. So I decided the hell with them and ate the corn myself.

Now this sort of thing must be the result of a very definite boycott, or, in its more aggressive stage, an anti-Benchley campaign. Left to myself, I would have only the very friend-liest feelings for pigeons (it is too late now, but I might once have been won over). But having been put on my mettle, there is nothing that I can do now but fight back. Whatever I may be, I am not yellow.

Here is my plan. I know that I am alone in this fight, for most people like pigeons, or, at any rate, are not antagonized by them. But single-handed I will take up the cudgels, and I hope that, when they grow up, my boys will carry on the battle on every cornice and every campus in the land.

Whenever I meet a pigeon, whether it be on my own win-dow sill or walking across a public park, I will stop still and place my hands on my hips and wait. If the pigeon wants to make the first move and attack me, I will definitely strike back, even to the extent of hitting it with my open palm and knocking it senseless (not a very difficult feat, I should think, as they seem to have very little sense).

If they prefer to fight it out by innuendo and sneering, I will fight it out by innuendo and sneering. I have worked up a noise which I can make in my throat which is just as un-pleasant sounding as theirs. I will even take advantage of my God-given power of speech and will say: "Well, what do you want to make of it, you waddling, cooing so-and-sos?" I will glare at them just as they glare at me, and if they come within reach of my foot, so help me, St. Francis, I will kick at them. *And* the next pigeon that strolls in across my window ledge when I am just awakening, I will catch with an especially prepared trap and will drag into my room, there to punch the living daylights out of him.

I know that this sounds very cruel and very much as if I

The next pigeon that strolls in across my window ledge when I am just awakening, I will catch and drag into my room, there to punch the living daylights out of him.

were an animal hater. As a matter of fact, I am such a friend of animals in general that I am practically penniless at the advanced age of eighty-three.

I have been known to take in dogs who were obviously imposters and put them through college. I am a sucker for kittens, even though I know that one day they will grow into cats who will betray and traduce me. I have even been known to pat a tiger cub, which accounts for my writing this article with my left hand.

But as far as pigeons go, I am through. It is a war to the death, and I have a horrible feeling that the pigeons are going to win.

Sporting Life in America:
Following the Porter

HAVING someone carry your bag for you is a form of sport which has only comparatively recently found favor in America. It has come with the effemination of our race and the vogue of cuffs attached to the shirt.

When I was a boy (and I remember President Franklin Pierce saying, "What a Boy!" too) to let a porter carry your bag was practically the same as saying: "My next imitation will be of Miss Jenny Lind, the Swedish Nightingale." No man who could whistle or chin himself would think of it. In the old days before these newfangled steam cars started raising Old Ned with our apple orchards with their shower of sparks, I have seen men knock a porter down for even reaching for their valises. The only people who would consider such a thing were veterans of the Mexican War who had lost both arms above the elbow or traveling salesmen for pipe-organ concerns. The traveling salesmen could let a porter take one end of the pipe organ without incurring the sneers of their fellow travelers.

But nowadays it is a pretty unattractive porter who can't wheedle a great hulking man out of his brief case, even if he is just crossing a platform to take another train. And I am secretly glad of this change in the standards of virility; for, frankly, my arms used to get awfully tired in the old days.

221

This was due, in part, to the fact that any suitcase I ever buy always weighs a minimum of sixty pounds without anything in it. It is something about belonging to *me* that makes a suitcase put on weight. I lift other people's suitcases and they are like thistledown. But mine, with perhaps two collars and a tube of shaving cream in it, immediately swells up and behaves like the corner stone of a twenty-story building. I know that this is not just my imagination, because several people have tried to steal my suitcase and have complained to me about its being so heavy.

But even now I still have a slightly guilty feeling as I walk up the runway with a porter going on ahead with my bags. I try to look as if I were not with him, or as if he had snatched up my luggage by mistake and I were trying to catch him to take it myself. If it is very obvious that he is with me, I carry my right arm as if I had just hurt it badly. You can't blame a cripple for not carrying his own bag.

It is not only the impression that I must be making on other people that worries me. I feel a little guilty about the porter. If the bag is very heavy (as it always is, and not from what you think, either) I start out with a slightly incoherent apology to him, like: "You'll find that pretty heavy, I'm afraid," or "Don't do this if you don't really feel like it." Sometimes I tell him what I have in the bag, so that he will understand. "Books," I say, timidly. (He never believes this.) I have even been so specific, if the thing was very heavy, as to tell him that I was carrying home a law digest and a copy of the *Home Book of Verse* for a friend. If this doesn't seem to be making him feel any better, I add, "—and shoetrees. They make a bag heavy." Several times I have worked myself up into such a state of sympathy for the man that I have taken one handle of the bag myself. There is one bag in particular that worries me. It is what the French refer to as a *grand valise* and I don't know what I was thinking of when I bought it. Standing on a station platform it looks like a small rhinoceros crouching for a spring, and I have seen porters run ten feet to one side of it rather than be called upon to lift it.

It holds a great deal more than I have got to put into it, including two small boys, but even with my modest equipment it has to be lifted on and off boats with a crane. There is a story about Louis XVI having hidden his horse in it during the early days of the Revolution, but I rather doubt that, as there would have been no place for the horse to breathe through. However, the fact remains that I don't know what I was thinking of.

Now, this bag is all right when I am abroad, for the porters over there are accustomed to carrying anything up to and including a medium-sized garage. They hitch it to a strap with another load the same size on the other end, fling it over their shoulders, perspire freely, and trot off. I would be very glad to feel sorry for them, but they don't seem to mind it at all. It is an older civilization, I guess.

But in the United States I am very uneasy about this bag. I apologize to the porter who puts it on the train and feel that I have to give him enough extra to endow a Negro college in his home town. I start worrying about getting it into a taxi long before the train has pulled into the station, and I run over in my mind a few pleasantries with which I can assuage the porter on the other end. "Pretty heavy, eh? And I don't drink, either! Aha-ha-ha-ha!" or "Maybe I'd better get a trunk, eh?" None of these ever go very big, I may add.

It usually ends up by my being so self-conscious about the thing that I carry it myself. There are two ways of doing this: one is to carry it by the handles, but that way it crashes heavily against the side of the leg and eventually throws me; the other method is to hoist it up on the shoulder and stagger along under it. This is not much better, for then it not only cocks my hat over my eye but completely shuts off my vision from the other eye, so that many times I have walked head on into another train or collided with passengers. I have even caught up with passengers going in the same direction and smashed into them from behind. And the combined weight of my body and the bag, going at a fair clip, is sufficient to capsize and badly bruise a woman or a small man.

Taxi drivers are not very nice about my bag, either. When confronted with the problem of where to put it in the cab, they often make remarks such as: "Why don't we put the cab on top of the bag and drag it through the streets?" or "Where are the elephants?" With my bag tucked on the front seat beside him, a taxi driver had to lean out over the other side and drive with one knee. And nobody feels sadder about it than I do. Of all people to have a bag like that, I am the worst, because I am so sensititive.

It is not only with railway porters that I am ill at ease. I feel very guilty about asking moving men to carry bureaus and bookcases downstairs. I have a bookcase which I sold to a man three years ago which is still standing in my room because I could not get up the courage to ask anyone to move it for me. I know that there are men who make it their business to lift heavy articles of furniture, but this is a *terribly* heavy bookcase. The first six weeks after I sold it I used to sit and look at it and say to myself: "I really ought to get that over to Thurston right away." But I couldn't seem to feel right about getting anyone to do it.

I tried hitching it along the floor myself, but I couldn't even get it away from the spot where it had always been. So then I tried forgetting about it, and would look quickly away every time my eyes rested on it. Thurston asked me about it once, and I said that I had been trying to get a moving man to take it but that there was a strike on. I tried draping it with a sheet, so that I wouldn't have to look at it, but that did not good. The sheet just made it worse.

About a year ago I gave Thurston his money back and said that I had decided to keep the bookcase, but I really don't want it. Perhaps some moving man will see this confession and will come up some day and ask me if I don't want some especially heavy furniture moved. If he *asked* me, I couldn't feel guilty about it, could I? But I can tell him right now that it is heavier than he thinks, and I won't blame him if he drops it on the stairs, and I would rather not watch, if he doesn't mind.

It makes it very difficult to be afraid to impose on porters and yet not be able to carry things yourself. Perhaps the best thing to do would be just not to own any heavy things, and to buy whatever clothes and shoes I need in the town I happen to be in. Or perhaps it would be better yet not to go anywhere, and just sit in my room.

Take a Letter, Please

PROBABLY one of the most potent causes of a war in the world's history (this shapes up like a pretty broad statement, but my attorney tells me that I have adequate proofs) has been the giving out of statements, sometimes by mistake, which the giver-out is too proud to take back. A king or a dictator, a little behind in his phrase-making, has pulled a quick one like, "Beyond the Alps lies Italy," *"L'Etat, c'est moi,"* or "Never give a sucker an even break," and then has had to go through with it to save his face. A great many times all the trouble could have been avoided if the original speech-maker had been willing to say: "I guess I must have been cockeyed. I don't remember having said any such thing."

That is one reason why I am afraid to dictate a letter. I probably couldn't start a war between any nations worth noticing, but I could get myself into an awful jam. There is something about a stenographer sitting with pencil poised waiting for my next word which throws me into a mild panic. Anybody, in order to be a secretary or even a stenographer, has got to have a certain amount of concentrative power and a good common-school education. This means that while they are sitting there waiting for a word or two, they are passing judgment on me; for my own education, although lengthy, is what you might call "sketchy." Almost any stenographer could write a better letter than I can.

With this uppermost in my mind I sit down with a young lady facing me and try to sound businesslike. "Take a letter, please, Miss Keegle," I say. Miss Keegle always seems to be an exceptionally intelligent young lady, and always has the appearance of disapproving of me right at the start.

The first part of the letter goes like wildfire. I have the name and address of the man right in front of me. "To Mr. Alfred W. Manvogle, Room 113, Butchers' and Bakers' Bank Building, St. Louis." So far, so very good. Miss Keegle is obviously impressed.

" 'My-er-dear Mr. Manvogle,' or rather, I guess—'Dear Sir. *(Confidential aside to Miss Keegle:* I don't know him at all. *Miss Keegle nods, as if to say,* What of it?) In reply to your letter of September 11th *(long pause to figure out just what the reply is going to be. I should have thought this out before).* In reply to your letter of September 11th would say that, although I agree with you on the main principles of your argument *(I don't agree with him at all, but am saying this in order to give the girl something to write down),* I feel that—er—I feel that—ah—(This is awful!)—I feel that it would be better if your Mr. Cramsey and I could get together again some afternoon this week. (I *don't* want to see Mr. Cramsey again, and I haven't got any afternoon this week that I can see him, but I have got to say *some*thing. This girl has been waiting there fifteen minutes already.) I—er—or rather *you*—ah—seem to be laboring under the delusion—'No, I guess cross that out. Ah—'Your ideas about how we should go ahead in this matter—'No, I guess never mind that. (I should really get some sort of instrument to dictate into—but then think of the records I would waste!) Where was I, Miss Keegle?"

Miss Keegle says that that I really wasn't anywhere.

In desperation I continue, in a much more belligerent mood than I otherwise would have been, simply to get the thing over with: "I don't see how we can get together on this thing unless you are willing to listen to reason."

Miss Keegle reminds me that I have already said that I would like to talk to Mr. Cramsey again. Which do I mean?

"Cross that out about Mr. Cramsey. I don't want to see

him. I don't want to see anybody. I want to get this whole thing out of the way. Just send the letter as it is, Miss Keegle—and thank you."

Miss Keegle then goes away, and a letter goes out to Mr. Manvogle which gives quite the wrong impression of my attitude in the matter. If Mr. Manvogle were France and I were the United States, there would be a war, simply because I blurted out something, under the harassing fear of Miss Keegle, which I really didn't mean. Of course, I should have to stand by my guns when the matter came up before the World Court, and I should expect all the young men of the country to stand by my guns with me. Or, perhaps, I should expect them to stand by *their* guns while I dictated some more letters.

Of course, one can correct a letter when it comes back from the typist, but, after correcting a few letters until they looked

PETER ARNO

Simply because I blurted out something under the harassing fear of Miss Keegle.

like a manuscript of Victor Hugo's, with long sentences written out in the margin running upward and long sentences
on the end of a string running downward from the middle
of the sheet, I have given up postdictation correction, and
just sign my name. In fact, I have given up dictation entirely,
and write out my letters long-hand, to be copied by anybody
who can read them. I am thinking now of giving up writing
letters.

But this giving out snap judgments and snap answers, simply because somebody is waiting and making you very nervous, is a very dangerous business. This is especially true if
the language in use happens to be one with which you are
unfamiliar. If given plenty of time to mutter the thing over
to myself, and perhaps write it out on a little card, I can
understand what a Frenchman is saying to me. But when he
rattles it off like mad (and show me a Frenchman who doesn't)
and is obviously impatient for an answer, I am quite likely
to commit myself to something I don't want to do, just out
of sheer nervousness.

I once got into a French barber's chair (no small feat in
itself) and asked, in French which I had rehearsed out in the
corridor for five minutes before entering, for a shave. During
the process the barber said something to me which, because
of its rising inflection at the end, I took to be a question. In
fact, it was one of those questions which seem to demand an
answer in the affirmative, like "It's a nice day, isn't it?" or "Is
the razor all right?" (And, by the way, did anyone ever answer
this last question by saying that the razor *wasn't* all right?) So
I said, *"Oui, oui!"* out from my lather and shut my eyes again.
In about a half a second my hair was on fire. At the same
moment, a boy rushed up from the back of the shop and
started taking my shirt off.

I realized that I had said *"oui"* to the wrong thing, but was
ashamed to admit it. So I clung to my chair and took my
beating. It seems that, in addition to having agreed to have
my hair singed, I had got myself in for a treatment of congestion of the lungs (French barbers still maintain the old medieval office of surgeon and will treat you for anything up

PETER ARNO

*In about half a second . . . . I realized that I had said "oui"
to the wrong thing.*

to, and including, the birth of a small child), and before I
got out of the chair, I had had four little cups burnt on the
small of my back so that they hung there by force of suction
(all the air having been drawn out by flaming cotton, a charming process known as *"vendouse,"* which I had mistaken for
"vendeuse," which means "saleslady"). At least, I know enough
now to say *"non"* to everything. I may miss a little fun, but I
am playing safe.

It doesn't have to be a foreign language to cause misun-
derstanding. I can answer questions that I don't understand

in English just as easily and get into just as much trouble. It all comes from not wanting to ask for a repeat, especially after the second time. I have signed up for hotel rooms with Italian gardens attached and Roman swimming pools adjoining, simply because the man at the desk muttered something as I signed my name which I took to be a little pleasantry calling for a genial, "Yes, indeedy" in reply. I have bought suits with belts in the back, hats with green feathers in them, and shoes which would throw a Chinese lady on her face, all because I misunderstood the clerk and didn't have the nerve to crawl. If I were just learning about life, I would try to correct this fault. But it is a little late now. The best thing that I can do is bluff the thing out, and make believe each time that I am getting exactly what I wanted. But, as we noted in the beginning, that is one of the reasons nations get themselves mixed up in wars. And I certainly don't want to have another war until we get the last one paid for. It is quite a problem.

"Over the Top"

ONE of the most disastrous effects of the late war (you remember the late war, surely) was the success of the five Liberty Loan drives. These drives bred within our nation a race of four-minute speakers and drive experts which threatens to push most of the remaining population into the sea. At least one-fifth of the country's citizens are now spending their time trying to exhort money out of the other four-fifths.

Until the war and the Liberty Loan campaigns, whenever a hospital or boys' club needed money they made up a modest budget and went around quietly to the houses of wealthy citizens with a gentlemanly plea for assistance. They were very careful not to get the wealthy citizen up from the dinner table on their calls, because he might get cross and not suscribe. And at the close of the campaign they printed a little list of subscribers and headed it "Our Good Friends." In other words, they knew their place.

Then came the war (the same war we referred to above). The government needed money and the Treasury Department organized gigantic squads of publicity experts, public speakers, sob sisters, and organization men to whip the nation in line. It was probably the only time in the history of the country when all its publicity experts and newspaper reporters had jobs.

231

What happened was that thousands of perfectly terrible speakers got the idea that they were good, thousands of very bad executives got the idea that they could put the thing over with a bang, and just short of a million terrifically futile copy writers began to think of themselves as agitators of the public mind. They did not realize that what sold Liberty Bonds was the war and several thousand guys in France, and not Mr. Harrison M. Greeble, coming out in front of the curtain at the Bijou Dream Theater between reels and holding one chubby fist aloft calling on Heaven to witness that his Cause was Just.

Well, the war was over—or, at any rate, we thought it was over at the time. And what was left? Mr. Greeble was left, with a hunger for exhorting in front of a curtain. Mrs. Malvey was left, with a God-given gift of organization for money-raising purposes. Mr. Henry Rolls Turbin was left, large in the conviction that he could sway great masses of people with his editorial matter and an occasional appearance on a public rostrum.

And for properties, there remained several hundred gigantic thermometers, used for indicating the progress of the campaign, and several hundred monster dials, for the same exciting purpose. Then, of course, the customary amount of bunting and horns, and a few paper caps with mottoes in them for no purpose whatever.

What to do with these? What to do with Mr. Greeble and Mrs. Malvey and Mr. Turbin, and the monster thermometers? Throw them away?

But no! Here was too much talent, too much inspirational force, to allow it to die out with the coming of peace. Surely there must be some other things to raise money for! Surely our citizenry couldn't be allowed to save up a few pennies against that silly old rainy day we hear so much about. The people had got into the custom of contributing money. They couldn't be permitted to sink back into their old soft ways of putting it in the bank.

So, when it came time for the Mount McKenzie Bicycle Hospital to raise its yearly $25,000, the directors had a meeting and decided that, in view of the success of the Fifth

Liberty Loan drive in Lindport, it was only fair that the Bicycle Hospital should come next. So they engaged a drive expert from out of town to come in and look the ground over.

The drive expert came, accompanied by a corps of assistants, including copy writers, camera men, poster artists, and rubbers. They pitched a big tent on the Common and began making topographical maps. They surveyed the surrounding country, measured all the public buildings, looked in at the people's kitchen windows and had everybody vaccinated.

Then the expert submitted a report advising that, instead of trying to raise the customary $25,000, the hospital should go out for a $3,000,000 endowment, the campaign to embrace all of Weekover County. As the expert said, "If they will stand for $25,000, they will stand for $3,000,000. It is simply a question of posters."

So the board of the Mount McKenzie Bicycle Hospital voted to go ahead with the proposition. With $3,000,000 they could build a new hospital, with modern, up-to-date repair shops for wornout bicycles, experimental laboratories for new bicycles, trade schools for bicycle dealers and a restroom for the woman employees, if they should ever decide to employ any women. What was left over from the $3,000,000 they could put in the bank for anything that might come up, picnics or anything at all.

For the purposes of the campaign the expert brought up a fresh detachment of shock troops from the rear. Each of these had assigned to him the organization of one particular household in town, until every household was covered.

The organizer moved right into the house he was assigned to, and proceeded to pep things up. He appointed the father a four-minute speaker, the mother head of the Knitting and Bandage Corps, the young son in charge of poster display for the house, and the young daughter to act as usher at the family mass meetings. Thus every house in town was organized within itself, and each given a certain quota to raise within itself to help swell the total.

Outside of each house was placed a big thermometer, and, as the amount increased day by day, the young daughter was allowed to go out and punch up the indicator, appropriate ceremonies accompanying this service.

Posters were drawn and stuck up over the town. One showed an old man wheeling a broken-down bicycle up a hill toward the sunset. It read: "Don't Let This Old Man Hurt Himself Because of Faulty Gearing." Another showed a young man looking sadly out at a window, with the legend: "Where Is *Your* Bicycle?" Then there were the customary slogans: "Get Behind and Push!" "Over the Top for Our Bicycles!" and "Hermanstown Takes Care of Its Bicycles. Don't Make Lindport a Piker City!"

The newspapers were flooded with copy from the publicity department of the drive, Sunday stories on "The Progress of the Bicycle Since 1876," "Did Cleopatra Own the First Bicycle?" and "An Old Bicycle Tells Its Story."

Just as it began to look as if the campaign were going to flop a man dressed as Paul Revere rode down Main Street waving a check.

In the news columns there were accounts of the progress of the drive in the various households, which little girl was ahead in the contest to sell dolls' slippers, which little boy had won the day's bean shooting, and what the principal of the Wurdle High School said to the pupils about not kicking bicycles that they saw standing against curbings.

Then there were photographs of the committee in charge of the drive, the women's auxiliary committee, the "Junior Drivers" and the members of the Speakers' Bureau. During the progress of the drive the city of Paris, France, fell in and crushed two-thirds of its inhabitants, but the story was relegated to the second page under "Cable Dispatches" because the front page was devoted to the news of the next-to-last day of the drive.

On the day before the drive ended the excitement was intense. Only $2,350,000 had been raised. The thermometers were quivering with excitement and the schools were shut down at noon. Little groups of people stood on the street corners discussing the impending catastrophe. Would Lindport fail? A house-to-house canvass was made by the Boys' Brigade, dressed up as little bandits, armed with real guns loaded with real bullets, which they aimed at people and demanded just fifty more dollars. It was all in fun, of course, but several citizens who refused were shot down like dogs.

Then, just as it began to look as if the campaign were going to flop at $2,740,000, a man dressed as Paul Revere rode down Main Street waving a check for $250,000 from Senator Herman J. Mooter, which the committee had had up its sleeve all the time, waiting for a grand-stand finish.

So the $3,000,000 was raised for the Mount McKenzie Bicycle Hospital, and the citizens of Lindport could look everybody but their bankers in the face. And next month, stirred by the success of the Hospital Drive, the Lindport Girls' Outdoor Club began one for $5,000,000 to help fix up outdoors.

A great many of these drives are legitimate enough, but the methods used in putting them over are easily adaptable for any purposes whatsoever. This playing on the community or club spirit to build a new wing to a gymnasium can be overdone. In colleges and schools is it particularly heinous.

Let us say that the Feeta Theta Psi decides that their old house hasn't got enough pool tables, so they set out to build a new house. Each graduate is appealed to in a manner which implies that if he doesn't come across he will go down in history as "Old Crosspatch." But the graduates can take care of themselves. Lots of them would just as soon go down in history as "Old Crosspatch" and save the five hundred dollars.

It is the undergraduates who are bulldozed into spending father's money by the threat that if they do not come up to scratch in their allotments there is grave danger that the free institutions of the United States of America will crumble before December, and that the work of Washington, Lincoln, and Rutherford B. Hayes will have gone for nothing. The poor kids, coerced to the point of hysteria by the drive committee, sign up for enough of the Old Man's money to put them through Graduate School.

Something is wrong somewhere.

But before we close, I want to say a few words on behalf of the fund which we at the Snow Shoe League are trying to raise to keep the snow here longer in the winter. We need only $10,000,000 and we have a promise from an anonymous snowshoer of $5,000,000 if we can raise the other $5,000,000 by the next snowfall.

Now, this is not a fly-by-night scheme and would really do a whole lot of good, and I hope that each and every one of you who read this will sit right down and make out a good, big check and send it to me.

LET'S GET TOGETHER ON THIS! LET'S GO!

Good Luck,
and Try and Get It

You may think that you are not superstitious. But would you walk under a burning building? Would you hold a hammer in your left hand and bring it down on your right? Would you light three bank notes with one match? Probably not. But do you know why?

Most of the superstitions which we have today date back to the Middle Ages, when superstition *was* something. In the Middle Ages they were superstition-poor, they had so much. For several centuries there a man couldn't stoop over to lace up his shoon (Middle-Aged word for "shoes") in the morning without first throwing salt over his shoulder and wetting his finger in a distillation of wolfsbane.

For every single thing they did in those days they had to do three other things first, and by the end of the day you know that runs into time. Often they never could get started on the real business at hand because they were so occupied in warding off the evil eye, and a man who really took care of himself and ran no chances might very well starve to death before he got through his warding-off exercises.

For instance, there was a thing called a mandrake root which was considered practically infallible for keeping naughty spirits at bay; but you had to go out and dig your own mandrake root. You couldn't say to your little boy while you were dressing: "Run out into the garden and pull up daddy's mandrake root for him this morning." You had to go out and dig it yourself. Furthermore, you had to dig it at midnight, or under just the right conditions of the moon, or it was no good. And, just to make things harder, you had to be deaf; otherwise you could hear the mandrake root shriek when you pulled it up, and if you once heard that you would fall down dead.

People used to tie the root to a dog and then whistle from a safe distance where they couldn't hear the root complain. The dog would pull up the root in answering the whistle (as dirty a trick as ever was played on Man's Best Friend), hear the deadly scream, and fall down dead in his tracks. Then the mandrake digger would rush up, grab the root, and tear off to the office. But by this time his office was probably in the hands of the sheriff, or the water had overflowed the tub and dripped down into the room below, and there he was stuck with a mandrake root and a bill for $115.00.

Of course today we know that there is no such thing as bad luck, but just the same there is no sense in making a fool of yourself. If, simply by walking around a ladder, you can humor some little gnome into not dogging your footsteps all day with a red-hot pea-shooter, then why be narrow-minded? Walk around the ladder, even though you laughingly say to yourself that you are spoiling that little gnome by being so indulgent. What harm can come from walking around the ladder, unless possibly you slip off into the gutter and sprain your ankle?

The reason why we feel an instinctive urge not to walk under a ladder is fairly interesting (only fairly) and perhaps it would be just as well if I told it to you. If you are superstitious about hearing stories about how superstitions arose, wet your right thumb and turn this page over once.

It seems that when William the Conqueror (or Lief the Unlucky, as he was known in the Greek version of the fable) first landed in England (you know the date as well as I do—1215 Magna Charta) he was very nervous for fear that a Certain Party had followed him from Normandy (his real reason for leaving). Every night he used to take a walk around

What harm can come from walking around the ladder, unless you slip into the gutter?

the ramparts of his castle "just to get a breath of fresh air" as he said, but as he had had nothing but fresh air all day he fooled nobody. What he really was doing was taking a look to make sure that this Certain Party was not snooping around trying to find a way into the castle to get some evidence on him.

One night he came upon a ladder placed up against the wall and, thinking to trap the intruder, he stood under this ladder, very close up against the stonework, to see if he could hear without being seen.

It wasn't a ladder at all, however (he was pretty unfamiliar with the layout of the castle, having just come from Normandy), but a part of the drawbridge mechanism, and just at that moment the man in charge opened up the portcullis and pulled up the bridge to let in one of the menials who had been in town to a dance, and William the Conqueror was catapulted over backward into the moat (from which all the water had been drawn that very evening to make room for fresh) and wrenched his back very badly.

From that day on he gave orders for his bodyguard never to let him walk under a ladder *unless he was sure it was a ladder*. Gradually this last provision was dropped from the command and it became known as "William's Folly" to walk under *any* ladder. Gradually the "William's Folly" was dropped, and it became just a sap thing to do anyway. But we do not realize that the *original* form of this superstition was, "Don't walk under a ladder unless you are sure that it *is* a ladder!" So, you see, we have just been overcautious all these years.

The practice among athletic teams of carrying along monkeys or owls as mascots comes from a very old custom of monkeys and owls carrying along athletic teams as mascots. The word mascot comes from the French *mascotte*, meaning little witch, but practically nobody today carries around a little witch to bring him good luck.

In fact, a little witch would be a liability today, for it would mean just one more mouth to feed and one more railroad ticket to buy, even though you could probably get her on for half fare. But other things, usually inanimate, have taken the place of the little witch, and a great many people have odds and ends of crockery and bric-a-brac which they would not be without on any venture involving luck. These are sometimes called amulets, and range anywhere from a "lucky penny" (any penny at all is pretty lucky these days) to a small bust of some famous man.

I once heard of a man who was carrying a trunk downstairs when a messenger boy came up to him and gave him a note

PADEREWSKI

He considered the trunk his "lucky piece" and was afraid to go anywhere without it.

saying he had won a raffle. From that day on he considered the trunk his "lucky piece" and was afraid to go anywhere without it. This caused him no end of inconvenience and people stopped asking him to parties. But he still persisted in dragging the trunk with him wherever he went, always looking for another messenger boy to come up with another message of good cheer. He finally hurt himself quite seriously, so that he couldn't take the trunk with him any more, and then he just stayed home with the trunk.

Thus we see that even in this enlightened day and age the old medieval superstitions still persist in some form or another. Some of us go on feeling that if we sign our name on a little piece of paper, or check, we can get money from it. Others are perfectly convinced that if they go into a polling booth and push down a button they are having a part in running the government.

If it isn't one sort of superstition it is another—and sometimes it is both.

Is the Sea Serpent
a Myth or a Mythter?

Now that people are back from the seashore again we can scrutinize those reports on sea serpents! Coming after reports on budgets, taxes, and the increase in pellagra, a good sea serpent report is a relief. At least there is some ground for argument about a sea serpent.

There was, for instance, the famous serpent seen by the members of the crew of the schooner *Mrs. Ella B. Margolies* off Gloucester in 1896. I will set down the excerpt from the ship's log for what it is worth (closing price .003):

"On Board *Mrs. Ella B. Margolies.* August 6, 1896. Lat. 24° 57′ S., long. 16 ft. E. . . . Brooklyn-8; St. Louis-4. . . . Am. T. & T. 20½.

"In the 4 to 6 watch, at about 5 o'clock, we observed a most remarkable fish on our lee quarter, crossing the stern in a S.W. direction. The appearance of the head, which with the back fin (or upper leg) was the only portion of the animal visible, was something similar to that of a rabbit, only without the ears. It (the animal) pursued a steady undeviating course, keeping its head horizontal with the surface of the water except when it turned to look backward as if it were flirting with something.

"Once a small pennant was raised just above where the tail should be, a pennant which, according to the code of the sea, signified 'Owner on Board.' "

This same animal was seen from points along the shore at Gloucester and Bass Rock, and officials of the Odd Creatures Society took the trouble to investigate. The answers given by Roger Bivalve, a fisherman living in a lobster trap on Point Pixie, are representative as well as enlightening.

Q. When did you first see the animal?
A. I should say shortly after falling down on the rocks in front of my place.
Q. At what distance?
A. Once it was in my lap. Other times about fifty yards out.
Q. What was its general appearance?
A. Something awful.
Q. Did it appear jointed or serpentine?
A. Serpentine, by all means.
Q. Describe its eyes and mouth.
A. Well, its eyes were beautiful. I thought for a while that I was in love with it. Its mouth was more mocking than anything, which gave me the tip-off.
Q. Had it fins or legs, and where?
A. Do I have to answer that?
Q. Did it make any sound or noise?
A. I should say it was more of a cackle, or perhaps a laugh. I know I didn't like it.
Q. Do you drink?
A. Only medicinally, and then never after I fall over.

It is too bad that there should be this suspicion of excess drinking attached to reports of sea serpents, because I myself have a story which might help solve a great many problems in marine mystery, but I fear the effect it might have on my children's opinion of me.

Oh, well, I might as well get it off my chest! . . . I am not a drinking man by nature, and although on this particular day I had rubbed a little alcohol into my hair to keep the flies away, I have every reason to believe that I was in full possession of my senses. (I don't suppose that I can say *full* possession, for I have three more payments to make before

PADEREWSKI

they are really mine.) I had been talking to an old friend whom I hadn't seen for years, and the next time we looked at the clock it was Friday; so I said: "Well, Harry, what do you say we call it a week and knock off?" Harry was agreeable, so we went and bought two hats to put on so that we wouldn't have to go home bareheaded.

I know that this sounds fishy, but just as sure as I am standing here at this minute, I looked down the length of the hat store, and there, right by the little door where the clerks went in and out, something caught my eye—no mean trick in itself, as my eye was not in a roving mood right then, as I was concentrating on a brown fedora which I fortunately did not buy. It was as if something with a long tail had just disappeared around the corner of the door.

I thought nothing of it at first, thinking that it was probably a salesman who had a long tail and who was going about his business. But the more I thought it over the stranger it seemed to me that I had not noticed a salesman with a long tail before, as we had been in the shop several hours by this time.

So I excused myself politely and tiptoed down to the door where I had seen the disappearing object. It was quite a long walk, as I got into another store by mistake and had to inquire my way back, but soon I reached the rear of the original hat store and looked out into the workroom. There, stretched across an ironing board where they had been reblocking old derbies, I saw a sight which made my blood run cold.

Beginning at one end of the ironing board and stretching across it and off the other end into the window—

I guess that I was right in the first place. I never should have begun to tell it. You wouldn't understand!

Swat the Tsk-Tsk Midge!

AMONG the least flashy, and least interesting, of the movements looking toward the betterment of the human race comes our intensive campaign in the Uganda for the elimination of the tsk-tsk midge, or Hassenway's crab-fly. The tsk-tsk midge (or Hassenway's crab-fly) is something like the tsetse fly, except that it uses the hyphen. It is a very tiny fly, with plain features, and was first discovered by Dr. Ambercus Hassenway while he was looking for something else.

For a long time the residents of the Uganda had been conscious of the fact that *some*thing was wrong with them, but couldn't quite decide what it was. They were nervous and fidgety and likely to break down and cry if you pointed a finger at them, until it finally got so that they would just walk about all day rubbing two sticks together and looking out of the corners of their eyes at people. This was bad for business.

It was not until Dr. Hassenway isolated the tsk-tsk midge and had a good talk with it that the Ugandans realized what the trouble was. They had been accepting the tsk-tsk midges all along, thinking that they were caraway seeds and rather liking them. Dr. Hassenway pointed out their error and showed them that this little animal was probably the cause of all their *malaise,* and, in recognition of his services to them, they insisted on renaming the tsk-tsk midge Hassenway's crab-fly. Dr. Hassenway protested that he really had done nothing

247

to deserve this honor, that he already had had an oak tree blight named after him ("Hassenway's leaf-itch"), and that he was going home in a couple of days anyway. But the natives insisted, and Hassenway's crab-fly it was.

Then began the campaign to eliminate it. Dr. Hassenway is said to have remarked, a little bitterly: "Why bother to change its name if you are going to eliminate it right away?" But he took the thing in good part and entered into the game with a will. In fact, it was he who threw the first midge in the opening battle.

The first thing to do was, obviously, to discover the personal habits of the tsk-tsk and try to upset them. It was discovered (probably by Dr. Hassenway, as he was the only one in the Uganda at the time who knew how to read and write or even part his hair) that the tsk-tsk midge was dependent on a certain set of antennæ, cleverly concealed under a sort of raglan-like coat, for its pleasure in biting people. The bite of the tsk-tsk midge, by the way, is barely noticeable at the time of biting. The victim merely feels that he has forgotten something. It is not until later that he begins to rub two sticks together and look out of the corners of his eyes. And, by then, it is too late.

Now, in order to remove these antennæ, or "antlers," it is necessary to get the tsk-tsk midge into an awkward position, such as a big bonfire or a printing press. He must be convinced that he is among friends, and then set upon a rather nasty trick, if you ask me. The difficulty comes in locating the midge, for he is (I don't know why I keep referring to the midge as "he." "Midge" is certainly a girl's name.)—it is— able to change its color, and even its shape, at the drop of a hat. This completely confused Dr. Hassenway.

The next complication to arise in this mammoth battle of man against midge was the discovery of the fact that the female midge did not lay eggs but *bought* them from a sort of common egg supply. (If I am not making myself clear to you, you have nothing on me. I am, frankly, in a panic about the thing.) All that we know *is* that the female midge, when she wants to hatch a couple of million eggs, goes to the corner egg place and, in exchange for some bits of old ·moss and acorn ends, gets the required number of larvæ. These she takes home and puts into a quick oven, and, in fifteen or twenty minutes, there you are, bitten by a whole new set of tsk-tsk midges. The only way to fight this sort of thing was, obviously, to close up the egg supply stations. Try and do it, however.

The problem called for outside help. Dr. Hassenway cabled to America, imploring the authorities to start a drive in behalf of this humanitarian campaign, and, as a result of a whirlwind publicity avalanche, the good people of that country sent an expedition of five scientists to the Uganda with instructions to stay there. These scientists, under leadership of Dr. Joe Glatz, set out on October 12, 1929, and, so far as anyone has ever found out, never arrived.

So far, so good. The tsk-tsk midges had, by this time, so firmly entrenched themselves in the more tender sections of the Uganda that the natives were looking up timetables and planning business trips into the interior. It was a young Ugandan, Tanganyika Tangan (yika) by name, who finally came forward with a plan which was destined at least to postpone this hegira and to give his countrymen a good night's sleep.

Tangkanyika was a college man (Harvard, 1915) who had returned to his native land on a visit after graduation and had never got around to putting on his collar again. He saw the crisis and he decided that it was up to him to meet it. So he called a council of chiefs and told them that, unless they worked up some way to get rid of this devastating pest (pointing, by mistake, to his father), the country would be the laughingstock of the civilized world. "A people of our caliber," he said, "a people of our traditions, do not go on forever being bitten by tsk-tsk midges." (There were cries of "Hassenway's crab-flies!" from the Extreme Left, but he frowned them down.)

He then brought out some maps and charts which he had left over from his botany course at Harvard and showed them that, for every tsk-tsk midge which was born, 300,000 Ugandan babies woke up in the night and asked for a drink of water. He showed them that Dr. Hassenway had been doing all the work and that nothing had come of it (Dr. Hassenway was on his sabbatical at the time, a fact which was noticed only when Tanganyika mentioned it), and that if the Uganda was to have any national pride left, the tsk-tsk midge must go. Then he threw himself on the ground in a tribal doze.

It was, at this time, what is known as "the rainy season" in the Uganda, which means that everybody had lost interest. Everybody, that is, except the midges, and they were working in three shifts. Tanganyika tried to start grass fires, with a view to burning the midge nests, but succeeded only in burning his fingers badly. He instituted a spraying contest, in which the youths on the left side of the village street tried to spray more poison around than the youths on the right side of the street, with the result that the youths on both sides of the street were made violently ill. In fact, he tried everything known to science, but the only thing that happened was that the next litter of tsk-tsk midges was larger and had better color.

This is where the matter stands now. Dr. Hassenway and Tanganyika are both at French Lick Springs and don't seem to care any more. The tsk-tsk midges are having the time of their lives. The only ones who are concerned in the elimination of this little animal are the scientists, and I don't know how much longer their interest can be held. I am issuing this as a sort of appeal that Something Be Done!

PETER ARNO

The Railroad Problem

I UNDERSTAND that there is a big plan on foot to consolidate the railways of this country into four large systems. This doesn't interest me much, as I walk almost everywhere I go. (I discovered that I was putting on quite a bit of weight and was told that walking was fine for that sort of thing, but, since making the resolution to walk everywhere I go, I find that I just don't *go* anywhere. As a result, I have gained six pounds and never felt better in my life.)

However, there must be people who use the railroads or they wouldn't keep blowing those whistles all the time. And it is in behalf of these people that I would like to make a few suggestions to the new consolidated systems, suggestions based on my experiences when I used to be a traveler myself. I jotted down notes of them at the time, but notes made on a moving train are not always very legible the next day, and I am afraid that I shall have to guess at most of them (especially those written with the pen in the club car) and rely on my memory for the rest.

What I want to know is—what are they going to do about the heating systems? In the new arrangement, something very drastic has got to be done about running those steam pipes under my individual berth. I have tried every berth from Lower One to Upper Fourteen on every line in the

country except the Montour and the Detroit, Toledo & Iron-
ton, and in every damned one of them I was the central point
for the heating system of the whole train.

It wouldn't be so bad if, when I had finally accommodated
myself to lying beside a steam pipe by throwing off all the
flannel pads which serve as blankets and going to sleep like
Diana at the Bath (oh, well, not *exactly* like Diana but near
enough for the purpose of *this* story), they didn't then run
ammonia through that very pipe and set up a refrigerating
system along about four in the morning. They might at least
make up their minds as to whether they want to roast or
freeze me. It's this constant vacillating that upsets me.

Now in this new system of railroads, while they are deciding
so many questions, they might as well decide about me. I will
be a good sport about it, whatever they say. But I *do* want to
know what the plan is. Is it to roast or freeze Benchley? Then
I can make my own plans accordingly.

And while they are at it, they might work up some system
of instruction which would eliminate new engineers taking
their driving lessons on night runs. As I have figured it out,
this is the way the thing is worked now:

The regular engineer takes the train until about three in
the morning. Then the new man gets aboard and is shown
the throttles and is instructed about how to put on his overalls
and gloves. If the system is working well, this is the first time
the new man has ever been near an engine in his life. A
porter then comes rushing up from back in the train and
announces: "O.K., boys! Benchley is asleep! Let-er ride!"

At this point the instructor tells the new man to start her
up easy. The man, with that same enthusiasm which makes
a beginner in automobile driving stall the engine right off
the bat, starts "her" up as if he were trying to take off in a
helicopter and rise right up off the ground. The result is that
all the cars in the train follow for the distance of one foot
and then crash together, forming one composite car.

"No, no, no, Joe!" shouts the instructor, laughing. "Take
her easy! Let her in slowly. Look, let me show you!" So he
does it, and the cars unscramble themselves and stand trem-
bling, waiting for the next crash. I myself have, by this time,

PETER ARNO

The occupant of Lower Two finds himself in Lower Fourteen.

sat bolt upright in my berth in spite of a broken collar bone. It is not until I have snuggled down again that the novice up in the cab tries his hand again. This time he is a little better and gets the train ahead about ten feet before he forgets what to do next, grows panicky, and jams on his emergency. I venture to say that, on his second try, he sends me a good four inches into the headboard of the berth.

"At-a-boy, Joe!" encourages his mentor. "You'll learn in no time. Now, just give her one more bang and then I'll take it over. You've had enough for one night."

So Joe has one more, or maybe two more bangs and then goes back to take his first lesson in coupling and uncoupling. This is no small job to undertake for the first time in the dark, and he does awfully well under the circumstances. All that he does is to drive the Anastasia into the Bellerophon so far that the occupant of the Lower Two in the first-named car finds himself in bed with the occupant of Lower Fourteen in the second. Not bad for a starter, Joe. You'll be a brakeman *and* an engineer before you know it. (I take it for granted that it is the same pupil who is driving the engine and coupling the cars. There couldn't be *two* men like that on one train.)

Now, if there can be no way devised under the new system

to have these new boys try out their lessons in some school in the yards, using dummy trains instead of real ones full of real passengers, then the least that the roads can do is to have the lesson hour come during the day when people are sitting upright and have a little resistance power. When these crashes come in the daytime (and they do, they do) you can at least brace yourself and look out of the window to see whether or not the train has landed in the branches of a tree. The new railroad systems should recognize that there is a time for work and a time for play and that four A.M. is *not* the time for romping among the younger engineers.

There are one or two other points which ought to be brought out in this little petition, points which the roads would do well to take to heart if steam travel is ever to supplant flying as a mode of transportation.

(1) Those two men who shout under my window whenever a train comes to a halt in a station during the night. I have heard what they have to say, and it really isn't worth shouting. One of them is named Mac, in case the officials want to go into this thing any further.

(2) The piling up of bags in the vestibule by the porters on day trains. In the old days we used to carry our bags out ourselves, and, irksome as it was, we at least got out of the train. As it is today, the train has been in the station a good half hour before the porter has dug into the mountain of suitcases in the vestibule so that it is low enough for a man on a burro to climb over it. The roads should either add this half hour to their running time on the time-tables (Ar. N.Y. 4:30. Disembark N.Y. 4:55) or else cut a hole in the roof to let out those passengers who have other connections to make.

(3) The polish used by porters in shining shoes. This should either be made of *real* gum so that it will attract articles of value, like coins and buttons, or of real polish so that the shoes will shine. As it is, the shoes neither shine nor are they sticky enough to attract anything more tangible than dust and fluff.

Here again it is a case in which the roads must make up their mind. Before they can amalgamate they must make up their mind on a lot of things. I have already made up mine.

"Accustomed as I Am—"

IT can't really be that there are fewer banquets being held than in the old days. It is probably that I myself am attending fewer. I know that was my intention several years ago, and I must be living up to it. It makes me very proud to think that at least one thing that I set out to do in my life I have done. I have attended fewer banquets.

But, just as when your own headache stops you think that there are no such things as headaches in the world, so now that I have stopped going to banquets it seems to me that the practice is dying out. I see notices in the newspapers that a testimonial dinner has been given to Lucius J. Geeney, or that the convening salesmen of the A.A.O.U.A.A.A. have got together for one final address by the "Big Boss" over the coffee cups filled with cigarette ends, but I don't read them. Oh, *how* I don't read them! I should say that there was no reading matter in the world, including the Koran in the original, which is so unread by me as the newspaper accounts of banquet speeches. But they tell me that, even under this handicap, they are still going on.

The bitterness on my part arises from two rather dark splotches in my past. I used to be a newspaper reporter, and, not being a particularly valuable one, I was sent every night to cover whatever banquet there might be at the old Waldorf or at the Astor. My records show that I attended ninety-two banquets in one winter, which meant that I listened to about three hundred and sixty-eight after-dinner speeches during that time, all of them beginning "I shall not take much of your time tonight," and ending, forty-five minutes later, with "but I have already taken too much of your time."

Finally, unable to control myself any longer, I began mocking after-dinner speakers. I worked up some after-dinner speeches of my own, built along the conventional lines, and wormed my way into banquet programs, where I would deliver them in hopes of offending some of the old boys who had tortured me for so long. But, instead of flying into a

PETER ARNO

"Louder and funnier!"

rage, they drafted me into their ranks, and the first thing I knew, instead of waging war on after-dinner speakers I found that I was one myself! Tie that for irony!

It took me quite a long time to realize that I was actually a professional banqueteer and not an amateur crusader against banquets. I began to suspect the truth when I started getting letters from chairmen of banquet committees in Pennsylvania or Missouri suggesting that I come and make a speech before the Men's Club of the Rumbold Association or at the annual dinner of the Assistant Bankers' Club, adding: "We haven't very much money in our treasury, but you would be our guest for the duration of your stay in town and we can assure you of a royal good time." Then I knew that I was really a member of the Journeymen Talkers, and a great flush of shame swept my brow. I was hoist by my own, or, at any rate, a borrowed petard.

Imagine my predicament. (All right, *don't* then! I'll tell it to you.) Having stood all the after-dinner speeches that I could as a reporter, I now had to listen to a lot more, including my own. I tried to make mine so insulting that I would be thrown out of the union. I tried to impress it on my brothers in the bond of boredom that I was *against* them and not with them. But they were so busy running over their own speeches in their minds, or so firmly convinced that what they had just said was beyond being kidded, that water on a duck's back was a permanent institution compared with my weak lampoons. It was then that I admitted myself licked, and withdrew from the field.

But, during my brief membership in the ranks of the Coldstream Guards, I learned to have a little pity for them in their chosen calling. Not much, but a little. They have a pretty tough fight at times. Of course, they wouldn't be making speeches if they didn't want to (the exceptions being those poor wretches who get roped into the thing against their wills and bend four coffee spoons and crumble up eight bits of bread in terror before they are called upon), but also entertainment committees wouldn't have asked them if they weren't wanted. So the entertainment committees are equally to blame and probably more so. Now that we have got rid of

the open saloon, I recommend that we get rid of all entertainment committees. They are a menace to the nation.

Granted that the speaker has been asked, even urged, to
make a speech. Granted that he really loves doing it. What
does he do for his money besides bore the living life out of
his audience? He has to eat broiled jumbo squab *bonne femme,*
combination salad *Henri,* and raspberry *baiser* in a paper cuff,
talking with a strange master of ceremonies at his left who
is so nervous about his part of the program that he eats his
notes instead of his celery and gives the impression of being
very cross with the guest. He (the speaker) is asked, at the
last minute, by someone who comes up behind his chair en-
veloped in an aroma of rye, to insert in his speech some funny
crack at Harry Pastwick, P-a-s-t-w-i-c-k, who has just been
appointed Sales Manager. He is introduced by the nervous
master of ceremonies as somebody else or in terms which
indicate that the master of ceremonies is only vaguely familiar
with his name and record and cares less. And then he begins
his speech.

That is, he begins as soon as thirty or thirty-five guests have
scraped their way out of the banquet hall to the gentlemen's
room, and thirty or thirty-five more have scraped their way
back to their seats. He begins as soon as the boys at Table
48 in the back of the room have stopped Kentucky Moon,
and as soon as the representative from the Third Sales District has been convinced that if he stays under the table he
will catch cold. And he begins without waiting for the waiters
to get fifteen hundred coffee cups quiet.

"Mr. Chairman, fellow guests, members of the American
Association of Aromatics: When your chairman asked me to
speak to you tonight, I felt somewhat in the position of the
Scotchman who, when asked—"

At this point one of the members, probably technically in
the right, but distinctly out of order, yells, "Louder and funnier!" There is probably no more devastating or bloodcur-
dling cry in the world to a man who is on his feet trying to
make a speech. There can be no answer, only a sickly smile.
A sensitive man will sit down then and there, but sensitive
men aren't usually up making speeches. As for the man who

yells "Louder and funnier!" he ought to be made to get up himself and be funny. The only trouble is that he probably would love it.

I realize that this isn't much punishment to subject a man to for talking forty minutes overtime, but, as I figure it out, both sides get only what is coming to them. The speaker knows what he is in for when he agrees to make a speech. And if the banqueteers, after all the experience they have had, don't know what they are in for when they attend a banquet, then they deserve what they are getting. This thing has been going on for years. It has always been the same, and it probably always will be. Very young boys may be excused and pitied for attending their first banquet, but after that, they have nobody but themselves to blame.

Look at me. I stopped going, and see how happy I am!

Happy Childhood Tales

WE have had so many stories lately dealing with the sordid facts of life, about kitchen sinks and lynchings and young girls thrown out into the streets by mean old farmers who live in horsehair trunks, to say nothing of incidental subjects, such as gin and cold oatmeal and unfortunate people who have only one glove apiece, that a reaction is taking place in the mind of the reading public and a demand is going up for some of the fanciful happy tales of our youth.

"Enough of these stories of crime and unhappiness!" the people are crying. "Tell us again some of the ancient myths of an older day, the gay little legends on which we were brought up before the world grew grim and sordid."

And so, my little readers, I am going to try to recall to you some of the charming fairy tales, or, at any rate, to make up some like them, and I hope that after this little trip back into the Never-Never Land of our youth those little cheeks of yours will be blooming again and that you will shut your traps. For, after all, there must be *some* good in the world, else why were erasers put on the ends of lead pencils?

ENDREMIA AND LIASON
(From the Greek Mythology)

ENDREMIA was the daughter of Polygaminous, the God of

260

Ensilage, and Reba, the Goddess of Licorice. She was the child of a most unhappy union, it later turned out, for when she was a tiny child her father struck her mother with an anvil and turned himself into a lily pad to avoid the vengeance of Jove. But Jove was too sly for Polygaminous and struck him with a bolt of lightning the size of the Merchants Bank Building which threw him completely off his balance so that he toppled over into a chasm and was dashed to death.

In the meantime, Little Endremia found herself alone in the world with nobody but Endrocine, the Goddess of Lettuce, and her son Bilas, the God of Gum Arabic, to look after her. But, as Polygaminous (her father; have you forgotten so soon, you dope?) had turned Endremia into a mushroom before he turned himself into a lily pad, neither of her guardians knew who she was, so their protection did her no good.

But Jove had not so soon forgotten the daughter of his favorite (Reba), and appeared to her one night in the shape of a mushroom gatherer. He asked her how she would like to get off that tree (she was one of those mushrooms which grow on trees) and get into his basket. Endremia, not knowing that it was Jove who was asking her, said not much. Whereupon Jove unloosed his mighty wrath and struck down the whole tree with a bolt of lightning which he had brought with him in case Endremia wouldn't listen to reason.

This is why it is never safe to eat the mushrooms which grow on trees, or to refuse to get into Jove's basket.

MILGRIG AND THE TREE WILFS
(Something like Hans Christian Andersen)

ONCE upon a time there was a little girl named Milgrig, believe it or not. She lived in the middle of the deep dark forest with her three ugly sisters and their husbands, who were charcoal burners. Every night the three ugly sisters used to take little Milgrig and pull out a strand of her golden hair, so that by the time she was thirteen years old she looked something awful. And after the three sisters had pulled out her hair, their three husbands (I forgot to tell you that the three husbands were even uglier than the three sisters and much nastier) would stick pins into little Milgrig until she looked like a war map.

Milgrig wasn't particularly crazy about going, but a prince is a prince, and she knew enough to keep her mouth shut.

HERBERT F. ROESE

One night, when little Milgrig was so full of pins that she couldn't see straight, a fairy prince came riding up to the door of the charcoal burners' hut and asked if he had lost his way.

"How should I know?" replied the oldest sister, who was uglier than all the rest. "What was your way?"

"My way was to the king's castle," replied the prince, "and I must get there before midnight, for my father is torturing my mother with red-hot irons."

"Your father sounds like a good egg," replied the oldest husband, who was uglier than all the rest. "We must ask him down some night."

The prince, however, did not think that this was very funny and asked if little Milgrig might not be allowed to show him the way to the castle.

The ugly husbands and sisters, thinking that Milgrig would not know the way and would get the prince lost in the forest, agreed heartily to this suggestion, and the pins were pulled out of Milgrig to make it possible for her to walk.

"Good luck and a happy landing!" they all called out after the two young people as they set forth on their perilous journey.

But the prince was no fool, and knew his way through the forest as well as you or I do (better, I'll wager), and he took little Milgrig to the palace just as fast as his palfrey would carry him.

She wasn't particularly crazy about going, but a prince is a prince, and she knew enough to keep her mouth shut.

When they reached the palace and the prince found that his father had already killed his mother, he turned to little Milgrig and said:

"Now you are queen."

At this, little Milgrig was very pleased and immediately dispatched messengers to the charcoal burners' hut, where her three ugly sisters and three still uglier brothers-in-law were burned alive in a slow fire. Little Milgrig and the prince, happy in this termination to their little affair, lived happily ever after.

And so now, my readers, you must toddle off to bed, for we have had an evening with the happy, happy story-tellers of an earlier day and have had a vacation, for one night at least, from the drab, unpleasant sordidness of present-day writing.

Yarns of an Insurance Man

I WAS talking with an old friend of mine, an insurance man, the other day (oh, well, maybe it wasn't quite the other day—just before America entered the war, it was) and trying to convince him that it would be bad business for his company to write me one of those twenty-payment-life policies (with time-and-a-half for overtime), when he suddenly turned to me and said: "Old man, did I ever tell you some of the strange accidents that insurance men run up against?"

I told him that he *had*, and tried to change the subject. But he was in a mood to be entertaining, whether he entertained or not, so I drew his chair up to the fire (hoping he would fall in) and he began: "You would hardly believe some of the unusual accidents which an insurance company is called upon to settle for," he said jogging me slightly to awaken me, for I had traveled all day on horseback and was dog-tired.

"Whazzat?" I asked, starting up.

"I say you would hardly believe some of the unusual accidents that an insurance company is called upon to settle for," he repeated. "But, whether you will hardly believe them or not, I have a good mind to tell you. It will do you no harm to know how the other half lives."

"Did it ever occur to you that I *am* the other half?" I countered, falling asleep.

He ignored my sally. (By the way, I wonder what's become of Sally.) "I remember once being called out in the dead of night to go and investigate a case where a client claimed to have thrown his collar bone out by trying to pull a Pullman blanket up around his shoulders during a cold night on the ride from Bagdad, California, to Los Angeles. He was—"

"But I thought that it was never cold in California," I said in my inimitable way.

"That is why we were suspicious. Our Callifornia man said that this would be impossible unless the man had caught cold somewhere in the East and brought it with him to California. 'An ordinary chill, incident to an attack of grippe contracted in the East' was the way his report read. But the fact remained that the man *had* thrown his shoulder out and was in a hospital.

"So I hopped aboard a west-bound covered wagon, and, after various exciting adventures with the Indians in the Santa Fe station of Albuquerque (from which I emerged with a dozen bows and arrows and three Indian blankets at the unbelievable price of $150), I arrived at the hospital where our man was presenting his claim."

"And did the queen's archers win the tournament, daddy?" I asked, awakening from my doze.

"There was yet another case," he continued, "which involved the claim of a man who was run over by a glacier. He was a botanist, traveling in Switzerland, and had found a very rare species of edelweiss growing in a cranny near the Mer de Glace. It was impossible to pull it up by the roots, so he lay down on his stomach, with his back to the glacier, to examine its structure. As he lay there he got to daydreaming of what would have happened if he had married that girl and stayed in Utica when he was young, and from there got to reminiscing about the different sorts of candy he used to buy when a kid, the licorice sticks, hore-hound, wine cups, and all the rest, and, although his ribs got a little lame from lying on them, he got so wrapped up in his reveries that he didn't notice the glacier creeping up on him. He felt something crowding him slightly, but thought nothing of it at the time, attributing it to nervousness on his part. It was in this way that the river of ice finally ran over him and jammed one hip quite badly, to say nothing of giving him chilblains and quite a fright."

"I should think that an affair like that would come under the head of occupational disease," I said, nodding my head sagely. "Wouldn't his employers be responsible?"

"He had no employers. He was a botanist in for himself," said my friend. (I call him my friend, although I would gladly have been rid of him.)

"I understood you to say that he was a man trying to pull his blanket up around his shoulders on a Pullman," I said, in some (but not much) surprise.

"That, my friend, is another story which I will tell you sometime. Right now I want to cap the climax of my last yarn with the rather comical one about a certain Elwood M. Rovish, age 42, who asked reimbursement for damages suffered from ostrich-bane."

"Ostrich-bane?" I could hardly keep myself from asking— but I did.

"Mr. Rovish had been attending a class dinner and had started home about four A.M. on a steam roller which happened to be standing for the night in a near-by roadway. At nine o'clock the next morning he was awakened by a ring at his doorbell, and, on opening the door, he was confronted by a man who said:

" 'Here is your ostrich.'

"Mr. Rovish said, as nicely as he could for the aspirin which was in his mouth, that he thought there must be some mistake, as he owned no ostrich, being a bachelor and living alone in a two-room apartment.

" 'Oh yes you do own an ostrich,' replied the man. 'You bought him last night.'

"Well, to turn an anecdote into a long story, it transpired that Mr. Rovish on his way home had alighted from his steam roller at an ostrich farm, climbed over the fence, and mounted one of the fancier animals for a brisk ride about the place. The bird had put up quite a fight, with the result that the bird had been quite badly damaged as to plumage and pride. The owner had rushed out and insisted that, since Mr. Rovish seemed so fond of the ostrich, it would be well if he paid for it, and a sale was effected then and there, with the man agreeing to deliver the animal at Mr. Rovish's the next day. And here he was."

"I am fascinated," I said.

"As the man would, under no conditions, take the damaged bird back, Mr. Rovish was obliged to take it up into his two-room apartment, where, in the course of a week or so, it ate most of his shirts out of his bureau drawer and in general distressed his new owner and made it impossible for him to sleep. He then applied to his local agent for reimbursement on the grounds of 'ostrich-bane,' against which, unfortunately for us, he had been foresighted enough to insure himself. But I thought that it was a rather amusing story, and that you would be glad to hear it."

"*You* thought," I said. "Well, it wasn't. But before you go (and you *are* going, aren't you, old chap?) there is one thing I would like to insure myself against."

"And what is that?" said the agent, all smiles and policy forms.

"Against insurance agents!" I fairly screamed. "And against just such losses of time as I have just suffered."

And I'll be darned if he didn't write me out the policy.

The Pincus Wall Paintings

THAT human nature has, unfortunately, not changed very much in the last four thousand years is shown by the recently discovered wall drawings in the ruins at Pincus on the little island of Maxl, near Greece. They are just as lousy drawings as a great many people make today.

The island of Maxl, and its promontory Pincus, was, as so few of my readers know, the scene of the ancient mythological battle between Kybos and the Mixthos. The Mixthos, as even fewer of you know, was that unpleasant animal of Greek mythology which had ears but no head, which gave it an aimless appearance but helped it greatly in its rather devilish work of bumping into things. (It is from this vicious bumping into things on the part of the Mixthos that we get our verb "to mixthos" or to bump into things.)

If it had not been for the fact that it had no head, the Mixthos would have been half man, half beaver. With no head, however, it couldn't really be half much of anything. This made it very self-conscious.

According to the legend, which I am now telling you, Kybos, who was a youth living in Pincus, determined that the Mixthos must go. How he rented a small boat and went out to the rock on which the animal lived, and how he finally, after eight years of splashing about in the water, killed the

268

That the girls of Pincus behaved very much like the girls of today is seen in the fresco.

monster and freed Pincus, is a story which I have little energy and no interest to recount for you. Which is doubtless all right with you, too.

If you will take your map of Greece and turn up the lower left-hand corner so that it touches the upper right-hand corner, and then will tear the whole thing into small bits, you will see where the ancient site of Pincus was. The ancient site was later changed (because, as one of the local wags said, "It was *such* a site!") and is now located at a point more inland and away from the trolley line. It is here that the excavations have been going on under the direction of Dr. Lorp of the

British Eden Musée, and it was here that the wall drawings were discovered, much to everyone's disappointment.

The drawings were made on the walls of a house which seems to have been more of a small cart or express wagon. On account of its small size, several members of the expedition expressed doubt that it really was a house, holding the view that a house should be large enough to allow a full-sized man at least to wedge his hip into it.

"I think that we are making a mistake in calling this thing a house," writes Prof. Enoch to his wife in England, "and many of us are threatening to return home if Dr. Lorp does not give up his madcap idea that it is. How did it come out about the insurance on the sofa? I wrote to the Indemnity and Assurance pople and told them—" But I guess that we are getting into the dull part of Prof. Enoch's letter to his wife.

All that we are interested in are the wall drawings—and we are not so gosh-darned interested in those.

Since, however, the head of the expedition persists in calling the find a "house," we are justified in calling the boards which inclose it "walls" and the drawings on those boards "wall drawings." If we begin to question and doubt now, at this late date, we shall have nothing to work on at all. The Pincus Wall Paintings is the subject of our paper, and the Pincus Wall Paintings it is going to be.

The drawings themselves were evidently made with an old chocolate lozenge by one of the smaller and less deft of the children who frequented the neighborhood. The lozenge was probably well wet in the mouth of the artist, and then seized between the thumb and other thumb and worked up and down and forward and back until the drawing was completed. Some sort of fixative, such as a corn muffin, was then spread over the whole thing, and it was allowed to stand for weeks before being looked at. A great many times people forgot to look at it at all.

The fresco on one side of the wall shows one of the old Pincusian games in which only the young men and the girls over fifty took part. It evidently had to do with an ox, and, from the fresco drawing, consisted of dancing round the ox until the creature became so mortified and fidgety that he got to crying. As soon as the ox started to cry the boys and girls threw rather heavy flower bulbs at him, and the game broke up in a riot of color with several people getting sick.

That the girls of Pincus behaved very much like the girls of today is seen in the fresco showing the girls of Pincus behaving very much like the girls of today. Here we see that they too had their hair-pullings and face-liftings, for the young ladies depicted on these ancient walls seem to be just about as miserable as their sisters of the twentieth century. The only difference was that in Pincus they wore their lipsticks,

HERBERT F. ROESE

Kybos, a youth living in Pincus, determined that the Mixthos must go.

powder puffs, and bath sponges on a chain around their necks instead of carrying them and spilling them from a so-called "compact" every eight minutes.

In the drawing in question the artist has shown us several of the young bloods of the day standing on the corner, by what corresponded to the Pincus Pharmacy and Fountain Lunch, giving the *keemos* (or "one time over") to the girls as they pass by on their way to nowhere in particular unless they get a break.

Unfortunately, the entire right end of this picture has been broken off by the four thousand years of thumbing it has had, and so we are unable to see the next corner and find out exactly what happend. Even if the missing piece were right in the next room, I doubt if I, for one, would get up to go in and see it.

Close to these wall frescoes, in the same hole, the excavators found a rare old bit of Pincusian belt buckle—or perhaps it is just an amalgam filling for an old Pincusian tooth. At any rate, it shows the skill of the ancient workmen in fashioning things out of metal for which there could be no possible use. Brides of today think they have a tough time trying to figure out what some of their wedding presents are for, but a glance over a collection of *objets d'art* unearthed in these old Greek towns makes one wonder how the brides of those days ever set up housekeeping at all. Maybe that is why so many of these strange little articles are found buried in the ground. The groom probably took them all out the week after the wedding and slyly dropped them in a hole in the garden.

What About Business?

I HAVE been asked (by a couple of small boys and a wire-haired fox terrier) to summarize briefly my views on the Business and Financial Outlook for 1931. I would have done this long ago, together with the other financial and business experts, but I wanted first to wait and see if there really was going to *be* a 1931 or not.

Just because a year has started off with a January and February is no sign that it is going to continue on indefinitely through the rest of the months.

But, as it looks now, we are in for a year which will be known as 1931. Just what else it will be known as remains to be seen, but I have got a good name all worked up for it if it turns out to be like 1930. However, I am not here to talk dirty. I am here to outline the economic forces and currents which have contributed to the present business and financial situation and to predict their course during the year which is now well on its way. In doing this I will stick pretty closely to the formula followed by the 2,300,000 experts who have already preceded me in this prognostication. I haven't read them all, but I got a fairly close idea of what they were driving at.

As I understand it (which is just about *that* much—or perhaps even *that* much), there are several causes which are responsible for the depression of 1930 and which I will list in the order of their legibility on my note pad:

Overproduction, a breakdown in artificial control over commodity prices, maladjustments in gold distribution, overproduction, deflation, subnormal thyroid secretion (or Platt's Disease"), too much vermouth, deflation, excess of charts with black lines, excess of charts with red lines, and overproduction. Let us make these up, one by one, and then drop dead.

First, overproduction. In 1925 (which brings us down to 1927) we exported this commodity to the extent of twenty-four billion bushels, obviously too much. In 1929 this had been increased by sixty-eight bushels, or one bushel for each of the sixty-eight states in the Union. This increase, together with a simultaneous *decrease* in deflation, or consumer resistance, brought about a situation in which the world's markets found themselves faced with what amounted to, in round numbers, a pretty pickle.

Thus we see that this shortsighted policy of increasing production and, at the same time, *de*creasing inflation (or Platt's Disease) brought on a crisis in distribution (or deflation) which naturally led to speculation in "shorts" (lobsters under six inches in length which are supposed, according to the Law, to be thrown back when caught. "Shorts," however, have much sweeter meat than the larger lobsters and it is often a great temptation to cheat just a teeny-weeny bit and take them home. They are delicious when served with melted butter).

The fall in silver which accompanied this ridiculous state of affairs naturally cut the purchasing power of the Far East, except in those countries where lozenges are used as legal tender. And with the purchasing power of the Far East diminished, and the importation of old rugs and punk from the Far East increasing, it is little wonder that people got so that they didn't know whether they were coming or going. Often they were doing both.

I am afraid that I can't be of much help to this discussion in the matter of gold and silver supply. I never quite caught on to what the hell it was all about.

We hear that there is a shortage of gold or an oversupply

of gold; that France has all the gold or that the United States has all the gold. What gold? I don't mean to insinuate anything, but how did France *get* all this gold if she shouldn't have it? Where did she get it from? And what does she do with it when she gets it? And who cares, so long as there are plenty of good, crisp bank notes in circulation?

Give me a bank note any time. Then you aren't so likely to give it away under the impression that it is a lucky penny. I once gave a neighbor's little boy a lucky penny which was so lucky that he got five dollars for it at the bank. The whole system is rotten to the core.

But to return to our business forecast. (If you don't want to return, there are books and magazines on the table in the anteroom, and we will be right out in a few minutes.) I look for the following changes in our economic system which should radically alter conditions for the better:

(1) There will be, if I have anything to say about it, a remedy for overproduction in the marked decrease in the manufacture of greeting cards, shirts that go on over the head, auto busses, gin-and-orange-juice cocktails, war books, washroom boys, seed rolls, tops to toothpaste tubes, art furniture, automatic elevators, paper matches. (I am rather sorry now that I began this list. There are so many things, and they are so difficult to remember.)

(2) In 1931 I look for a decided betterment in the relation of bond to stock yields. That is, of stock to bond yields. The ratio, as near as I can make it out without my glasses, is 4.7% as compared to 5.76%. (These figures are as of July, 1930, and what a hot month *that* was! I was at the seashore, and never got out of my bathing suit once, except to go in bathing.) Now this ratio, together with the increase in deflation and the *de*crease in *in*flation which must inevitably come about with the unfortunate and unpleasant distribution of gold which exists at the present moment (mentioning no names, but it begins with "F" and is a country noted for its dancing and light wines), will tend to break down the artificial control of commodity prices and possibly restore public confidence to a point where people will dare to go out into the street and perhaps walk one block under police escort.

It is often a great temptation to cheat just a teeny-weeny bit and take them home.

PETER ARNO

(3) Money will be less scarce. By this I do not mean that you and I will have *more* money, or that it will be any less scarce when you look inside your wallet when the dinner check comes. There seems to be another kind of money that the bank handles. It is "plentiful," or it is "scarce," or it is "cheap," or it is "high."

Personally, I have never been able to get hold of any cheap money. If I want five dollars, it always costs me five dollars to get it, or, at any rate, a check for five dollars made out to "Cash" (which may, or may not, be the same thing). I never could figure out whether "cheap" money meant that a five-dollar bill cost only four dollars and sixty cents to buy, or that it was in bad condition, with torn edges and little strings hanging from it so that it *looked* cheap. At any rate, whatever "cheap" money means to bankers, five dollars is always five dollars to me. And a hundred dollars is a godsend.

However, in a forecast of this sort, one must always say that money will be less scarce—so here goes: Money will be less scarce.

(4) Now about wheat. Wheat seems to have a lot to do with world conditions, although with so many people trying to reduce weight, I should think that it would be less important now than it was in 1900. Here again, like the money the banks use, the wheat referred to in the quotations must be another kind of wheat than that which goes into those delicious hot rolls we have at home. (Did you ever try dunking hot rolls in maple sirup? When you get down to the crisp brown part it just doesn't seem as if you could bear it.) The wheat we hear about in the financial quotations never comes in bundles of less than a million bushels, which, frankly, sounds a little unappetizing. When you get up into figures like that with just plain wheat, you run the risk of just sounding silly.

In fact, I am not sure that the whole financial and business structure on which our system is founded is not silly, with its billions of bushels and billions of gold bars and nothing to show for it.

I am working on a plan now whereby we scrap the whole thing and begin all over again, with a checking account for ten thousand dollars in my name in some good bank. With a head start like that I ought to be able to get my own affairs cleaned up, and with my own affairs cleaned up I am sure that world affairs would look a lot rosier.

Indian Fakirs
• Exposed •

INDIA! What mysteries does the very mention of its name not bring to mind? (Answer: Mysteries of the Deep, Mysteries of the Arctic Wastes, the Lizzie Borden Mystery, and Sweet Mystery of Life.)

Chief among the mysteries of India reported by returning travelers, aside from that of how the natives keep those little loin cloths up, is the so-called "rope trick," so called because it is a trick done with a rope. The rope trick is so famous the world over that it would be just a waste of time to report its details here. Follows a complete report of its details:

The fakir takes a coil of rope from the ground, swings it above his head, and throws one end of it into the air. His assistant then climbs upon his shoulders, seizes the rope, and proceeds to climb up it until he disappears into the sky. On a clear day the trick cannot be done; neither is it very successful if the assistant gets sick at great heights. In the meantime, the audience has been sitting around in a circle about the fakir, murmuring, "Oh!" and "Ah!" with several wise ones muttering, "Mirrors."

On the face of it, this is a pretty good trick; at least it sounds better than the one that I do by pulling a card off the bottom of the pack when someone says, "Stop!" But, in reality, the rope trick is nothing but a hoax. Let me explain how it is done.

Previous to beginning the trick, the fakir has asked his audience to inhale and exhale deeply, occasionally stopping breathing entirely for a space of perhaps ten or fifteen minutes. Now, it is a well known physiological fact that an excess of oxygen in the blood removes the carbon dioxide and makes possible temporary hallucinations. It is in such chemical states that a man gives a head waiter five dollars or asks a woman to marry him.

If he can be made to do these things, it ought to be a cinch to make him think he sees a rope go up in the air. The effect is something the same as that of eight old-fashioned rye cocktails, and is about six dollars less expensive. As with the cocktails, there is always the chance that you will topple over behind the bookcase and be a subject for the emergency wrecking crew. But you are still six dollars to the good and haven't had to bother with all those pieces of orange and sugar.

When his audience is in the proper state of oxygen poisoning, so that their eyes are nicely crossed and they are starting to hum "I'se Been Working on the Railroad" in harmony, the fakir throws his rope up. In the meantime, a large cloud of smoke has been sent up from a near-by bonfire which the patients have not noticed (the World's Fair could be on fire and they wouldn't notice it) and from the roof of a house in the background, also unnoticed, an accomplice has thrown a lasso to catch the top of the fakir's rope. It thus is easy for the assistant to climb up from the fakir's shoulders and disappear into the cloud of smoke on to the roof, where he receives his fifty cents.

(I say that it is easy. I really don't see how it is done, even now that I have explained it to you. Furthermore, I don't see why, if the fakir has got his audience into this state of autointoxication, it is necessary to use a rope at all. Why doesn't he just say, "O-o-o-o, see the big rope!" and then go home, leaving his spectators to fight it out among themselves as they sober up? Oh, well, it's none of my business. All I am supposed to do is to explain how it is done.)

Another favorite trick of the Indian fakirs is to charm snakes by playing on some reed instrument until the snake sways in time to the music. In order to do this trick it is first

HERBERT F. ROESE

His assistant then climbs upon his shoulders, seizes the rope, and proceeds to climb up it.

necessary to overcome any aversion you may have to snakes.

It would never do for a snake charmer to run screaming whenever a snake was brought anywhere near him. This qualification lets out quite a number of people from the profession. However, like the lady in the story (The story: A lady and here husband, married some twenty-five years, were attending a snake-charming performance in a side show. The snake charmer on the platform offered fifty dollars to anyone in the audience who would come up and perform tricks with the prize cobra of the collection. Much to the husband's terror, his wife volunteered, went up on the platform, and proceeded to win the money by making the huge reptile look silly. When she came back to her seat, he asked her, with some asperity, why, in the twenty-five years of their married life, she had never told him that she was a snake charmer. To which quite natural question the wife replied, equally quite naturally, "You never asked me.")—like the lady in the story, there may be some among us who have the gift and have not not been using it, chiefly because we have not known any good tricks. Here is one:

The cobra is placed in front of the charmer in a sitting position and is confronted with a reed which makes a rather dismal sort of music. The chances are very good that the snake will become so depressed by the wailing that it will refuse to go on with the trick unless the music stops. In this case, you will have got credit for taking the heart out of the reptile, at any rate. In the event that it stays put and shows any interest at all, you must keep swaying back and forth in time to the music as you play. The snake, who has it in mind to strike out at you eventually, will sway back and forth with you, in order to keep in good striking range. This will look as if the snake were keeping time to the music, when all the while it will be *you* who are keeping time and the snake who is following you.

Just how the trick ends, I have never found out. I guess you just keep on playing and swaying.

The "mango-tree miracle" is another which has mystified travelers for many years. This consists of planting a mango seed in full view of the audience and in a few minutes growing a full sized mango tree.

There is a cloth placed over the spot on the ground from which the mango tree is supposed to grow, and the magician keeps patting the ground around the cloth, with some idea of helping nature along with massage.

If the magician reaches in under the cloth with every pat, carrying some large object concealed in a paper bag, you may suspect that he is putting in a mango plant under your very eyes and that it is really not growing out of the ground at all. If he doesn't touch the cloth at all, but just stands back and lets you watch the tree grow, inch by inch, under the covering, then I don't know *what* you are going to think.

I am sure that I can't help you.

There are other stunts performed by Indian fakirs which

are not exactly tricks, because they are right there before your eyes when you meet the fakir. For example, there is one man who has had his arm tied up straight in the air for so many years that it is all shrunken and rigid and practically of no use as an arm. The nails are very long and he doesn't seem to care.

This is apparently on the level, because no one is going to do a trick which takes five or ten years each time to finish.

In concluding this little summary of Indian mysteries, let me say that *I* have never been to India, or talked with anyone who has ever seen the tricks done, and that I don't believe that any of them ever *are* done.

HERBERT F. ROESE

She went up on the platform and proceeded to win the money by making the huge reptile look silly.

Bunk Banquets

A GROUP of bankers and national leaders got together the other night and started a Big Movement for Economy All Down the Line. It was pretty impressive. They said that the first problem before the country today [applause] was the elimination of waste—waste in expenditures, waste in time, and waste in the hearts of his countrymen. [No laughter, but some slight applause from the speaker's two cousins.]

And how did these prophets of Economy crying out in the wilderness elect to assemble this momentous conclave? What agency did they pick to get their views before the public? A banquet. A banquet, which is, in itself, the great symbol of American waste today.

There are certain banquets which it is probably hopeless to try to forestall. Trade conventions, associated college clubs, visiting conventions, all more or less demand a culminating celebration of some sort, and a banquet is the only thing that our national imagination seems capable of devising. But there are banquets which have not even the justification of *cameraderie* or the brotherhood of selling the same line of goods. These mysterious festivals are usually the result of an enterprise about as spontaneous as the building of the East River Bridge. They are cold-blooded frame-ups, and are, in the language of the after-dinner encomium tosser, "the result of

283

the vision and foresight and business sagacity of one man."

This one man is usually someone who has tried several dozen other jobs since the war, each with a certain amount of financial success but each of such a nature as to allow of a more or less temporary employment. This one man then, being nothing if not astute, realizes the fondness of the American public for cheering and the even greater fondness of American public men for being cheered. So he makes himself up a title, such as "The American Academy of Natural and Applied Arts," buys himself a new dress suit, has letterheads printed, and opens up an office in Room 1175, Hucksters' Bank Building.

The next step is the location of a client. He has practically the entire volume of *Who's Who* to choose from, for there is at least one man on every page who is just crazy to have a banquet given for him. So, running his finger at random down the first page he opens to, he lights on the name of "Thomas Merkin Wilney, Author," or "Norman L. Heglit, Theatrical Producer." Let us say that, the weather being what it is, Mr. Norman L. Heglit seems to be the best bet.

The next day Mr. Heglit is approached. How would he like to have a big testimonial dinner given by "The American Academy of Natural and Applied Arts"? Without ever having heard of "The American Academy of Natural and Applied Arts" before, Mr. Heglit says, "Fine." Our *entrepreneur* thinks that he can fix it, if Mr. Heglit will pay for the printing. Out of the printing appropriation will come the cost of the banquet hall, lighting, dinner, service, bunting, and a slight commission for the *entrepreneur* for all his trouble. Mr. Heglit does a little calculating on the back of an envelope and decides that it would be worth it.

So "The American Academy of Natural and Applied Arts" goes back to his office in Room 1175 Hucksters' Bank Building and dictates the following letter to a list of prominent men and women throughout the land:

DEAR ———
As you probably know know, the American Academy of Natural and Applied Arts is giving, on the evening

of November the sixth, a testimonial dinner to Norman L. Heglit, the eminent theatrical producer, in recognition of his twenty-five years of distinguished service in behalf of American theater. We would esteem it a great favor if you lend your name to the honorary committee in charge of this event. This will involve the expenditure of no time on your part. Etc.

H. G. WAMSLEY,
For the Committee.

    The distinguished ladies and gentlemen who receive this letter have never heard of the "American Academy of Natural and Applied Arts" or of H. G. Wamsley, but they have heard of Norman L. Heglit, and the name of the society sounds all right and what's the worst that can happen to them? They do not even have to go to the dinner. So enough of them accept the honor to make quite a respectable-looking letterhead.

    On this letterhead Mr. Wamsley writes a selected list of prominent speakers, actors, producers and wits, and signing

ROY ROHN

Conventions, college clubs, visiting dignitaries, all demand a culminating celebration, and a banquet is the only thing that our national imagination seems capable of devising.

it again, "For the Committee," asks them to dinner as the committee's guests, and will they just say a few words?

Here again the speakers are rather in the dark, but the names of the committee are impressive, and they have heard of Mr. Heglit and they all like to get up at a banquet table and "say a few words"; so a goodly number of them fall, and the layout is complete.

All that remains is for Mr. Wamsley to send out the invitations heavy again with the names of the honorary committee and startling with its promised array of notable speakers, all of which is placed at the disposal of the lucky invitee at five dollars a throw.

And then the miracle happens. Hundreds of otherwise sensible citizens, flattered at receiving an invitation from so distinguished a committee and nervously eager to hear the prominent speech-makers in this line-up, make out a check for five dollars and send it to Mr. Wamsley, treasurer of the American Academy of Natural and Applied Arts. And, on the night of November sixth, they leave comfortable homes and assemble in droves to listen to five or six representatives of the liberal arts lose all track of the time.

The net result is that Mr. H. G. ("American Academy of Natural and Applied Arts") Wamsley makes out a fat deposit slip downstairs in the Hucksters' Bank, Mr. Norman L. Heglit is richer by a large amount of publicity and "good will," and each of the suckers is out a cool five checker-berries.

In the same class of nonfraternal get-togethers are the banquets arranged by the various leagues of one kind or another. On these occasions the thrill comes in sitting at a table with one person whom you knew in school and trying to pick out the celebrities who are advertised as being present.

"I think that's Rupert Hughes," you whisper to your neighber, and in return for this information he tells you that he thinks that woman in the black dress is Kathleen Norris. It transpires later that the two are George M. Wass, press agent for Forget-Me-Not Films, Inc., and Miss Ida Rolly, press agent for the hotel, respectively.

You cannot blame Mr. H. G. Wamsley for organizing banquets any more than you can blame James J. Hill for organizing that great big railroad that he organized, but all over the country there are people getting up dinners who don't even get a dime out of it. And they certainly can't get any fun out of it. And if they don't get any fun out of it, who does?

The whole thing is very confusing.

Laughter and Applause

WHEN radio came into general use (I can remember the first electric light, too—or, rather, the first electric light we ever had in our house. It had probably been done somewhere else before), it looked for a while as if broadcasting was going to put a stop to the old-fashioned scarf dance which public speakers had been indulging in under the head of public speaking. When a speaker could face his audience and flash those fiery black eyes or shake those wavy locks and get the business-like sex appeal into play, it didn't make much difference what his speech consisted of. He could be saying "Hill-dill-come-over-the-hill-or-else-I'll-catch-you-standing-still" and his audience wouldn't know the difference. A great many elections were won in this manner.

It certainly seemed that radio would put a stop to all this. When a man gets up in front of a microphone it doesn't make any difference whether he has got great, big, brown eyes or no eyes at all. Unless he cares what the musicians think, he doesn't even have to shave. But his talk has got to be worth listening to or there is going to be a general turning of dials all over the civilized world, leaving him hanging in the middle of a four-syllable word. Or, at least, that is what we all hoped would be the result. I am not so sure now.

A while ago I listened in on a speech being made in London by George Bernard Shaw, who is a clever guy, too. He was

288

introducing Professor Einstein at some banquet or some-thing—possibly a handout for the unemployed. I couldn't hear what Professor Einstein said, because just at that time the nest of field mice which live in my radio set began gnawing their way out, getting a couple of beavers to help them. But I did hear Mr. Shaw, and I heard the effect he was having on his audience. There is an old superstition that the English are slow at getting a joke, but I want to tell you that the Englishmen at that banquet were in a laughing mood which bordered on nervous hysteria. They were laughing at com-mas. All Mr. Shaw had to do was to say, "And, furthermore —" and the house came down. Of all the push-over audiences I have ever heard, they had the least gag resistance.

What they would have done if they had heard a *real* gag is rather terrifying to think about. Blood vessels would have been bursting like toy balloons and the salvage of collar but-tons and dress ties which would have flown to the floor might easily have filled twelve baskets.

I thought at first that something (more than usual) was wrong with my radio, and that I wasn't getting the last few words of the witty sallies which were being received with such a din. But the next day the papers carried the Shaw speech verbatim, and I found to my horror that I had heard every word. Here is a sample of what set London by the ears that night, with my own italics to indicate its effect on the listeners:

MR. SHAW: "Ladies and gentlemen *(laughter)*: When my friend Mr. Wells asked me to take this duty, I could not help wondering whether he realized the honor he was conferring upon me *(prolonged laughter)*, and whether I was able to dis-charge it adequately. *(Three minutes of hysteria.)* I felt I could only do my best. *(Crashing applause.)* Here in London we are still a great factor, but no doubt presently that will be trans-ferred to the United States. *(The first real gag, throwing the place into pandemonium.)* . . . We have a string of great fin-anciers, great diplomats, and even occasionally an author *(intermission while half a dozen listeners with weak hearts are carried out)*, and we make pictures as we talk." *(Complete collapse of roof, as the diners beat each other in a frenzy.)*

I did hear Mr. Shaw, and I heard the effect he was having on his audience. They were laughing at commas.

This, then, was the opening of Mr. Shaw's speech, and I had, with my own ears, heard what it was doing to the hand-picked audience in front of him. There were two possible explanations: first, that it was over my head; and, second, that the entire London group had been up in Room 211 before the banquet commenced and were cockeyed drunk.

I like a laugh as well as anyone, and I am accustomed to laugh loudly at Mr. Shaw's plays, occasionally because I am amused, but more often because by laughing at Mr. Shaw's plays one lets the rest of the audience know that one is on the inside and gets the subtler meanings. But as I listened to the speech of the great man on this occasion, I felt that what few giggles I might be able to throw out would be so inadequate in the face of what was going on in London that I had much better just listen quietly and mind my own business.

Now this sound effect of an audience in a fever heat of enthusiasm is what is going to save radio speakers. And it has given rise to an entirely new trade, the professional Applause-Donor or Audience-Sitter. They sit in the radio studio—at so much a sit—and on signal from a director, laugh, sob, or beat their hands together. If a really good effect is desired they can be induced to ring cowbells and twirl policemen's rattles. It is barely possible that Mr. Shaw had a couple of hundred of these at work for him.

I once made a speech over the radio (there must have been a ship sinking at sea that night, for I never could find anyone who heard it) and, when I entered the studio, I was surprised to see about fifteen people of assorted ages and get-ups sitting very grimly over against the wall. I thought at first that they constituted some choir or team of Swiss bell ringers who were going to follow me on the program, but the announcer told me that they were my audience and that, whenever he gave the signal, they would burst into laughter and applause so that my larger audience in radioland would think that they were listening in on a wow. All that this did was to make me nervous. Furthermore, I could feel that my professional laughers had taken an immediate and instinctive dislike to me.

I began my speech, after a few salvos of applause from the benches, and for the first couple of times, on signal from the overseer, got a pretty fair assortment of laughs. But as the gags kept getting thinner and thinner I detected a feeling of mutiny stirring through the ranks of my professional audience, and the director had harder and harder work to get anything resembling a genuine-sounding laugh out of his crew.

He was furious, but, owing to the necessity for silence, was unable to bawl them out or even say, "Come on now, louder!" At last the revolt broke and, just as he had given the signal for a round of laughter and applause, three of the workers got up and tiptoed from the room, automatically resigning from their jobs as they went. Even my paid audience was walking out on me. They were followed by a half a dozen others, who evidently felt that, money or no money, there was such a thing as personal pride, even in their profession. By the time I had finished there was only one of the claque left, and she was asleep.

The announcer told me, when we got outside, that such a thing had never happened before, and that the company would start a suit against the mutineers the next day, as they were all under contract. He added that it might be better if I left the building by the back entrance, where he would have a cab waiting for me to duck into. I promised that the next time I made a radio speech I would bring my own applause-donors, relatives of mine, if possible, but he said that we would discuss that when the time came.

So whenever you hear a speech over the air which seems to be knocking the audience cold, you needn't feel that it is your fault if you don't like it yourself. Just picture a row of disgruntled workers sitting against the wall of the studio, muttering under their breaths.

It doesn't seem possible that Mr. Shaw could have hired so many "supers" as there seemed to have been at this London dinner, but the unemployment situation in London is much worse that it is here and you can probably get people to do anything for money. I'd like to get about a dozen of them over here for my next radio appearance. I'd be a riot.

First—Catch Your Criminal

WITH the increase in crime during the last decade has come a corresponding increase in crime prevention. Or perhaps it is vice versa. At any rate, we are awfully busy down at our laboratory trying to find out who is a criminal and who isn't. (You can imagine the surprise of the head of our Research Department the other day when he reacted to one of his own tests, thereby proving himself to be a "lingoidphrensic" type, or man-eating shark. He immediately resigned his portfolio and gave himself up to the authorities; but as he is seventy-one years old, they didn't want him.)

Our theory of crime prevention has a strictly psychological basis, but we will listen to anything. It is our idea to take the criminal *before* he becomes a criminal and to chivvy him about the laboratory until he is too tired and disgusted to commit the crime. A great many times we have converted potential criminals into hermits and deep-sea divers by making them want to get away from it all and just be alone. The man who runs the lighthouse at Salt Mackerel, Maine, is one of our graduates. He won't even let people bring him newspapers.

This man is a rather interesting case of a reformed "rhombusmanic," or "inverted nail-biter" type; that is, instead of wanting to bite his own nails he wanted to bite other people's. Perhaps I should say that his *tendencies* were in that direction,

293

for we caught him before he had really started on anything that could be called a career in that field. Following was our course of experimentation: Mr. X, as we will call him (although his real name is Mr. Y), was a patient in the Nursing Home on City Island, having been brought there suffering from a three days' beard. He had been shaved, and was lying in his cot rubbing his chin with the tips of his fingers, when discovered by our Dr. Altschu, who was browsing about among the charity patients looking for types. Dr. Altschu immediately detected in Mr. X the indications of a rhombusmanic (low frontal elevation, pendent ear lobes, and absence of pupils in the eyes) and effected a transfer of the patient from the Nursing Home to the Crime Prevention laboratory. We gave a third baseman in exchange.

Once in the laboratory, Mr. X was put into a hot bath with a rubber walrus and told to get himself nice and clean. He was then dressed in a suit of blue denim and taken into the

HERBERT F. ROESE

Dr. Altschu detected in Mr. X the indications of a rhombusmanic and effected a transfer of the patient.

Chart Room, where he was seated in an easy-chair (or what he thought was an easy-chair) and told to watch the words that were thrown on the screen in front of him.

As a matter of fact, the chair was a special invention of Dr. Altschu's, with a delicate registering device concealed in the arms and an invisible wire stretching across the patient's neck, so that each fluctuation in his breathing and each quickening of his pulse was registered. Also the wire across the neck gradually choked him until he jumped up yelling: "Let's get the hell out of here!" At this point another registering device, which had in some unaccountable way become attached to his ankles to indicate ankle fluctuation, became suddenly rigid and threw him to the ground, where his weight and preference in flowers were taken simultaneously.

The room was then darkened and a series of jokes were flashed on the screen. It was the patient's reactions to these jokes, as indicated on a dial in the Control Room, which determined just which type of rhombusmanic he belonged to. (There are three types of rhombusmanic—the A type, or introvert; the B type, or extrovert; and the D type, or Old Man River. There used to be a C type, or Life on the Oregon Trail; but we had to drop it, as it began to edge over into the lower thermo-depressive type, which gets us into Juggling and Sleight of Hand.)

There was considerable confusion in the case of X, however, as he would not laugh at *any* of the jokes which were flashed on the screen. He just sat and asked when the news reel came on. We couldn't get him to react to the slightest degree, and the man in the Control Room kept popping his head out and saying: "O.K.! Start 'er up!" But X wouldn't start.

We tried the one about the man who had three daughters that he wanted to get married, the one about the Scotchman, the Irishman, and the Jew, and the one ending: "Lie down; do you want to make a fool out of the doctor?" But all that X would do was to keep asking about the news reel and saying: "I like Mickey Mouse." This in itself was significant, but we couldn't decide of what.

So we took Mr. X out of the Joke Registration Room and

put him in the Blank-Filling-Out Clinic. We set great store by our blanks, or questionnaires, especially the pink ones. If we can get a patient to fill out one of our pink questionnaires, answering every question without once dashing it to the floor and screaming, "Of all the damned nonsense!" we feel that we have done a lot toward the preservation of Society. So far we haven't been able to find one patient who could keep his temper long enough to answer every question on the sheet. This makes it difficult to keep our records straight.

Mr. X was no exception to the rule, even though we began him on the blue questionnaire. His aversion to the questions, however, took the form of frivolity and sneering, which is even harder to cope with than rage. For example, the first question on the blue form was: "You are *(a)* Mohammed, *(b)* Disraeli, *(c)* Mussolini, *(d)* yourself. Cross out the wrong ones." On this the only name that X would cross out was Mussolini's, because he said Mussolini was the only one who was wrong. To all the other questions he answered simply "Yes" or else drew a thumb-nail sketch of a sailboat and labeled it, "My vacation sport."

It was obvious that X was no ordinary rhombusmanic, but it was equally obvious that he ought not to be allowed at large with as many questionnaires as are being put out today. Here was a man who was evidently in a way to become either a menace to Society or else darned good company. We couldn't decide which, so we subjected him to further tests. By this time we had him in the Cutting and Binding Room.

Here he had little electric bulbs flashed before his eyes and was told to say the first word which popped into his mind at each flash. All he would say was "Ooops!" every time. He was told to shut his eyes and twirl around on his heel three times and then walk straight and place his finger on the center of a wall chart. He shut his eyes as we told him but kept on twirling round and round without stopping, maintaining that he liked it. When he was finally persuaded to stop, he walked forward and stuck his finger in Dr. Altschu's mouth, keeping on until Dr. Altschu gagged.

By the time the patient was beginning to get restless, and

Mr. X was put into a hot bath with a rubber walrus and told to get himself nice and clean.

we of the examining staff were frankly upset. So we came right out and asked him frankly if he didn't think that he might possibly be a criminal in the making, and he said that he was sure of it. In fact, he said it was only a question of minutes before he killed us all.

It was then that he asked us if we thought we could get

him a job as a lighthouse keeper where he wouldn't have to see anyone ever again, and the position at Salt Mackerel Rock was found for him.

It is along these lines that we are trying to build our system of crime prevention, on the theory that, if we can catch the criminal before he commits the crime, there will be no crime. What we need right now, however, are more experimental chairs and lots more colored bulbs.

When the State Plays Papa

I WILL string along with the radicals on most of their plans for betterment. But there is one item on their schedule which I cannot go for at all. I refer to the raising of children by the state. I don't think that the state quite realizes what it is letting itself in for.

Of course a great many mothers and fathers are unfit to raise children beyond the spitting-up stage, and probably most of the crime and maladjustments of today are due to parents having bought ten-year-old suits for fourteen-year-old boys. But even with the state functioning perfectly I can see nothing but confusion in its attempting to bring up children. I can see nothing but confusion in bringing up children anyway.

Let us suppose, just to drive ourselves crazy, that all children are taken from their parents at the age of two, which is about the age when modern educators begin making children express themselves, whether the children want to express themselves or not. ("Now, Henry Martin Manning, Junior—you go right upstairs and express yourself before you can sit down at the table!") The two-year-olds, on being packed off, bag and baggage, to the State Department of Nurseries and Child Culture, are registered and filed under "Worries." For, with the taking over the children, the state will have to give up worrying about budgets, deficits, or even counter-revolutions. The kiddies will take up practically all of its time.

In the matter of bathing, for instance. The chairman of the State Bath-Giving Commission will have to be a pretty husky guy who doesn't mind getting a little wet himself. He will not be able to keep his assistants very long unless this is to be a real dictatorship. Giving a three-year-old child a bath is a job that most governments would not want to take on. A peep into the first annual report of the State Bath-Giving Commission will disclose a paragraph like the following:

> Owing to our limited facilities and the difficulty of obtaining competent labor, the department has made a rather poor showing on the year. Baths were attempted on 14,395 children. Baths completed: 75. Injuries to state officials incurred by slipping and striking chin on edge of tub: 8,390. State officials drenched: 14,395. State officials drowned: 11.
>
> If this work is to be continued next year, completely new equipment will have to be bought, including elbow guards and knee pads for the employees, together with a larger and more efficient model face cloth. If the department's appropriation cannot be increased, it is the opinion of the chairman that the project should be abandoned. (As a matter of fact, the chairman is resigning anyway.)

Of course the whole thing will have to be divided up into subcommittees, and there will be work enough for one whole subcommittee in picking up toys and spoons thrown on the floor by children sitting on high chairs. Here is another committee I do not want to be on. *Some*body has got to pick them up, presumably the state. We shall probably get a condition where the official who is supposed to pick up thrown rattles will pass the buck to an underling, who will pass it on to somebody else, with the result that the rattle lies on the floor by the high chair and the child flies into a rage. This is not going to look very pretty for state conntrol, especially if a lot

PADEREWSKI

"We do not seem to be able to break Marian of the habit of sticking out her tongue at the officials."

of children fly into rages at once.

This attempt to raise children as a party pledge is going to make the party in power very vulnerable at each election. The anti-Communist candidate, speaking before a group of enraged parents on the street corner, can say:

"And, furthermore, voters of the Eighth Ward, what sort of children are our friends turning out? I will tell you. I had occasion the other day to invite one of the state's children into my house for supper, and I may say that I have never seen a ruder little brat in my whole life. I don't know what his guardians are thinking of to let him run wild the way he does. His knuckles were dirty, he didn't answer when spoken to, and, as I said to my wife, if he were a child of mine I would have taken him over my knee and given him a good hiding. If those women at the state nursery would play a little less bridge and pay more attention to their children—our children—we wouldn't have so many disrespectful little hoodlums growing up into unmangageable pests. This condition of things cannot go on a day longer!"

Perhaps it would be just as well to *let* the first Communist government take the kiddies over and then sit back and wait. Pretty soon the parents would find themselves being called to the telephone and asked: "What did you use to do to make Albert eat his peas?" Or, "We do not seem to be able to break Marian of the habit of sticking out her tongue at the officials and saying 'Nya-a-aya!' Did you ever have that trouble with her?"

As it is, state officials are none too efficient. They don't do very well by the roads, and they made quite a botch of prohibition enforcement. There would be slight chance for graft in raising of children; in fact, it would cost them a tidy sum in pennies for slot machines and odd dimes to fill up dime banks.

"Fall In!"

It may be because I do not run as fast, or as often, as I used to, but I seem to be way behind on my parades. It must be almost a year since I saw one, and then I was in it myself. I don't mean that I started out marching in it, but I got caught up in it and became confused and had to march several blocks before I could get out. It was horrible.

But in spite of the fact that I haven't been out watching them go by, I know that there have been parades, because I have heard the bands. Nothing makes a man feel older than to hear a band coming up the street and not to have the impulse to rush downstairs and out on to the sidewalk. I guess that this symptom of senility comes on after about twenty-five years of rushing downstairs and out on to the sidewalk only to find that it is the Reuben Lodge of the local Order of Reindeer marching by in brown sack suits and derby hats. After a while, this sort of disappointment makes a cynic of a person.

I think that not only was the last parade I ran after made up of men in brown sack suits and derby hats, but the *band* had on brown sack suits as well! That definitely crushed me, and now I wouldn't even take my head out of my hand (where it is most of the time) to look out the window at the finest band music that could pass my house. . . . Well, I might just *look*.

The American people, however, are still pretty unswerving in their allegiance to any organization which feels like walking up and down the street to music. And as for the police and city officials, they will go out of their way to help make it a gala occasion.

Our municipalities spend thousands of dollars and tear out great handfuls of hair trying to figure out some way of relieving traffic congestion. They arrest pedestrians who don't hold out their hands when making a left turn, and chase automobilists who go straight ahead when they should go around in a circle. They arrange red lights and green lights and orange-by-southeast and blue-by-southwest lights, with systems of bells which only a Swiss bell ringer can understand, and all in an attempt to straighten out the tangle in our streets which modern automotive civilization has brought down upon us.

And yet, let the National Association of Cyclone Underwriters petition for a permit to march up the main street of the city and throw traffic into a five-hour chaos, and not only do they get their permit but the police get out their riot machine guns and help them to spread confusion. There is a flaw somewhere.

In the old days parading was more simple. If the morning paper announced that the circus or the local cavalry troop was to start their parade at the Fair Grounds at 10 A.M., the entire route, all the way along Main Street, through Elm, up Center and down Walnut, would be cleared by 9:45, and the sidewalks lined with expectant throngs hours before the marshals had arrived at the starting point.

"It said in the paper that they would pass by the City Hall about ten-twenty," was the whisper which ran along the curbing. "That would bring them along here about ten-twenty-five." The smaller children would start crying shortly after ten-five, and the older ones would begin darting out into the street and tripping over their balloons by ten-fifteen. One would hardly have believed it possible for children to get so smeared with molasses and popcorn in fifteen minutes. In

PETER ARNO

The parade hadn't even started yet, owing to the man who carried the front end of the drum being unable to get up.

fact, one would hardly have believed it possible for there to have been so many children, and so unattractive.

"Listen, Norman, mamma'll take you right home this minute if you don't stand up here on the sidewalk. Come *here!*" But Norman, knowing that mamma wouldn't give up her place on the curbing for anything short of a cash bonus, was never impressed. And neither was Evelyn, Harold, Stanley, or Ralph, Junior. They knew that until that parade had gone by mamma was as good as planted right there, no matter what they did. So they did it.

Then, as the minutes dragged by and no parade appeared, the parents would join their children in little abortive excursions out into the middle of the street to look in the direction of the Fair Grounds. By this time all traffic had entirely disappeared from Main Street, which meant that Dakin's Fish Market was making its deliveries over another route and that it would be noon before McCann & Stodder got their groceries around.

Every now and again some of the older boys would yell: "Here they come!"—at which children would be yanked in from gutters and hats would topple off as their owners tried to crane their necks to see. But these false alarms soon ceased to have their effect, especially as someone who lived across the street from the Fair Grounds telephoned down that the parade hadn't even started yet, owing to one of the horses refusing to get up or the man who carried the front end of the drum being unable to get up. When this word had been passed around, everyone sat down on the curbing and waited, the comical ones pretending to go to sleep, the more serious-minded ones finishing what they had brought along to eat.

But no one went home. And no traffic passed through the restricted area. It was probably eleven or eleven-thirty before the band was finally heard in the distance and the excitement, for the eighth consecutive time, reached a fever heat. But it made no difference to anyone how long they waited. In those days, *nothing* made any difference to anyone. And civilization is supposed to progress!

Today a parade is no joke. Next to a big fire, there is probably nothing worse than a parade for jamming things up. There are still a lot of people who will wait on a curbing for hours to see one, but there are also a lot of people who *can't* wait on a curbing for hours. Today there are trains to be caught and dates to be kept, and a man who has to catch a train or keep a date never seems to enter into this parade spirit—not when he is held by the necktie and prevented from crossing the street by a large cop while phalanx after phalanx of strangers wearing red sashes and carrying bamboo canes shuffle past. To have one section of a city's populace lining the streets cheering and another section held in check by the police, fuming, is a state of affairs which tends to civic unrest.

Then there is the question of saluting the colors. In the old days, two flags were enough for one parade, and it was a pleasure, not unaccompanied by a thrill, to doff the hat. But today, when every chapter of an organization representing every state in the Union carries the national banner, the thing loses a little of its impressiveness. It is better just to keep your hat in your hand and perhaps genuflect a little at each passing flag.

Of course, if you are in an office and have work to do, there is an almost irresistible urge to rush to the window and hang out whenever a band is heard. I used to do that myself until I got an office over a radio store. For the first two months, every time I heard the martial strains of "Under the Double Eagle" coming from the street below, I would drop everything and tear to the window. It took me two months to discover that the band music came from the loud-speaker projecting from the store below.

It is too bad that the parade as an institution has lost its glamour. If I were police commissioner I would issue parade permits only to those organizations which wore brilliant red coats or could promise to ride camels. Then they would be worth watching. If they could be induced both to wear red coats and ride camels, I might be induced to march with them.

For, in spite of my aversion to parades in general, I have always had a sneaking feeling that I could cut rather a dashing figure in one myself.

Sporting Life in America:
Watching

· ————————————————— ·

IF there is one sport which we Americans go in for whole-heartedly it is the grand old outdoor exercise of "watching." By "watching" is not meant "kibitzing," for a kibitzer takes things more personally than does a watcher. A kibitzer gets very close to whatever he is watching, usually a game of cards. Sometimes he is almost in the cards. Sometimes he even gets hit.

The watcher, on the other hand, is more or less detached and does his observing from a distance, as, for instance, a railing surrounding a building excavation. He offers no advice, as the kibitzer does. He doesn't understand much about what is going on down in the excavation. His game is more gazing than really watching. After a certain period of time he seems to have crossed the border between human beings and plant life and become a form of fungus. This is our watcher.

The most common watching-fields are found around the above-mentioned cellar excavations. Just dig a hole in the ground big enough for a donkey engine to chug around in, surround it with a fence to keep people from dropping in, and you will in three minutes have a crowd of busy Americans (oh, the rush and bustle of this money-mad land!) settled along the railing, who will follow the project through to the bitter end. If the hole is big enough, and you set some com-

PETER ARNO

Excavation-watchers, as a class, are very conscientious sportsmen.

pressed-air drills to work, you will have half the population of the town fascinated to the point of stupor.

The rules of the game of watching, or unprofessional observation, are fairly simple. The watcher takes his position leaning against a wooden fence, resting the elbows on the top rail with the body inclined out into the sidewalk at an angle of perhaps twenty degrees. (There is an Australian game in which the players' bodies rest at a forty-degree angle, but in this game the player is supposed to sleep part of the time. There is no sleeping among American watchers, no siree!)

Once in position, the player fixes his eyes on some one object in the excavation below and follows it carefully. This object is known as the "quarry." It may be either a workman, a chunk of rock, or the revolving wheel of an engine. As it moves about, either under its own steam or by some outside force, the player keeps careful watch of it until it has stopped. This counts him ten. If he loses sight of it somewhere in its course, either because of defective vision or because it gets behind some intervening object, he loses ten. If he can find two or more quarries which he can watch all at once, he becomes a master-watcher and may wear a gold eyeball on his watch-chain. The game is over when one watcher has got a thousand points, but as it begins again immediately, the result is not noticeable to passers-by.

Excavation-watchers, as a class, are very conscientious sportsmen. You very seldom catch them watching anything else when they are on an excavation job. Fire engines may go by in the street behind their backs, old ladies may faint over their very heels, and even a man with a sidewalk stand of bouncing dolls may take up his position on the curb across the street, but the cellar-hole boys stick to their post without ever so much as batting an eyelash. In fact, the eyelash-batting average of some of the old-timers has gone as low as .005 in a busy season.

They are also not averse to night work. If the boss decides that the job requires coming back after supper and digging by the light of flares and torches, the watchers are on hand without a word of complaint and may even bring along a couple of friends as helpers. I myself have been caught up by the spirit of the game at night and, in amateur circles, am known as something of a speed demon at night-excavation-watching. My eyes are a little weak for daytime work, but when the flares are throwing their hellish light over the jagged walls of rock and the little men are darting about like demons in purgatory (it must be the mystic in me that is fascinated) I find it hard to pass by without giving at least fifteen or twenty minutes of my time to a general survey of the scene. One night I became so enthralled by the inferno-like spectacle that I allowed my top hat to fall into the abyss, where naturally it was lost and will probably turn up in a hundred years or so embedded in the wall of the foundations. This will cause no end of speculation among archæologists, for it had my initials in it and they will know that I never went in much for building, even in my heyday. "Jack-of-all-trades-and-master-of-none" will probably be the sobriquet under which I shall go down in history as a result of this little incident. And even then they won't quite understand what I was doing laying foundations in a silk hat.

Once the framework of the building is up and the wooden observation bridge removed, the game of watching becomes a little more difficult. The players may then move on to the next excavation or get jobs in offices across the street where they can carry on their watching from the windows. In several offices where I have worked I should say that at least two-thirds of the office force had been recruited from the ranks of old excavation-watchers who had come up from the wooden bridge to keep an eye on the job as it progressed. It had become almost a religious frenzy with them. Give them a desk by a window overlooking a new building across the way and put a sheet of figures in their hands to be checked up and copied by four o'clock, and long before that time they will have had six large steel girders in place and twenty red-hot bolts tossed through the air, to say nothing of having assisted at the raising and lowering of a temporary elevator at least forty times. If it is possible to place a water cooler by the window which commands the best view of the construction work, you will soon have everybody playing the game.

Of course, excavation- and construction-watching is not the only form this recreation takes. There are also drug-store windows. There is more variety in drug-store window-watching, but it attracts a slightly more superficial crowd than an excavation. Their hearts aren't in it, and they stop and pass by with perhaps only a ten- or fifteen-minute wait. This is probably because of the frivolous nature of the exhibits.

A train of cars made out of coughdrop boxes running round and round in a circle may be all right for a quarter of an hour's fun, but it isn't getting buildings built. A man may profitably spend a few hours a week watching a red ball disappear in a mound of peanuts, but the human brain demands a little more to work on.

Of course, if there happens to be a man in the window demonstrating a strap which holds the trousers up and keeps the shoes on at the same time, *then* it would be worth while to stick around a bit. This comes under the head of scientific investigation. An hour would not be too much to devote to

An hour would not be too much to devote to this.

this, especially if you have a bundle to deliver or an appointment to keep in half an hour.

Unfortunately, however, window-demonstrating seems to be dying out as a trade. I don't think that I have seen a man standing in a window in his underclothes for over a year. There are still a few ladies who do legerdemain with day-beds, but that doesn't strictly come under the head of scientific research. Everyone knows how to work a day-bed by now. What we want is to see a new way to open a corkscrew, or a combination cuff and spat. Where have all those men gone who used to hold up three fingers at you through the glass, meaning that three times they had tried to break a watch crystal and now admitted themselves hopelessly defeated? Where are those martyrs to health who used to allow themselves to be shaken to a froth by electric vibrators? Wherever they are, they are holding up the wheels of window-watching, one of the noblest of America's outdoor games.

Special Anthropological Extra!

WE do not want to get the public too excited, and then have to let them down, but we think we've found something in the Gobi Desert. By "we" I mean our little anthropological expedition which set out eight years ago to hunt for relics of Ancient Man, got stuck for seven years in Paris what with one thing and another, and now have, at last, reached our destination and goal. We arrived at the Gobi Desert last night. Early this morning we found something. Now, mind you, we do not want to say just yet that it is valuable from an anthropological point of view. But we do know this: if it *isn't* valuable from an anthropological point of view, it certainly isn't valuable from any other. It looks awful.

Our expedition started out from New York with twelve people, including four red caps, a cameraman, a sound man (with a sound machine for making talking pictures in case we should dig up anything that could talk), Dr. Reeby, who is in charge of the badges and hats, and myself. The other four people decided to come along at the last minute, and I don't know who they are. Somebody Dr. Reeby met at dinner that night, I guess.

Then, after we got to Paris and found that we weren't going to be able to get away to the Gobi Desert for some time (we really *didn't* think that it would be seven years, however), we added a few more people to the party, until we finally had about two hundred. This was one of the things which held us up, getting passports for all those extra people. Passports and extra sandwiches.

Then, too, the Springs were lovely in Paris. We landed there just as the horse-chestnut trees were beginning to blossom, and you know how hard it is to leave Paris when the horse-chestnut trees are in bloom. The funny part of it was that they seemed to stay in bloom all of that year and part of the next. By then we had worn out a lot of our clothes and had to have new ones made, and there were fittings and things to be gone through with, and then the horse-chestnut trees were in bloom again. In the meantime, we were accumulating people.

When at last, after seven years, we were ready to leave Paris for the Gobi Desert, Dr. Reeby had a three-year-old child who, unfortunately, had to be left behind. This caused quite a little hard feeling, Dr. Reeby maintaining that if some of the people already signed up were to be allowed to go, he saw no reason why his three-year-old child couldn't. We finally convinced him that it would be impractical, by pointing out that the child would have nobody to play with and might grow up to be near-sighted and perhaps have a camel-fixation, to say nothing of getting full of sand all the time. So the child was placed in the French Senate, where he would have playmates and good food, and we were off!

And now we come to the interesting part of our trip. As soon as we had reached the border of the Gobi Desert we unpacked, washed up, and started digging immediately before dinner. It was quite a sight to see all two hundred and thirty of us digging like mad, all intent on discovering something of interest for the Museum and the motion-picture company. Some of the party dug so fast and so deep that they had themselves completely out of sight inside of an hour and had to be pulled out by natives. Several, I am afraid, never did get out, as there weren't quite enough natives to go around. We haven't definitely checked up yet, or called the roll, but I think that the missing ones are some of those we picked up in Paris, in which case we may just let it go at calling the roll.

Early this morning we found something.

It was Lieut. Raffus, the cameraman, who came upon the first "find." Owing his inability to think of the word "Eureka!" it was quite some time before he could make his discovery known, but when he did, you may be sure that each and every one of us dropped his pick and ran over to Lieut. Raffus' excavation. The object which he held up (and dropped almost immediately, saying "Ugh!") seemed to be a sort of mat, or perhaps I should say muff, or perhaps I might even better say nothing. It was about a foot square, if you can call anything which is rather rounded "square," and was in a state of fossilization which would have made you laugh.

"It is a part of the Pliocene stratum (circa 500,000 years B.C.)," I was the first, and only one, to cry.

"Don't be so sure," replied Dr. Reeby. "You haven't looked on the other side yet." Dr. Reeby is the careful one in our little party. I will bust his nose some day.

However, we turned it over rather gingerly, and there, on the other side, was embroidered some sort of inscription. (See Fig. 15.)

"Pleistocene that somewhere before," said the sound man, who is always getting off comical cracks, and the laughter at this one was so general that the inscription was forgotten for the time being. In fact, it is only now that I have come to the writing of my report and daybook, that I remember that we really got nowhere in figuring it out. It is in a bag under the table on which I am writing, but I had much rather not pick it out to examine it. One never can tell where such things have been.

But we do know this: The thing is very, very old, or else, naturally, very unattractive. Most of the things found in the Gobi Desert are of the Pliocene Age (the difference between Pliocene and Pleistocene is that Pliocene has not so many letters in it and sounds like a mistake when you say it), and I see no reason for not allocating this discovery in this period. I don't know who is going to contradict us, as we don't intend showing it to anybody except a few personal friends at home.

The question now is: Shall we call it a day? We have really been here only about half a day, but we have been away from New York for eight years, and that is a pretty long time. The time in Paris shouldn't really count, for we had lots of fun there, but, after all, an expedition is an expedition, and there are movies to be made. The movie company is going to be awfully cross if we come back with a lot of shots of the Arc de Triomphe and Zelli's and only one or two of the Gobi Desert.

So what we think we had better do is stick around here for a couple of weeks, maybe working up a little story which will make a good picture. I wish now that we had brought Dr. Reeby's little boy along, because shots of children always go big and we could show him, in close-up, crying because a camel is drinking his milk or perhaps singing "Anchors A-weigh!" (By the way, I hope that these *are* camels we have here. I haven't looked closely.)

The plan now is that we should not go back by way of Paris. We have seen enough of Paris for one expedition, and a lot of us have never been to Hong Kong. If we go back by way of Hong Kong, that ought to land us in New York in perhaps three years (there are no horse-chestnut trees in Hong Kong,

PETER ARNO

It hardly seems possible, does it?

I hear), which will make it an even eleven years away from home. Gosh, it will seem good to get back!

In my next radio, I will tell just what we found out about our discovery. If it should turn out to be merely what it looks like, then I suppose we shall have to stick around until we find something else. But I see no reason why we can't make it sound good enough to make it worthwhile having sent us out. The picture rights alone ought to be worth plenty.

Dr. Reeby has just come in and says that our hieroglyphic expert says that the inscription reads: "Deliver no more milk until further notice." Just think! Five hundred thousand years B.C. people were going away on vacations and leaving notes to milkmen! It hardly seems possible, does it?

Well, I guess that means that we don't have to dig any more. So it's off to Home and Hurrah for Science!

A Trip to Spirit Land

In all the recent talk about spirits and spiritism (by "recent" I mean the past three hundred and fifty years) I have maintained what amounts to a complete silence, chiefly because I have been eating crackers a great deal of the time and couldn't talk, but also because I saw no reason for my giving away those secrets of spirit communication which have, in my day, made me known from Maine to New Hampshire as "the Goat of Ghosts." Now, however, I feel that society should know how it has been duped, boop—doopa—duped, in fact.

I first began my experiments with spiritism in 1909 while sitting in the dark with a young lady who later turned out to be not my wife. Watches with phosphorescent dials had just come into use and I had one of the few in town. In fact, I had one of the few watches in town, most of the residents still sticking to the old-fashioned hourglass as being more handy. I had just moved my watch up to my nose to take a look at it in the dark, as I realized that it was time to go beddie-bye, when the young lady, seeing a phosphorescent blob of light make its way like a comet through the dark at her side, screamed, "There's a ghost in the room!" and fainted heavily.

It was some time before I could get out from under her, and even more time before I realized what it was that had

319

given her such a fright; but, once it became clear to me, I knew that I had here the makings of a great little racket. So, stepping across her prostrate body, I went out into the world to become a medium, or, in the technical language of the craft, a medium stout.

Not many people realize how easy it is to fake spirit manifestations. For example, there was the famous case of one Dr. Rariborou, well known in London during the first decade of the century as a highly successful medium and eye-ear-nose-throat man. He combined his medical practice with his occult powers by making spirits play tambourines in people's throats while he was working on them. This not only mystified his patients but made them pretty irritable, so he had to give it up in the end and devoted all his time to séances.

Dr. Rariborou, or, as he afterward became known, "Dr." Rariborou, was famous for his "flying leg" trick, or "foot messages." This was a highly mystifying manifestation, even to Dr. Rariborou, although he knew exactly how it was done. The client was seated in a darkened room, after having examined the medium to make sure that he was securely bound with surgeon's tape to his assistant, who was, in turn, chained to the wall of the room. The room was then hermetically sealed, so that it got rather unbearable along about four o'clock.

Having made sure that everything was shipshape (one of those old medieval prison ships you read about—I don't), the client sat in a chair and held fast on to the knee of Dr. Rariborou. Sometimes they would sit this way for hours, if Dr. Rariborou happened to like the client. Otherwise, the séance would begin immediately with a message to the doctor from his control, an old Indian named Mike. Mike would tell the doctor that someone wanted to talk to the client, usually someone of whom the client had never heard, whereupon a ghostly leg would be seen flying through the air, delivering a smart kick with its foot on the side of the client's head. Almost simultaneously a kick would be received on the other side of the head, which would pretty well rock the client groggy. His chair would then be pulled out from under him and a pail of water be upset over his shoulders.

At the same time a spirit mandolin, suspended in mid-air, would play Ethelbert Nevin's "Narcissus" in double time, with not too expert fingering on the high notes.

This astounded, and bruised, a number of clients, and the doctor's reputation grew apace. The funny part of it was that practically every client who was thus maltreated had no difficulty in recalling some deceased friend or relative who might be glad to treat him in this manner. They all took it for granted that they were getting only what was coming to them from someone who was dead. They would say, as they picked themselves up after the séance: "I guess that must have been Dolly," or, "Sure, I know who *that* was, all right. It was Joe." All of which does not speak very well for human society as it is constituted today.

His chair would then be pulled out from under him and a pail of water be upset over his shoulders.

Now for the explanation of how this "flying leg" trick was done. It was one of my favorites when I was at the zenith of my powers. The medium is strapped, as we saw, by surgeon's tape, to his assistant, who is in turn chained to the wall. When the lights are put out, the medium using the one knee which is free from the grasp of the client, presses a concealed spring in the chairs on which he is sitting, which releases the entire side of the room to which the assistant is chained.

The assistant, with nothing to bother him now but the loose wall hanging to his wrists and the medium who is strapped to him, seizes an artificial leg which has been covered with phosphorescent paint and belabors the client with it as we have seen. With one foot he releases a spring which pulls the chair out from under the victim, and with the other foot releases another spring which upsets the pail of water. By this time the client doesn't know or care much what goes on.

Meanwhile the medium, still strapped to the assistant, brings out a mandolin pick which he has had concealed in his cheek and plays a phosphorescent mandolin which has been lowered by a second assistant from the ceiling to a point directly in front of his mouth. "Narcissus" calls for very little fretwork on the mandolin, being played mostly on the open strings, but what little fingering there is to be done is easily handled by the tip of the medium's nose which he has trained especially for this work. You can do it yourself some time, unless you happen not to like "Narcissus" as a tune. I myself got pretty darned sick of it after five or six years, which was one of the reasons I gave up holding séances.

Another famous medium, whose fakes are now generally recognized, was Mme. Wayhoo, an East Indian woman from New Bedford, Massachusetts, whose father was one of the old New Bedford whales. Her specialty was spirit writing, and her chief claim to integrity was that she herself could neither read nor write. (As a matter of fact, she was a graduate of Radcliffe, according to the gossips.) The person desirous of getting in touch with deceased relatives would go into a darkened room and ask questions of Mme. Wayhoo, such as, "Is it in this room? Is it animal, vegetable, or mineral? Did you file an income-tax return in 1930 and, if so, were you married or single at that time?"

To these questions the medium would reply nothing, until the questioner got rather jittery as a result of sitting in a dark room and asking questions into the blackness with no replies. Just as some form of mental breakdown was about to take place, the medium would scratch on a slate with a slate pencil, at the revolting sound of which the client would leap into the air and rush from the room screaming. On returning, he or she would find that a message had been written on the slate, something lie "Out to lunch—back at 2:30," or a complete bowling score. I do not even have to explain how this was done.

I have in my files hundreds of other explanations of psychic phenomena, but I am saving them up for a debate. I also have some excellent rye whisky which I will let go for practically nothing to the right parties.

Around the World
with the Gypsy Jockey

Our movietone globe-trotting this week will take us to far-off Gukla, where the exotic odors of the East mingle with the sound of temple bells and bits of old string to blend into one bewitching symphony, a never-to-be-forgotten idyl in the memory of the traveler from the West. And two dozen of your best eggs.

As in our former travelogues, we shall be conducted by a man who, because of his romantic wanderings in and out of all the lands of the earth, as well as upstairs in grandma's house, has become known as "The Gypsy Jockey." I need hardly introduce to you, therefore, Colonel Michington Mea, "The Gypsy Jockey," who will conduct you through the movietone to far-off Gukla where (see first paragraph).

Well, my dear cinema audience, here we are at the ends of the earth, or, at any rate, one end. The first shot shows us paddling up the West Okash River on our way to far-off Gukla, and those little heads and things that you see bobbing up and down in the water are my own little heads and things that I had just discarded after a night of drinking the native punch or Kewa—and I think that you would agree with me that "punch" is just the word for it. Rather a distressing sight, isn't it? I don't know which was the more distressing, the heads I discarded or the one I kept on my shoulders. None of them was in the least satisfactory.

Now we are coming to the bend in the river from which we may see a vista of Gukla, with its toylike pagodas and strange monuments to unknown deities. Truly a wonderful sight, unless by chance, we happen to be looking in quite the wrong direction. Gukla is a city which is many hundreds of years old and is built entirely on bamboo piles about the water. Perhaps you will wonder why, when the town was built, it was not built on dry land along the river bank instead of on poles in the water. The natives themselves often wonder that, too, but it is too late to do anything about it.

Here we are, landing at Gukla, and you will notice the hundreds of natives who have come down to the landing to watch us. What funny costumes! (I am referring to *our* costumes and not those of the natives, who, as you will see if you are not skittish about such matters, wear no costumes at all.) That little old man who is waving something at us is an uncle merchant trying to sell us his uncle. There is a great deal of trading in uncles in Gukla, although this particular year the market is unusually small, owing to the unparalleled hoarding on the part of the aunts.

And now we climb the road from the river bank to the top of an old hill where stands this perfect example of a Gukla temple, built in the Fourth Century After Krinkjka—everything here is dated as before or after Krinjka, the God of Summer Squash—which would make it the third century before the Reign of the Butterfly Cocoon, or about 1896 in our language.

As you will see, it is a perfect example of 1896 architecture, with French roofs and lace curtains and a cast-iron dog on the lawn. The only flaw in this temple, as a show piece, is that it was built indoors in the contractor's workshop, with the result that, when it was moved out to its present site, the top had to be tipped slightly to the left in order to get it out through the door. It is still, however, pretty ugly.

There is a legend about this temple, which I resolved to investigate and, if possible, to photograph for my movietone travelogue. According to the story which the more intoxicated of the natives tell each other, there was once a princess

Colonel Michington Mea.

named Mah Patoola who lived there, dedicated to the service of Krinjka. This meant that all the days of her life she had to sit at an upstairs window and look out at the river below, making believe that she expected to see a lover come paddling by in a canoe. This made it very dull for the princess, for she knew as well as anyone else that there was no lover and that it was doubtful if there was even a canoe. For the sake of the legend, however, she had to sit and look sad and every once in a while lean out of the window a little farther and mutter, "Where the hell can he be?"

Naturally, this got on the princess' nerves after ten or eleven years and one night she leaned so far out that her feet touched a trellis which ran from her window to the ground and, after three or four minutes of catching her skirt on nails and getting vines tangled around her neck, she was on the river's bank and off to town.

She never returned, and it is generally supposed among the natives that she was seized by remorse and came back to the cellar of the temple, where she still roams at night. There is another story, however, which has it that she met a boy from the U.S.S. *North Dakota* in the town that night and went with him to Bridgeport, Connecticut, where she still is living and running a doily shop.

Determined to find out the truth of one of these legends, I went up to the temple at midnight and climbed down into the cellar. Here you will see me, in the light of a couple of Kliegs we happened to have brought along, stumbling about among the ruins of old sofas and horsehair trunks which had been relegated to the storeroom by the princess' parents.

What was that at my right? I stopped short and had the cameras brought up. The sound of a woman sobbing! Fortunately the microphones were in good shape and our soundman said, "O.K." Gripping my revolver in one hand (for there is nothing more dangerous or treacherous than a sobbing princess), I pushed aside the debris and peered into the darkness from whence the sound came.

My native runners had all deserted me, for this was sacrilege that I was engaging in, and the penalty for sacrilege was fifteen minutes on the *suttee,* or funeral pyre. The *suttee* is usually reserved for widows, but, in the case of any one who had committed a sacrilege, a widow is moved over to make room and the culprit is given his fifteen minutes' penalty. After that he can get off or stay on, as he likes.

But I am getting away from my story, and here we are, all set with cameras and sound machines in the cellar of the Temple of Krinjka, with me looking everywhere for a sobbing princess. That is me—or is it I?—over there in the shadows stumbling—no, up again!—falling—no, by George!—by great good luck catching myself on an assistant director—here we go—what do you suppose we are going to find?—is this exciting or isn't it?—and now we come to the place where the sound is—and find—what is this?—well, of all things!—three of the cutest kittens you ever saw, with the old mother cat as proud as Punch and ready to give battle to anyone who disturbs her young ones in their play. Never mind, Pussy, we aren't going to hurt you—off with the lights!—cut! And here we are, out again in God's sunshine, none the worse for our exciting adventure.

And now we come to the last reel of our little travelogue, just as we are about to take the boats again and drift down the river to—who knows where? The sun is sinking over there behind temple towers and from the river bank comes the tinkle of old peasants grinding their teeth. What a beautiful sight! What a punk picture! The spell of the East!

Will it ever release us from its thralldom? Who knows? Who cares?

Ding-Dong School Bells

Or What the Boy Will Need

ALTHOUGH it hardly seems credible, it is almost time to begin packing the kiddies off to school again. Here they have been all summer, the rascals, tracking sand into the dining room, rolling Grandma about, and bringing in little playmates who have been exposed to mumps (when Daddy himself hasn't had mumps yet, and mumps for Daddy would be no fun), and in all kinds of ways cheering up the Old Manse to the point of bursting it asunder.

And now the school bells will be ringing again! A sure sign of the coming outbreak of education is the circulars which come in the mail from the clothing and general outfitting stores with lists of "required articles for the schoolboy and for the schoolgirl," just as if the schoolboy and the schoolgirl couldn't tell you themselves exactly what they are going to need—and more, too. Some day I want to get one of those list-compilers to come round and listen to my son and my daughter make out *their* lists. They will have him crying his heart out with chagrin inside of three minutes. "One rubber slicker," indeed! "One green slicker, one tan slicker, one old-rose slicker," is more like it. That is in case the rain comes in three different colors.

I can remember the time (by pressing my temples very hard and holding my breath) when the opening of school

329

meant simply buying a slate with a sponge tied to it and a box of colored crayons. No one, to my knowledge, ever used a slate and a sponge. They were simply a sentimental survival of an even earlier day which the man in the stationery store forced on children who were going to school. The colored crayons were, of course, for eating.

But we bought our slates and our sponges and our crayons (sometimes with a ruler for slapping purposes), and then never used them, for the school furnished all the pencils and pads of yellow paper which were necessary. One of the great releases of my grown-up life has been that I don't have to write on a yellow sheet of paper with blue lines ruled on it half an inch apart. I don't *like* to have to write my lines half an inch apart, and now that I am a great big man, I don't do it. That is one of the advantages of graduating from school.

Today, however, although the slate and the sponge have been removed from the list, there are plenty of "incidentals" even for those children who go to what are known as public schools. What with the increase in high-school fraternities and fixings, high school today resembles the boarding school of yesterday, the boarding school of today resembles the college of yesterday, and the college of today (let's see if I can keep this up) has turned the corner and resembles the public school of yesterday. Is that clear? Or shall we go over it just once again?

Of course, according to the clothing-store lists, once your child gets into a so-called private school (which means that no child who has killed an uncle, an aunt, or any nearer relative, can enter) he is in for an outfitting such as hasn't been seen since Byrd started for the South Pole. You wouldn't think that merely sleeping away from home, in a nation as strict as ours, would entail so many extra clothes for a child.

And not night clothes, either. A boy, when he is living at home, may just sit around the house reading and grousing all day, but the minute he gets away at school (according to the lists) he goes in for fox-hunting, elk-hunting, and whatever it is they hunt with falcons (Falcon hood, $45.50). Then for caber-tossing, you can get a good caber for $24, but the suit that you have to wear must be made by a Scottish tailor

One hat in a hatbox. Five hundred pairs of socks. One overcoat. One old model Ford.

out of regulation St. Andrews heather, made up into a smart model for $115.

As I remember my school requirements (I am both a public and a private school boy myself, having always changed schools just as the class in English in the new school was taking up

Silas Marner, with the result that it was the only book in the English language that I knew until I was eighteen—but, boy, did I know Silas Marner!), I would substitute a list something like the following in place of that sent out by the clothing store:

One sheet of note paper (with envelope to match) for letter home. This should do for the school year. Requests for money can be made by telegraph, collect.

Five hundred pairs of socks, one to be thrown away each day.

One hat, in a hatbox, the key of which will be left with the school principal for safekeeping until the end of the term.

One overcoat, to be left with the hatbox key, *unless* the overcoat is of raccoonskin, in which case it should be made adaptable for wear up to and including June 10.

One copy, in clear English translation, of each of the following books: The *Æneid, Odyssey, Immensée, La Fontaine's Fables* (be sure that this follows the original French; there are a lot of fancy English adaptations which will get you into trouble with words which aren't in the text), *Nathan the Wise,* and *Don Quixote.* There should be plenty of room between the lines in these books, to allow for the penciling in of a word now and then.

One rubber mouth appliance, for making the sound commonly known as "the bird."

One old model Ford, with space for comments in white paint.

One pipe, with perhaps an ounce of tobacco, for use about four times, then to be discarded or lost.

One pocket lighter, made to harmonize with the other bureau ornaments.

Three dozen shirts, with collars already frayed to save the laundry's time.

One very old T-shirt.

Three dozen neckties, for use of roommates.

One set of name tags, to be sewn on clothing to ensure roommate's getting them in return for clothing marked with roommate's name.

There is no sense in trying to provide handkerchiefs.

Here, then, Mr. Boy's Outfitter, is my list. I think that it takes care of everything. I am not prepared to go into as much detail as to the requirements for a girl's school, because my daughter (if I had one) is not old enough. But I don't want to get any more intimations that I am not doing right by my boy if I don't buy him a red hunting coat. If he wants a red hunting coat, he can let the sleeves of mine down an inch or so and wear that.

Around the World Backward

WHAT would all you boys and girls here today say if I were to come bursting into the room and cry out: "Huzza, huzza! We're going around the world! Get out your tippets and your warm undies, for we're off to Paris, Berlin, Russia, Manchuria, Japan, China, and far-away Tibet"? You would be pretty happy boys and girls, I guess, unless you happen to be the kind who like to stick around home.

And so was I happy, very, very happy, when a motion-picture director named Milestone (the master mind who directed *All Quiet on Western Front Page*) came crashing into my little study one day last winter and announced that I had been chosen to accompany him and Douglas Fairbanks on a vagabond spin around the hemispheres in search of material for a travel picture.

I could hardly believe that such good fortune had really come to poor little me—me what had always drawn my own carriage—but the Cinderella story is ever new and one never can tell what may happen, especially if one doesn't know.

So I dug out several old Russian costumes I had tucked away for just such an emergency, put some drops in my eyes to make them sparkle, and late that afternoon we were off, the Two and a Half Musketeers, for a gay, devil-may-care *tour du monde*, "the Great Adventure," as I dubbed it. Life, I

334

thought, must be like this.

It was not until the first day out on the clipper ship *Europa* that I realized what I was in for. I had always known Douglas Fairbanks in pictures as a bonny, bounding sort of chap, with a pleasant smile and considerable vitality, riding through the air on horses and carpets; but I had always, in my extreme sophistication, had an idea that most of the difficult feats were made in the studio by means of trick shots and doubles. It had never occurred to me that one man would be crazy enough really to do all those things. It certainly had never occurred to me that he would expect anyone else to do them with him.

I have never been, even in my palmiest days (now known as the Great Blizzard of 1888), an athlete. I used to stand in front of an open window and breathe deeply—oh, well, *pretty* deeply—and cheat a little on some bicep flexing, and, when I was very young and offensive, I used to bang a tennis ball up against the side of the house; but, thank God, several years ago I threw my left knee out by walking down a flight of phantom steps, and ever since then I have always been able to say, "My knee, you know!" whenever anyone suggested any exercise more violent than stooping over to pick up the morning paper.

In my ordinary course of life this sedentary principle of existence fits very well. But it is not good training for a jaunt with Douglas Fairbanks. I had no reason to know, when I adopted it, that I should ever be called upon to make a jaunt with Douglas Fairbanks, as that isn't one of the contingencies that the average man includes in his list of things to be prepared for. So when, on the first morning out, I was awakened by my cabin door being flung open and a lithe form in gray flannels and rubber-soled shoes hurtling through the air onto my bunk, I was inclined to treat the whole thing as one of those strange nightmares that one has just before awakening, and turned over to face the wall with a deprecatory wave of the hand. But it was not to be so.

"Come on, you old son of a gun," said America's Male Force. "Time to get up for a workout!"

"Where's my contract?" I asked through one eye. "Is there

"Come on," said America's Male Force. "Time to get up for a workout!"

anything in my contract about workouts? I'm a writer."

This designation of myself brought down a storm of derisive laughter, and I was placed upright on my feet and put into a tub of cold salt water. (I get sore even today as I write about it.) Mr. Fairbanks was accompanied on the trip by one "Chuck" Lewis, former All-American halfback and tissuebuilder, and a hard man to haggle with over details. Mr. Milestone, being a director, stayed in bed and thought up camera angles.

The first "workout" on deck consisted of a brisk dash along the straightaway, a snappy hurdling of the bar at the end up on to the superstructure, and a monkey-climb finish up the ladder on the forward stack, leaping from there to the after stack and a sheer drop to the deck, followed by a pyramid formation and a chord from the orchestra, "Ta-da-a-a-a!"

I myself got as far as the superstructure and halfway up

the first stack, at which point I stopped and gave the matter a little thought, did my drop right there, and ran and hid in a lifeboat. I should have stayed in that lifeboat. I see that now.

But I allowed myself to be dragged out, and the rest of the sea trip I spent trailing behind the pack. My shins took on the markings of two totem poles, my thighs turned an unpleasant blue from abrasions, and my one bad knee, which long since had ceased to be an excuse, was joined by the other knee in its infirmity.

Just before we landed in France we had what is technically known in movie circles as a "story conference." A "story conference" is where various people responsible for a motion picture get together and tell stories. This conference, how-ever, had a more practical angle, for we were to decide just what was to be done first in making this big travel film, for we couldn't very well begin shooting without some general idea in mind. That would be just silly.

"I'll tell you what we'll do," said Douglas, leaping to the back of the sofa and swinging back and forth on a porthole casing. "We'll go first to St. Moritz for the winter sports, skiing, bobsledding, breaking arms and legs, and all that. Then, once we are used to the cold, we can push on up into Russia, where I am sure they will let us jump around on the Kremlin and perhaps tear a few wolves to pieces. Manchuria may be a little bloody right now, what with the Sino-Japanese trouble, but we might be able to recruit a regiment from the vagabond Americans and English who are in the country and fight on one side or the other."

"Is there a dental corps in this war?" I asked. "I know a lot about teeth."

Douglas leaped from the porthole and landed on the bu-reau. "We've got you all assigned already," he laughed, a mocking, sinister laugh. "You're going to stick to me and do everything that I do, so that when we come to put the picture together you can write the dialogue. Funny cracks, you know. Making a gag of the whole thing."

"I see," I said quietly . . . .

On the return trip of the *Europa*, the man occupying Room
86 was surprised on the first night out to hear a scratching
from his bureau drawer. On opening it, he was even more
surprised to see me lying there; but being a man of considerable experience in traveling, he said nothing at the time.
On the third day out toward New York, I emerged and told
him my story. I even rolled up my trousers and showed him
my shins.

"I think you were very wise to do as you did," was all he
said.

I even rolled up my trousers and showed him my shins.

For the
Entertainment Committee

As a general thing, the average citizen is a pretty good sort, popular superstition to the contrary notwithstanding. He may not be a mine of wise cracks, and he may get fooled about eight times out of five, but, in general, he has a vague intention of doing the right thing in as decent a manner as possible. With one exception. And that is when he is made a member of an entertainment committee.

Henry W. Peak, let us say, has lived in his town for twenty years and has always respected property rights and had a fair amount of regard for the civil rights of his neighbors. That is, he wouldn't think of going into anyone's house at two in the morning and pulling him out of bed crying, "Get up, get up, you lazy head!" He wouldn't even ring his door bell, unless perhaps the house was on fire.

And yet let Mr. Peak be appointed to the entertainment committee in charge of giving the visiting Shriners a good time and he becomes a veritable fiend. Give Mrs. Peak the task of getting up a benefit for the district nurses and you would never recognize her as the gentle, ladylike creature who presides in so patrician a manner over the Peak household.

A wild light comes into the eyes of a member of an entertainment committee which old friends of the family will swear

they have never seen before. "Fanatic" would be a good word
for it, if there were such a word. Let's make such a word up!
"Fanatic."

To a man or woman trying to arrange an entertainment,
no matter if it be only something to entertain the kiddies on
a rainy afternoon, the entire world's business becomes sub-
ordinate to their task. Not only do they neglect their own
jobs, they demand that everyone else neglect his.

International conferences, the production of steel for the
world's markets, the writing of the novel of the age, or the
painting of an ocean liner, all must stop at a word from the
entertainment committee and the people who have been busy
at these minor pursuits must drop everything and "lend a
hand" in order to make this just the best show that was ever
put on in the Second Congregational Church. And anyone
who doesn't feel the same way is just a mean old thing.

Having served on entertainment committees, I know the
procedure. The committee at its first meeting is a trifle luke-
warm on the proposition, all except the chairman, who is
quite likely to be a go-getter.

"Now, this thing has been put into our hands," he says,
"and it is up to us! We've got to get up just a bully show!"

Just what there should be in this speech that should arouse
any enthusiasm in the members is difficult to say, but the fact
remains that it does. Gradually the flush of excitement creeps
into the faces of those present, and each becomes, for the
time being, a crusader.

"Now, whom can we get to take part?" asks the chairman.

With this the committee proceeds to shift the burden of
the entertainment from their own shoulders to those of a
half a dozen poor souls who don't even know that they are
under discussion.

"Well, there's always Eddie Fripp," suggests someone. "He's
got a peach of an act which he does with a screen and a
pointer. It's a sort of travelogue, and he takes you all around
these crazy places and explains them on the screen. He did
it at the Girls' Friendly last winter."

Then, before they have even asked Mr. Fripp if he can do

The committee shift the burden of the entertainment from their own shoulders to those of half a dozen poor souls who don't even know that they are under discussion.

it, there is a discussion as to whether or not it is the kind of act they want in the benefit. Mrs. Arthur Hamston inquires if it is clean. They don't want any questionable stuff, you know. Yes, someone will vouch for its being clean, so Mrs. Hamston is satisfied. Will he charge money for doing it? Oh, no! Eddie will be only too glad to do it for nothing. Mr. Reiss will answer that. So. Mr. Reiss is delegated to get Eddie Fripp to do his travelogue.

Then Georgia Ranson is proposed as being a very nice singer. She makes her living by singing, but she will surely be glad to do it for nothing for Mrs. Matoon. So Mrs. Matoon is assigned the task of getting Miss Ranson, dead or alive.

"Arthur Meacham used to do an awfully funny imitation of different kinds of birds," remembers Mrs. Pfaff. "He used to *look* like the birds, as I remember it."

"He's working in Chicago now," says someone who keeps up with the times.

"Oh, that's all right. I'll get him. What's a few hundred miles?"

This is said with quiet confidence by Mr. Tethrow. The latter is one of those business men who, when he sets out to do a thing, *does* it—whether it is worth doing or not.

And so it goes. The committee goes over the whole list of available entertainers in town and elects those lucky ones who are considered suitable for the occasion. It is decided that George Wesson will be allowed to do his card tricks, and that Arthur McKeag may do his song and dance act.

The idea never presents itself that perhaps George Wesson may have something else that he would rather do on the night of the benefit or that Arthur McKeag may not consider it such a favor to be allowed to contribute to the gayety. The malign spell of the entertainment is on them, and they expect every man, including England, to do his duty—and like it.

Once they have assigned the jobs of lining up the victims to various members of the committee the real dirty work begins. If you think that the zealots have been offensive in conclave, you ain't, as John L. Sullivan used to say, seen nothing yet. Like a pack of hounds turned loose on the scent, they start off down the street after their prey. Go get 'em, Prince! Atta boy, Major!

First, Mr. Tethrow puts in a long distance call to Chicago for Arthur Meacham. To these big business men long distance calls are nothing when a thing like this is at stake.

"Hello, Meacham? This is Tethrow talking. William Tethrow. Want you to come on and do your bird imitations for benefit next Wednesday. . . . Now, now. . . . We won't take no for an answer. . . . We've simply got to have you and you can't squeal out of it. No, sir! We mean business. Now, don't pull any of that stuff. . . . We'll pay your railroad fare one way and put you up at the club when you get here. . . . Oh, ditch the other party. . . . You don't have to go to that. . . . Oh, no, you don't. . . . Remember, now, we're counting on you. . . . Not another word now. . . . We're counting on you. . . . Good-by."

So Mr. Tethrow reports that he has called Meacham in Chicago, and that, although Meacham said he had something else to do that night, "he'll come all right, all right. I left it so he couldn't help himself."

The same tactics are used by the other members of the committee in their rounds of the entertainers. The theory they work on is that civilization has been striving all this time toward its culmination in the benefit next Wednesday and that the least that people can do is shut down their factories, close the schools, and declare a national holiday, with a special tax levied on each citizen as a contribution to the success of the affair.

In calling on out of town speakers or entertainers a member of the entertainment committee for anything—a banquet, benefit, or open forum—seems to consider the word "guest" a bait which the victim will be unable to resist.

"You will be our guest," seems to hold within its ample significance all that any normal man could possibly demand of life, even though he gives up a couple of days of his time, uses up a dress shirt, and perhaps pays his own railroad fare. The lure of being a guest of the entertainment committee, together with the high honor of being asked to contribute his services to the amusement of the members of the Booklovers' Guild or the Every Thursday Evening Club, is counted on to bring speakers and entertainers stampeding from all sections of the country.

This probably has a basis in fact. There are unquestionably people who are so fond of doing card tricks or making speeches that they would gladly walk to the place of amusement to do their stuff and ask no other recompense than an audience of half way attentive faces.

But this type is not common enough to justify a generalization, and for every one of these eager entertainers, there are hundreds of poor souls throughout the land who, because they once did something on the spur of the moment at a Grange meeting or a club dinner which met with the approval of their colleagues, have become engulfed in a whirlpool of eleemosynary activity which is not only distasteful but very expensive for them. And, as they seem always to be concomitantly easy-going, soft-hearted goofs who can't say "no," they become in time the plaything of hordes of ravenous entertainment committees throughout the district in which they are unfortunate to live.

The remedy lies nowhere. Just so long as people insist on being amused there will be entertainment committees, and just so long as there are entertainment committees there are going to be efficient committeemen, which means that everything else is expected to go by the board until a "bully good show" or a "crackerjack dinner" has been lined up.

But don't be surprised some day if you hear of an organization of hitherto charitable speakers, card tricksters, bird imitators, and singers, who, armed with machine guns, have taken up their position behind barricades in the city streets, waving aloft a banner bearing the defy: "Come On, You Entertainment Committee! Come On and Get It."

The Return of the Bicycle

A Conservative Huzza

WITH the complete collapse of the automobile as a means of transportation (I believe that I am correct in assuming that it has been a miserable fiasco and will soon be seen on our roads only in the form of heavy trucking vehicles or agricultural tanks), and with the failure to leave the ground of practically every airplane constructed in the last six months, thereby eliminating aviation as a factor in future travel, there remains but one solution to the problem of those of us who want to get from one place to another. We must go back to the bicycle.

We were fools ever to leave the bicycle. I remember being quoted at the time in *Handlebar and Sprocket,* the great bicycle journal of the day, as saying: "Mark my words, you horseless-carriage fiends and flying-machine bugs! The day will come when you will forsake your senseless toys, which will have not even the sanction of natural laws, and will come crawling back to the safety of the bicycle, begging to be given a ride, even on the handlebars."

Well, the day has come, and it is going to cost those people anywhere from fifty to seventy-five cents apiece if they want to ride on *my* handlebars. A dollar if they want to ring the bell themselves.

It was obvious from the start that the automobile and air-

345

plane were impractical. Any agencies of propulsion which depend upon tricky outside helps as gasoline, heavy motors, slip covers, and radiator caps are, on the face of it, no good for general use. And as for being dependent on wind and weather, the old-fashioned sailing ship was discarded because of that very drawback. The bicycle calls for nothing in the way of accessories except a pair of sturdy calves and a wire basket to carry lunch in. Gas? No, sir, thank you! Fog? Ha-ha! Spark plugs? Head winds? Indeed! It was hop on and away the devil take the hindmost! It will seem good to have those days back again.

Of course, there will be some die-hards who will insist for a while on pushing their old automobiles out on the roadway and blocking traffic with them. Such reactionaries must be dealt with summarily. The new code of traffic regulations should make it obligatory for those who wish to chug along in motor vehicles to keep close to the right-hand side of the road and to draw over into the gutter whenever a bicycle club riding five or more abreast wishes to pass. (Bicycle clubs have already begun springing up all over the country, reviving their old charters and buying new blazers.)

All motors giving off a carbon-monoxide exhaust or in any other way interfering with the vision or comfort of cyclists who happen to be behind them should be confiscated and the owner obliged to wheel his chassis home across the fields.

Any parking of motor vehicles which makes it impossible for cyclists to draw up to the curb should be done away with. If motorists want to leave their "cars" anywhere, let them leave them at home where they will be out of decent people's way. A set of rules along these lines would soon do away with what few automobiles may survive the debacle which is already drawing near.

I feel a more or less personal interest in this revolt against motor and air transportation because I have reason to believe that it is an ancestor of mine who is depicted in the oldest existing record of the cult of self-propulsion. In a stained-glass window in a church at Stoke Poges, Buckinghamshire, England, is shown the figure of a man astride a wheeled instrument, which students of bicycle pictures claim to be the

"And if you fall, you have farther to fall and just that much more fun and excitement."

PETER ARNO

earliest attempt by any artist to show self-cycling.

This man is apparently propelling himself by pressing his feet against the ground with a forward pushing movement, using the wheel more or less to lean against, with probably a little high-spirited coasting now and then. I have seen the window, and the man looks quite a lot like me, except for a full beard and a more nervous expression around the eyes. The name underneath the figure is in Gothic letters and very difficult to make out, but it certainly begins with a "Ben" and the rest seems to be something of a compromise between "wgaale" and "chhaalle."

Now, my people originally came from Wales (which in itself

would account for the spelling), and, for a man with a contraption like the one in the picture, a spin from Wales to Buckinghamshire would have been mere child's play. As I figure it out, this man Benwgaalle or Benchhaalle built his bicycle, took along some lunch, and pushed himself along to Stoke Poges, at which place he became a sort of local hero, like Lindbergh at Le Bourget, and a stained-glass window was made in his honor. I rather imagine that he stayed in Stoke Poges all the rest of his life, as he probably was pretty lame.

Having seen this evidence of the pioneering activities of my ancestor in self-propulsion, I took the trouble to look up the records of a man named Denis Johnson of Long Acre making an improvement on the original Benchley model, but the market price of the machine was so high that very few could afford it, and it became scornfully known as the "dandy horse." Pushing the feet against the ground was still the method of obtaining power, so the dandies of that day must have been a great deal more agile than dandy. In fact, at the end of a ride in the country it must have been hard to tell them from anyone else.

It was not until 1840 that the first real bicycle was constructed by Kirkpatrick McMillan of Dumfries, Scotland, who was immediately arrested for "furious driving on the roads." He probably got sulky after that and never left his house. But his soul went scorching on and the bicycle became a reality, with what was considered the last word in bicycle building in 1873.

It is not difficult to imagine the selling talk of the first agent for this model: "I'll tell you, Mr. Waterous. The trouble with the bicycle up to now has been that both wheels have been of the same size. Now, our 1873 model has a very radical departure in body building. The front wheel is *twice* the size of the back wheel, thereby eliminating all the jarring and bouncing of the other makes. You are also up a great deal higher and can see more of the surrounding country as you ride. And if you fall, you have farther to fall and just that much more fun and excitement.

"I need hardly tell you, Mr. Waterous, that the cyclist who

buys one of our models right now, before the price goes up, will never regret it and will be the most envied man in his neighborhood."

If he is alive today there probably is no more bitter person in the world than the inventor of the high-wheeled bicycle. He is probably still claiming that he was "crowded out" by the combine in 1855 when the high wheel was abolished and the "safety" introduced.

But it is the "safety" bicycle which has come to stay, and which is now about to sweep the flash-in-the-pan automobile from the roads and the unreliable airplane from the skies. The bicycle has been lying low all these years while the Wright brothers and Ford have been experimenting. We old cyclists have been keeping quiet and letting the fly-by-night innovations run their course. And now that our predictions are coming true, we are donning our trouser clips and pulling our caps over our eyes, crouched over our handlebars in silent expectation. At the word "Go!" we will sweep down the road, and it needs must be a nervy automobilist who will stand in our way.

The only trouble is that I can't find my bicycle.

What Does
·   Your Boy Read?   ·

ONE of the reasons children grow up so quickly these days
must be that the books which are written for grown-ups are
so much more fun to read than the so-called "juvenile
literature."

Most of the children's books today are designed to improve
the child's mind or inculcate in him a spirit of good clean
camel-hunting. Instead of heroes taking pot shots at Indians
or hiding gold in caves, we find the continent of South America as the hero of one modern child's book and the man who
discovered how to insulate copper wire as the hero of another. What inducement to read is there for a boy who has
spent a hard day at school and in the back lot? Now I ask
you!

There was such a hue and a cry about the old-fashioned
dime novel (which cost a nickel) that no self-respecting parent
today would allow his children to have one in the house; and
yet Frank and Dick Merriwell, and even Old and Young King
Brady, were as highly moral characters as, I venture to say,
any of the modern heroes who set out to get specimens of
quartz for the Museum and become president of the Inter-
urban Oil Company in the process. Old King Brady did chew
a little tobacco now and then, it is true; but most of the dime-
novel heroes were models of behavior which many a child of

350

today would do well to follow. I'll bet there are not more than six young men in the country now as well behaved and noble as Frank Merriwell used to be.

Take the following excerpts (imaginary but typical) from an old-time thriller and a new-fashioned "inspirational" book for children:

"Dick Montague turned and faced the four masked figures who confronted him and Elsie Maxwell as they stood, with their backs to the wall, in Old Indian Meg's cave. His eyes flashed fire as he rolled back one sleeve.

" 'Your names are unknown to me,' he said in a calm voice, 'but, unless my eyes deceive me, you are members of the Red Band which has been marauding the country hereabouts. I know you all to be cowards at heart, and although I am not one to pick a fight without justification, I will offer to knock down the first man who dares make a move toward this young lady here!'

"The four blackguards sneered in unison but there was something in Dick Montague's voice which inspired terror in their craven hearts.

" 'Come, son, have a cigarette and let's talk it over,' said one of them, taking a step forward.

"Crack! A blow on the face from Dick's fist felled him to the floor of the cave.

" 'Get up, you yellow dog!' said Dick (for it was indeed he). 'You know very well that I do not smoke cigarettes, otherwise I should not be able to lead the flying wedge on the Yale football team with such courage.'

"A second member of the gang stepped forward. 'You darned little whelp,' he muttered, 'I'll—'

"But before he could finish his sentence, he, too, lay sprawling on the ground, the victim of a second crashing blow delivered by the young athlete.

" 'Get up, you yellow dog,' said Dick, 'and the next time, mind your language when there is a lady about!' "

And now something from the "recommended reading list" for the kiddies, put forward by the National Society for the Drying up of Children's Books:

"Little Sir A. S. Eddington turned to his companions who

were clustered about the telescope.

" 'It was awfully good of you chaps to ask me here to look through your telescope,' he said, wiping off the eyepiece carefully, for you never can tell who has been looking through a telescope before you. 'I wonder if the rest of you boys know that the other name for the Milky Way is the Galaxy.'

" 'I knew it, but I had forgotten it,' said H. Spencer Jones, the little boy who was later to become head of the observatory at Edinburgh, but not until he had learned not to forget things.

If I were a child I would welcome bedtime.

" 'The Galaxy, or Milky Way,' continued little Sir Arthur, 'is perhaps three hundred thousand light-years in diameter. Think of that!'

" 'Do we *have* to think of that?' asked happy-go-lucky Dr. Arbuthnot. 'It makes me giddy!'

"There was a general laugh at this, but there were more serious matters to be attended to.

" 'The center of the system of globular clusters is in Sagittarius,' continued Arthur—

" 'In *what?*' asked someone incredulously.

" 'In a group of stars known as Sagittarius,' repeated Sir Arthur impatiently, 'so called because it means "the archer," as this group of stars used to be represented in the old days by the picture of an archer shooting an arrow.'

" 'Let's go out and shoot arrows *now*,' suggested Dr. Arbuthnot, and away they all went to shoot arrows."

Now, in this latter form of writing for children there is undoubtedly a great deal of valuable information, but if I were a child (and I sometimes wonder) I would welcome bedtime if that were all I had to sit up for.